LIES
and
FICTION
in the
ANCIENT WORLD

LIES
and
FICTION
in the
ANCIENT WORLD

Edited by
CHRISTOPHER GILL
and
T. P. WISEMAN

UNIVERSITY
of
EXETER
PRESS

First published 1993 by
University of Exeter Press
Reed Hall, Streatham Drive
Exeter, Devon EX4 4QR
UK
www.exeterpress.co.uk

Printed digitally since 2010

British Library Cataloguing in Publication Data
A catalogue record of this book is
available from the British Library

ISBN 978 0 85989 381 7

Typeset in 11/13pt Stempel Garamond
by Colin Bakké Typesetting, Exeter

Printed and bound by CPI Group (UK) Ltd,
Croydon, CR0 4YY

CONTENTS

Preface vii

Notes on Contributors x

Prologue:
MICHAEL WOOD xiii

Chapter One:
Lies, Fiction and Slander in Early Greek Poetry
E.L. BOWIE I

Chapter Two:
Plato on Falsehood—not Fiction
CHRISTOPHER GILL 38

Chapter Three:
Truth and Untruth in Herodotus and Thucydides
J.L. MOLES 88

Chapter Four:
Lying Historians: Seven Types of Mendacity
T.P. WISEMAN 122

Chapter Five:
Fiction, Bewitchment and Story Worlds: The Implications
of Claims to Truth in Apuleius
ANDREW LAIRD 147

CONTENTS

Chapter Six:
Make-Believe and Make Believe: The Fictionality of the
Greek Novels
J.R. MORGAN 175

Epilogue:
Towards an Account of the Ancient World's Concept
of Fictive Belief
D.C. FEENEY 230

Bibliography 245

Index of Passages from Ancient Authors 255

General Index 259

Preface

THE nature of the boundary between fact and fiction—indeed, the question whether there *is* a determinate boundary—is an important issue of contemporary debate among literary critics, historians, and philosophers. The debate has had its equivalent in classical studies too, coinciding with an upsurge of interest in the ancient novel, and in the rhetorical character of ancient historiography.

This collection of new essays focuses on the question of the relationship between ancient concepts and the modern distinction between fact and fiction: how far was 'lying' distinguished from 'fiction' in different periods and genres of antiquity? We are concerned both with the categories and distinctions which figure in explicit theorizing and programmatic statements and with those which seem to inform ancient practices of writing and reading.

The collection includes two chapters on archaic and classical Greece (poetry and philosophy), two on Greek and Roman historiography, and two on the Roman and Greek novels. Our aim has not been to provide systematic and comprehensive coverage, but rather to display the issues as they arise in a number of key authors and areas. However, the collection brings out certain recurring themes in ancient thinking on this topic, which are underlined here and by Michael Wood in the Prologue.

In the first two chapters, E.L. Bowie and Christopher Gill raise partly analogous questions about archaic Greek poetry and Platonic philosophy. Bowie asks to what extent the practice and self-presentation of archaic lyric and narrative poets implies an understanding of their project as fictional invention, as distinct from the propagation of collective memory or 'truth'. Gill asks to what extent Plato's theorizing about poetry in the *Republic*, as well as his own myth-making and dialogic practice, involves the delineation of a concept of fiction. The two chapters reach what look like opposite conclusions, Bowie stressing the presence of a pre-reflective interest in fictional invention, Gill arguing against the idea that Plato is concerned to analyse fictionality. However, this disagreement reflects a partial difference in the issue raised. Gill acknowledges that we can see in Platonic thinking and practice an implied recognition of what we call 'fiction'; what he denies is that this concept *matters* for Plato, in the way that the concepts of truth and falsity matter for him. It is also possible that the subsequent failure of antiquity to develop a clearly defined category of fiction (even when evolving a genre we see as being that of narrative fiction) reflects the persistence of the concerns underlying Plato's views, in particular, the concern with literature as a vehicle for shared truth rather than for the individual imagination.

The next two chapters bring out, in different ways, the interplay between 'literary' and 'historical' objectives in ancient historiography. By a close reading of the programmatic prefaces of Herodotus and Thucydides, J.L. Moles shows how these historians *both* see themselves as inheritors of the epic tradition—commemorating a great war and creatively interpreting its causal patterns—*and* insist on their innovative, non-poetic project of distinguishing factual truth from falsehood. T.P. Wiseman, focusing on Hellenistic and Roman historiography, identifies 'seven types of mendacity' in ancient historical writing, based on a combination of ancient comments on historical procedure and features which derive from ancient historiographical methods and modes of presentation. Like Moles, he stresses that the fusion of rhetorical and dramatic modes of exegesis with the distinctive historical project of truth-seeking enquiry makes it difficult to categorise ancient historiography in terms of either 'fact' or 'fiction'.

The relationship between historical and non-historical narrative is also a theme in the two chapters on the ancient novel. Andrew Laird, discussing Apuleius' *Metamorphoses*, suggests that fictional narratives, like factual ones, establish their claims to truth by constructing a 'story world' of ordinary experience. He illustrates this by showing how Apuleius' report of a magic metamorphosis is rendered at least half-credible as an account of the narrator's own 'bewitchment'. He suggests also that the 'bewitchment' of the psyche is one of the ways in which fiction was conceived in the ancient world. J.R. Morgan focuses on the paradox that the narrative modes (and implied reading practices) associated with the Greek novels imply an understanding of fiction which is nowhere fully articulated in ancient theory or criticism. He explains this paradox partly, like Gill, by a continuing cultural validation of communal truth rather than of private invention and pleasurable fantasy. But he also highlights the existence of ancient categories in which 'fiction' could be partly conceptualised; these include the historian's licence to expand the narrative by illustrative dialogue and incident, and the idea of rhetorical verisimilitude.

Morgan describes the characteristic narrative effect of the Greek novels as a combination of transparent, self-conscious artistry and realistic 'make-believe'. D.C. Feeney, in the Epilogue, also sees this duality, which both invites and limits the suspension of disbelief, as characteristic of ancient fiction—and indeed of fiction generally, as analysed by some contemporary theorists. So too Michael Wood, in the Prologue, sees the idea of fiction as a 'space of uncertainty' rather than a determinate category, and one which is as applicable to modern as to ancient thinking. In some other respects too, although our aim has been to chart the distinctive categories and dilemmas of the ancient thought-world, the overall effect may be, unexpectedly, to illuminate certain deep points of similarity with the contemporary thought-world, in which the distinction between fact and fiction has become such a problematic one.

The volume originated in a colloquium held at the University of Exeter in April 1991. Most of the chapters are revised versions of papers given there; Michael Wood and Andrew Laird, who also participated in the conference, wrote their contributions specifically for the book. The editors and contributors would like to thank all the participants in the colloquium for helping to generate a collaborative and constructive occasion, and for stimulating the publication of a volume which we hope will have the same qualities. Special thanks are due to Duncan Cloud, Michael Crawford, Richard Hunter, John Marincola, Louise Pratt, Victor Sage, Tony Woodman and Rosemary Wright. We should like also to acknowledge the financial assistance of the University of Exeter towards the costs of the conference; and to thank Juliette Hammond and Kerensa Pearson for typing the bibliography.

C.G.

T.P.W.

Notes on Contributors

E.L. BOWIE is E.P. Warren Praelector in Classics at Corpus Christi College, Oxford. He has written widely on early Greek lyric, elegiac and iambic poetry, and on Greek prose and poetry of the second and third centuries AD, including the Greek novel. He is preparing a commentary on Longus, *Daphnis and Chloe* for Cambridge University Press.

D.C. FEENEY is Associate Professor of Classics at the University of Wisconsin-Madison. He is author of *The Gods in Epic: Poets and Critics of the Classical Tradition* (Oxford, 1991), and has published articles on Latin poetry and on the Greek and Latin epic tradition.

CHRISTOPHER GILL is Senior Lecturer in Classics at the University of Exeter. He has written widely on Greek philosophy and litera-ture; publications include *Plato: the Atlantis Story*, with commen-tary (Bristol, 1980), a translation of Longus, *Daphnis and Chloe*, in *Collected Ancient Greek Novels*, ed. B.P. Reardon (Berkeley, 1989), and *The Person and the Human Mind: Issues in Ancient and Modern Philosophy*, ed. (Oxford, 1990).

J.R. MORGAN is Lecturer in Classics at the University College of Swansea. He has published a number of articles on ancient fiction, and translated Heliodorus' *Ethiopian Story* for *Collected Ancient Greek Novels*, ed. B.P. Reardon (Berkeley, 1989). Current projects include a commentary on the last two books of Heliodorus' novel, for Oxford University Press; an edition of Longus, *Daphnis and Chloe*, with translation and commentary, for Aris and Phillips; and a collection of essays on Greek fiction, co-edited with Richard Stoneman for Routledge.

ANDREW LAIRD is Lecturer in Classics at the University of Newcastle upon Tyne. His doctoral thesis is on the presentation of speeches in Latin literature, and he has published on the Roman novel and on *ekphrasis* in Classical literature.

J.L. MOLES is Lecturer in Classics at the University of Durham. He has written widely on ancient historiography, literature and philosophy; his publications include *Plutarch: Cicero*, with translation and commentary (Warminster, 1988).

T.P. WISEMAN is Professor of Classics at the University of Exeter. His books include *New Men in the Roman Senate* (Oxford, 1971), *Clio's Cosmetics* (Leicester, 1979), *Catullus and his World* (Cambridge, 1985), *Roman Studies* (Liverpool, 1987), and *Talking to Virgil* (Exeter, 1992).

MICHAEL WOOD is Professor of English Literature at the University of Exeter. His publications include *America in the Movies* (New York, 1989), *Garcia Marquez: One Hundred Years of Solitude* (New York, 1990), and the chapter on literary criticism (1910–40) in the *Columbia Literary History of the United States* (New York, 1990).

Prologue

Michael Wood

W E are accustomed to believing that fiction can tell both
truths and untruths, or that it may have nothing much to
do with either; but this curious and complicated notion is
unknown in many cultures and remains riddling and precarious even
where it is known, a mystery in its very familiarity. Poets have a
(highly visible) stake in the notion, but so do historians and
philosophers and scientists. So indeed does anyone who wishes to
distinguish literal truths from others, and to entertain both kinds.
The idea of fiction, true, false or free-falling, is intimately bound up
with figures of discourse such as metaphor and irony, and with
speculation and hypothesis, all the optative worlds of *what if*
and *as if*.

One of the consequences of this range of possibilities, this entang-
lement of fiction and truth, is that history, even of the most reliable
kind, can be seen to contain elements of fiction, while novels, ostensibly liberated into a world of literary invention, may serve as (often
minutely accurate) historical documents. Another consequence is
that the very chance of such crossovers becomes a philosophical
question, nimbly juggled with in *As You Like It*, where the
argument that 'the truest poetry is the most feigning' is part of a
seduction routine,[1] and brilliantly framed in Cervantes' complicated
jokes, in *Don Quixote*, about the variable truthfulness of lies.

The word 'fiction' is old, but not that old. It appears in English in
the late fourteenth century, a little earlier in French. Caxton in 1483

---

1. W. Shakespeare, *As You Like It*, Act 3, Scene 3, New Temple Shakespeare
(London, 1934), 49.

uses 'fyction and fayning' together, perhaps thinking of their common Latin root. Classical writers seem to have had no term that maps exactly on to our 'fiction', although they were acutely concerned with the question of truthful and untruthful lies. The title of this volume therefore names a double perspective: one that is recognizable within Greek and Roman culture and one that belongs to a much later moment of the European mind. The volume is concerned with the meeting, and occasionally the conflict, between these two perspectives.

Taken together, these essays aim to trace the extent and intensity of the ancient world's interest in these matters. The book has, I think, three main threads, which we might characterize as logical, epistemological and moral. The logical question concerns discursive oppositions in theory and practice: what sort of utterance or text is to be called fact or fiction, truth or lies, literal or figurative, and when and how these distinctions are to be made. The epistemological question takes the previous query as the identification of a space of uncertainty, a troubled or disputed site, an opportunity or an anxiety. Culturally licensed lies may be delightful, but do they also help to undermine knowledge, to take away the very ground of knowing? The moral question asks what is at stake when such delights and uncertainties are incurred, whether by poets or historians; what happens to persons and to cultures when issues of truth and falsehood are raised, resolved, left unresolved, found unresolvable? The modern term 'fiction' might in such a context seem not so much anachronistic as too comfortable, too secure in its confidence about what it is not, too sure of what the implied facts are.

A passage that recurs so often in this book that it amounts to a sort of *leitmotif* is the statement by Hesiod's Muses, in the *Theogony*, that 'we know how to tell many falsehoods that seem real: but we also know how to speak truth when we wish to' (27–8). Are they saying that they understand the nature of fiction or that they are skilful deceivers? And what do they mean by 'when we wish to'? Are they teasing Hesiod or is he teasing us? I do not need to add to the very good commentary these lines already receive here, but I do want to say that the muse of modern fiction, if there were one and if she could speak, would certainly make much the same declaration. She would mean, however, different things at different times: enigmatic in each case, but embracing different enigmas.

If she were the muse of Cervantes or Fielding, she would be

saying that both art and life are littered with fictions, that literary fictions mock and correct the other kind, and that reading novels may prepare us for reading the plausible snares of the world and history. If she were the muse of Balzac or Flaubert, she would be saying that the road to truth is through the very falsehoods she simulates so well, that for the attentive realist, as Flaubert said, everything one invents is true: the imaginary Madame Bovary weeps in a thousand real villages in France. If the muse were Proust's or Calvino's or Kundera's, she would be saying that realism is possible and has been hugely influential, but one can also tell the truth in fiction by other means, by understanding one's own metaphors, for example, or those of one's culture: even outright fables may be true once we have grasped their figurative significance. Is it only a historical irony that the most recent implication seems closest to the most ancient, the one in circulation long before the birth of anything resembling a novel?

All of the essays in the volume take up all three of the threads I have mentioned, at least implicitly, but particular threads are particularly visible in some places. The logical thread is dominant in the essays by E.L. Bowie, Christopher Gill and T.P. Wiseman, although the moral thread is also strong in Gill. Bowie finds an (unnamed) idea of fiction clearly in place in Hellenistic Greek writing, but suggests there are intimations of it much earlier; that Hesiod's Muses, for example, may be talking about types of poetry as well as about truth and falsehood. Gill argues that while most of the relevant modern discriminations are made in Plato, the distinction between fact and fiction is not; that what we call fiction is still governed in Plato by criteria of truthfulness, and has no equivalent of its modern autonomy. Wiseman identifies seven types of historical untruth, or rather seven characteristic arguments about how it arises—showing that Roman writers already knew that playfulness and theory, as Roland Barthes suggests in another context, are not always incompatible.[2] Seneca's ironic assumption that historians are all liars is a response, presumably, not only to their economies or extravagances with the truth but to their very assertions of truthfulness, their claim to be writing history at all.[3]

---

2. See *Roland Barthes par Roland Barthes* (Paris, 1975), 94.

3. *Quaestiones Naturales* 7.16.1f, noted by T.P. Wiseman in the first sentence of ch. 4 below.

The epistemological thread comes to the fore in the essays by J.L. Moles, Andrew Laird and J.R. Morgan, although the moral thread again lurks everywhere, and is explicitly theorized by Morgan. Moles looks at the literary and rhetorical manoeuvres of ancient historians, and the relation of these strategies to the various truth-claims being made. What emerges is a complex array of techniques and assumptions, a set of textual performances not easily to be classified in any ready-made box, even a box with the capacious name of 'literature' or 'history'. Laird explores the ambivalences of *The Golden Ass* about the reality of what it portrays, demonstrating that the text places itself on a border of uncertainty, posing a particular problematic of what we call 'fiction'. Morgan argues that the appeal of the ancient Greek novel rests on precisely the epistemological doubleness that so many later novels exploit: we believe what we know to be fabricated, behave as if truth were in question when we know it is not. D.C. Feeney's *Epilogue* picks up and takes much further the issues I am sketching here.

But how many meanings of 'fiction' are in play in this book? And how many meanings of 'lying'?

The second question is easier to answer, since the opposition between truth and falsehood seems quite straightforward and remarkably constant from culture to culture. There is, of course, plenty of argument everywhere about what is true or false, but there is also, wherever the terms are accepted as usable, considerable agreement about what they mean. Lies are whatever is not true, although we can classify them in a number of ways. We may wish to approve of certain forms of lie, and probably need to distinguish between intentional and unintentional untruths, between deception and ignorance or misinformation.

The first question, however, generates a flurry of quite different answers. Fiction is pure invention, any sort of fabrication. It is invention which knows it is invention; or which knows *and says* it is invention; or which, whatever it knows and says, *is known* to be invention. It is permissible or noble lying, licensed under quite specific cultural circumstances, and displays (sometimes) the linguistic or textual marks of its licence. It is not lying at all, but exempt from all notions of truth and falsehood, licensed in quite a different way. It is a form of double-think, a game of truth in which we pretend to forget that lies are lies; or in which the ordinary rules of truth and falsehood are both simulated and suspended. It is artistry, evidence of a design to please. It is interpretation, the sign of a shaping mind, present in all writing, historical and literary. It is hypothesis, neither lie nor fable but a narrative of things we cannot possibly (yet) know.

We do not need to resolve these meanings, and could not anyway. They are themselves part of the history and the continuing life of fiction, and of the world it inhabits. J.L. Austin speaks of the 'innumerable and unforeseeable demands of the world upon language',[4] and fiction, the word and the practice, is one of the ways in which we negotiate those demands. What does emerge from so rich a discussion is that the ambiguity and complexity of our thoughts on fiction are no accident. Western culture, ancient and modern, has urgently needed, alongside its capacity to distinguish truth from lies, a ground where such matters could not quickly be settled either way—where the issue was not suspended (on the contrary: promiscuously courted) but not laid to rest either.

The larger question, therefore, to which the essays in this volume offer such interesting and varied answers, is not only what truth and lies were in the ancient world, but what it can mean for a culture to be able to interrogate, to shift and mask, the boundaries of what it takes to be the truth. This would be to ask, in Michel Foucault's terms, about the 'conditions of possibility' of such concerns, but it would also be to alter Foucault's question. Foucault's 'archaeology' involves discovering 'the configurations which have given rise to the various forms of empirical knowledge'.[5] The consistently implied question here is what social structures, what patterns of consciousness and behaviour, are involved in the very possibility of *these* questions about truth and falsehood? It is like deducing from a joke not a meaning or a motive but a state of cultural play, or the nature of a social order. We ask: not what are the configurations or how do they appear, but what does it take for them to function, what world of assumptions do they require for their working?

It is possible that Austin's rather unlikely notion of 'unhappiness' may help us here. For Austin, when a performative occasion goes wrong in any way the utterance is 'not . . . false but in general unhappy': 'And for this reason we call the doctrine of *the things that*

---

4. J.L. Austin, *Sense and Sensibilia* (Oxford, 1964), 73.
5. M. Foucault, *Les mots et les choses* (Paris, 1966), 13.

can be and go wrong on the occasion of such utterances, the doctrine of the *Infelicities*.[6] Possible infelicities, Austin says, would be utterances made by someone who was 'joking' or 'writing a poem'.

> ... a performative utterance will, for example, be in a peculiar way hollow or void if said by an actor on the stage, or if introduced in a poem, or spoken in soliloquy. This applies in a similar manner to any and every utterance—a sea-change in special circumstances. Language in such circumstances is in special ways—intelligibly—used not seriously, but in ways *parasitic* upon its normal use—ways which fall under the doctrine of the *etiolations* of language.[7]

All but the most hard-headed philosophers and theorists have always been bothered by this famous passage. To call literature an etiolation of language seems even worse than calling it an infelicity, however particular and pragmatic the point of view may be in context. But Austin can be seen as back-handedly sketching a region where a cultural theory of fiction might develop.

The essays in this volume suggest, I think, that the interrogation of truthful and untruthful lies, the testing of non-literal ways of representing and misrepresenting knowledge, may be among the deepest and most necessary habits of a culture. Austin's 'special circumstances' and 'special ways' would, indeed, be different from what he calls 'normal use', but they would also cause us to redefine our notion of the normal. They themselves would be a crucial feature of normality, one of the ways in which (some) cultures go about their business. Fiction would not be a hindrance to doctrine but a major element in the expansion of it; not an etiolation of language but an aspect of what Wittgenstein would call the grammar of truth. This book offers a precise and copious exploration of the life of this grammar in the ancient world.

---

6. J.L. Austin, *How To Do Things With Words* (Oxford, 1965), 14.
7. Ibid., 22.

Chapter One

Lies, Fiction and Slander in Early Greek Poetry

E.L. BOWIE

I

OST first-order discourse is sent out into the world with
some presumption that statements and wishes are true and
that commands are a true reflection of wishes. A system
of verbal communication in which this was not so would soon break
down—as indeed would a non-verbal system of communication in
which signs could not be interpreted as, in most cases, true indi-
cators of assertions, wishes or commands. If I were to utter such
sentences as 'The tonic has run out', or 'I would like another gin',
or 'Please put in some more ice', in such a random way that there
was no way of my addressee knowing how she was expected to
react, I would rapidly exclude myself from the world of articulately-
speaking bread-eating and, indeed, gin-drinking mortals.

Of course, once this presumption is there, it can be exploited for
various purposes. On April 1st, statements are regularly made which
turn out to be false. The fact that there is a rule or expectation
concerning statements made on April 1st can help someone who
hears such a statement to assign an appropriate truth value to it.
More seriously, in certain societies, being systematically economical
with the truth and occasionally liberal with falsehood is a deliberate
and persistent strategy for ensuring that an individual or group
secure more than their due share of resources and respect. For
instance, within ancient society, this strategy has been detected by

I

Jack Winkler in Longus' portrayal of the world of the herdsmen in *Daphnis and Chloe*.[1]

In a society where the presumption of veracity is frequently abused for serious ends, special markers are required to reinstate it: hence such practices as oaths and self-imprecations. I take an example from a text to which I shall return for another purpose, the false tales of Odysseus after his return to Ithaca in *Odyssey* (*Od.*) 13, 14 and 19. At *Od.* 14.151 Odysseus, still incognito, assures Eumaeus that Odysseus will return

> but I shall tell you not just so, but with an oath

and he goes on to deprecate the teller of lies in words which impudently recall those of Achilles in *Iliad* (*Il.*) 9.312 where the covert target of the remark was Odysseus himself:

> for that man is as hateful to me as Hades' gates
> who yields to his poverty and utters words of deceit

Odysseus then gives a long account (167 lines) of his Cretan origins and his knowledge of Odysseus (*Od.* 14.192–359) beginning with the emphatic but trite claim to veracity

> therefore shall I tell you all this with great exactness.

But after this tale Odysseus again raises the stakes. If an oath does not persuade Eumaeus, what about a bargain (*rhētrē*) which can be sanctioned by the gods? If he tells the truth, he is to get clothes and safe passage to Doulichion; if Eumaeus' master does not come, Eumaeus may set his slaves on the lying beggar and hurl him over a cliff *pour encourager les autres* (*Od.* 14.391–400). Of course, Odysseus knows that he will win the wager, so his skin is safe; but he knows too that Eumaeus will not be called upon to honour his side of the bargain. The poet is playing with the irony that the consummate liar builds his claim to truth on something that *is* true, one of the few facts in a string of falsehoods.

---

1. J.J. Winkler, 'The Education of Chloe: Hidden Injuries of Sex' in *The Constraints of Desire* (New York, 1990), 101–146, at 107–111, 'The Constrained Life'.

Just as early Greek society had markers to emphasize that something said was true, so it had markers of a category of utterance different from normal, first-order utterance, utterance for which truth was either not being claimed at all or was not being claimed in the same way. In modern British society, there are many story-telling patterns used for telling jokes ('There was an Englishman, and Irishman and a Scotsman', etc.) which mark them as different from narratives of events which really happened.[2] There are also contexts in which an anecdote is not expected to be wholly or even largely true—when, for example, a preacher in a church begins 'I met a man on my way to the service today . . .'. In early Greek society there was at least one pattern which surely marked a story as making no claim to literal truth, namely the *ainos* or animal fable from which morals about man's conduct might be drawn. Our earliest examples are Hesiod, *Works and Days* 180ff. and Archilochus fr. 172ff. These are poetic genres; but the later 'Aesopic' development of the animal fable and Aristophanes' evidence for its telling in prose in a sympotic context (*Wasps* 1122ff.) can leave little doubt that such fables might be told orally and in prose and were not confined to verse genres. To some extent, then, 'I shall tell you an *ainos*' must have carried with it the same sort of caution as the modern British examples just cited.

But modern society also has a clearly identified and widely familiar category of 'literary fiction'. We are brought up to expect some written texts to fall into this category and we learn to look for the markers that signal it—though, as in real life, once there is a system, it invites subversion. How and when did this category develop? It seems to be widely agreed that it is recognized in the Greek world by the Hellenistic period, or perhaps even by the time Agathon composed the first attested dramatic work with an invented plot and an invented set of characters (the *Antheus*).[3] Have we any evidence that Greeks of the archaic period recognized something that stood between 'telling the truth' and 'lying', and, if they did, to what extent was that co-extensive with our developed concept 'fiction'?

---

2. For a less superficial discussion of the importance of context, see P. Bourdieu, *Esquisse d' une théorie de pratique* (Geneva, 1972), 244–5 with n. 6.

3. For the *Antheus* (or *Anthos*) see Aristotle, *Poetics* 1451b21–2.

One feature of archaic Greek literature that must be of great relevance is that all that has been preserved until well into the sixth century was composed in verse. Moreover—something that is in danger of being obscured by the fact that our almost invariable medium is the printed text—most was intended either to be sung to the accompaniment of music or to be delivered in some form of recitative. Even the one metrical form that may simply have been spoken, the iambic trimeter, must have sounded different from everyday discourse, while those sung and recited will have immediately advertised to their audiences that they were not to be identified with ordinary speech. In most genres, the difference will have been emphasized by their adoption of a different range of vocabulary or even of a dialect alien to the place of performance. In the case of some literary genres, a further signal that this was a different sort of utterance will have been given by the context of performance: the festivals, which were the context for some genres of choral lyric and (less integrally) for hexameter epic, the symposium which was the nursery of elegiac song and much lyric monody.

The quality of claims to truth, if any, of utterances in archaic poetic genres might a priori be expected to vary from one genre to another. In the following discussion I examine the presumptions apparently associated with the various archaic genres, working both from what we can know or conjecture about the role of that genre in society and from such evidence as I can discover within the texts themselves. I begin with a number of genres where it seems that, despite the difference in mode and context of utterance, the same sort of expectation of veracity obtains. I then consider some where, to my mind, there is a stronger presumption that the utterance makes no claim to truth. Only then do I turn to the most problematic cases.

II

1. *Oracles.* The case of oracles makes it clear that casting a prediction into hexameter verse might strengthen rather than diminish the expectation that an utterance of that form claimed to be true. Oracles from Delphi, Dodona or Didyma were treated by most Greeks as predicting what would happen, even if they were enveloped in an

ambiguity that made it hard to work out what that prediction actually was. They might, of course, be thought to be only of marginal relevance to the more central type of hexameter verse performance. Their claim to truth derives from the divine authority which guided or inspired priestesses or priests, not from the verse form into which they were cast by other officials of the oracles. The choice of the hexameter may have been partly due to the authoritative profile it had acquired in the hands of bards and, later, rhapsodes; but it would be unwise to attempt to argue that its choice also demonstrated an established expectation of veracity.

2. *Epitaphs and dedications.*   One other factor that may indeed have contributed to the choice of hexameters for oracles is the more mundane one that in the early archaic period it seems to have been treated as an all-purpose verse form, a role later assumed by the elegiac couplet. Among early inscribed texts, whether sepulchral or dedicatory, hexameters are used first and then outnumber elegiac couplets until the late sixth century. When both are in use there seem to be no general principles governing the choice of the one rather than the other, and, in all cases of 'real' epigrams, truthful communication of facts and evaluations is manifestly presumed. This presumption of truth is only overturned when, in the late sixth or early fifth century, 'literary' epigrams begin to appear, look-alikes which have the outward appearance of 'real' epigrams but which some further feature or circumstance demonstrates to be, as it were, imposters. A certain example of a 'real' epigram is that composed by Simonides for his friend the seer Megistias who died at Thermopylae.[4]

> Here famed Megistias is laid, whom once the Mede
> slew at the crossing of Spercheius' flood:
> this prophet clearly saw the Fates' attacking wings
> but did not stoop to leave the Spartan kings.

---

4. Herodotus 7.228.3 = D.L. Page, *Further Greek Epigrams* (*FGE*) (Cambridge, 1981), 'Simonides' 6.

An equally certain 'literary' epigram was also, improbably, ascribed to Simonides, a satirical couplet on the poet Timocreon:[5]

Much I drank, and much I ate, and much my fellow men
abused: now dead, Timocreon of Rhodes, I lie.

As Page (*ad loc.*) conjectures, this pseudo-epigram was presumably first sung at a symposium as the type of drinking song known as a *skolion*, and in that context there would be no doubt that it was an abusive exploitation of the epigram form: only on a written or printed page, torn from context, does its reader have to resort to its content to establish its real status. The formal similarity of types of utterance whose presumptions of truth are quite different is something that will recur.

3. *Narrative elegy.* By this I mean the class of long elegiac poems like Tyrtaeus' *Good Order* (*Eunomia*), Mimnermus' *Song of Smyrna* (*Smyrnēis*), Semonides' *Early Years of Samos* (*Archaiologia tōn Samiōn*), Xenophanes' poem *The Foundation of Colophon and Migration to Elea*, and perhaps the poem of Simonides on Plataea of which papyrus scraps have recently turned up and are now published by Peter Parsons in *Oxyrhynchus Papyri*.[6] I have discussed the evidence for this class of poem elsewhere and argued[7] that they dealt both with early 'mythical' events and more recent political and military history. Much of this later material will have fallen within the memory span of individuals in the audience and will therefore have invited the test of truth or falsehood. Recent events allowed new approaches. Witnesses could be called—this seems to happen in a fragment probably but not certainly from the *Song of Smyrna*:

---

5. Athenaeus 10.415F = *FGE*, 'Simonides' 37.
6. *P.Oxy.* 3965: it is also included in the second edition of M.L. West, *Iambi et Elegi Graeci* (*IEG*) vol. 2 (Oxford, 1992), frr. 10–17. The other poems are *IEG*, Tyrtaeus 1–4, Mimnermus 13, 13a and perhaps 9 and 14. For Semonides, see the Suda 4.363.1; for Xenophanes, see Diogenes Laertius 9.18.
7. 'Early Greek Elegy, Symposium and Public Festival', *Journal of Hellenic Studies* (*JHS*) 106 (1986), 13–35 ('Elegy'), at 27–34.

Not such do I learn him to have been from those forebears who
saw him routing the close-packed squadrons of Lydian cavalry
in the plain of the Hermos.

Mimnermus 14.2–4 West (W)

For such material, a precise time-scale can be indicated: it was the
grandfathers of Tyrtaeus' generation—*aichmētai paterōn hēmeterōn
pateres*—who fought for Messenia for 19 years, and in the 20th the
Messenians fled to Ithome (Tyrtaeus 5.6–8W).

On the other hand, the early material must have been drawn from
traditions which circulated without any such control or precision,
and will have depended upon what has been termed the *mémoire
collective*. They will have been in some ways comparable to the
stories developed in the *Iliad* and *Odyssey*. It is not surprising,
therefore, that features of heroic epic are discernible: an invocation
to the Muses by Mimermus (13W) very probably comes from the
Smyrnēis, and evidence for speeches certainly does (13aW). Unfortunately, our fragments do not reveal the extent or nature of divine
apparatus. The only involvement of gods in what survives is the
consultation of the Delphic oracle by the Spartan kings Theopompus
and Polydorus (Tyrtaeus 4W). This could stand in any historian and
cannot be a basis for inference about the intervention of gods of the
sort found in epic. Overall, on the available evidence, these poems
purveyed narratives which could reasonably claim to be a true
account of recent history but which could not be subject to the same
sort of checks in their presentation of the distant past. However, the
foundation and early history of cities were subjects where the collective memory may have known a generally accepted and authorised
version, and there are likely to have been stricter limits on the poets'
freedom than applied in Homeric epic or Attic tragedy. Even when
dealing with the early period, then, the poet may never have had
reason to see himself as inventing what he sang.

4. *Narrative in trochaic tetrameters and iambic trimeters.* A related
genre involved long political or military narrative in trochaic
tetrameters. Two large epigraphic texts from Paros, supplemented by
papyri and a few quotations, preserve the remains of long sections
of such tetrameters by Archilochus (88–104W, 105–113W). Most
indications suggest an account of recent events that purports to be
factual. Contemporary individuals are named (Peisistratus' son,

7

93a.4W) and even addressed, whether actually as addressees of the poem (Erxies 88W, cf. 89.28W; Glaucus 105W) or perhaps by apostrophe (again Glaucus, 96.1W).[8] The poet describes his own role in the battle and may credit his escape to Hermes (95.4–5W).[9] Other gods are also described, in Homeric terms, as playing a part in the action: Athena encourages (94.1–2W, 98.7–8W?); Zeus acts and resorts to his scales (98.13W, 91.30W); less specific Olympian involvement is invoked (94.6W, 96.1W).

Something similar is found in the iambic trimeters and trochaic tetrameters of Solon (32–40W). Here too, there is narrative of recent events, but it is focused wholly upon Solon's own political actions. Clearly, this narrative purports to narrate the truth, not lies or fiction, and Solon even calls Earth as witness to its truth (36.3–7W). Solon would be an unusual politician if it were wholly true; but it is clearly a version that he thought could be represented and defended as the truth. Most deviations from truth in this genre are to be treated as lies rather than any sort of fiction.

Of the sorts of poetry just reviewed it is most probable that the long narrative elegies were intended for a formal public occasion rather than for a small, informal symposium.[10] I suspect that this was also the case with iambic and tetrameter narratives, but I know of no evidence to determine their intended context of performance.

5. *Hexameter narrative epic.* With hexameter narrative epic about kings and heroes, we move into a much more contentious area. The context of performance is again likely to be formal and public; but the relation of the audience to the material is different, perhaps very different, from that where the subject is the early history of their own city. The singer of the *Iliad*, the *Odyssey* and of other poems in the Trojan and Theban cycles is indeed handling 'traditional' material, but we must imagine a much more complex tradition. The audience envisaged seems to be drawn not from one city or even from one Greek linguistic group but from cities both Ionian and

---

8. Conceivably, 96W comes from a poem addressed to Glaucus, like 105W and perhaps 131W; but its place in the Sosthenes inscription rather suggests it comes from the poem addressed to Erxies.

9. If Zieliński's conjecture (for which see West's apparatus) is correct.

10. See my argument in 'Elegy', 33–4.

Aeolian. Although individual characters in the poems may have links with the early history of some of these cities, the links will almost always have been through a few families who claimed to be their descendants. The limitations set upon a singer by the collective memory of one city will be much less constricting than in those set upon composition of a foundation poem for that city; and they may actually be in conflict with the collective memory of another city where he may perform or whose citizens may be present at a festival performance. A poet of hexameter narrative epic will thus have had greater opportunity for changing, by variation, supplementation or deletion, a story he had heard from another.[11]

It is also clear, on two counts, that such changes took place. First, most students of the epic tradition argue, plausibly, that the Homeric poems stand at the end of a tradition to which several 'generations' of singers have contributed. Parry and Lord's observations of Serbo-Croat oral poetry have shown that, in this tradition at least, one singer cannot exactly reproduce a song he has heard from another, though he may well claim to do so. Transmission, therefore, necessarily involves change. Second, unless we adopt the easily refutable hypothesis that an *Iliad* and an *Odyssey* of just the form in which we have these poems suddenly came fully-fledged into being generations before they were committed to writing, and were then passed down orally without change, we must concede that the poems we have are the end-products of several stages of development.

What awareness did the Greek singers of hexameter narrative epic have of such change, and to what extent, if any, should we see the process involved as a stage in the development of 'fiction'? In what follows, I argue that such changes should indeed be seen as a form of 'fiction', and that there are indications in the poems that their composers were aware that they were inventing significant portions of what they sang.

Of course, the principal and striking impression given by the poets is that their narratives are simply narratives of facts which have been communicated to them by the Muse or Muses. The poet does not

---

11. For a discussion of the ways in which the Kirghiz *akyn* adapts his narrative to his audiences and a convincing argument that Homer and bards presented within his poems do likewise, see J. Svenbro, *La parole et le marbre* (*Parole*) (Lund, 1976), 11–29.

appeal to any witnesses other than the Muses as sources or as corroboration of his story. The knowledge of the singer and of his Muse is coextensive. Although the Muse may be appealed to for special assistance at points where bravura performance impends, as before the Catalogue in *Iliad* 2, the Muse is never represented as supplementing or correcting the singer's tale. This goes hand in hand with the fact that the singer adopts the posture of omniscient narrator. There is no hint of those moves that we find much later, in Callimachus or in the novelists, to range the poet alongside historians and, in doing so, to confess ignorance about certain topics or to offer alternative explanations for some of the alleged events. It is a further corollary that there exists only the version that the singer is now telling. There is no hint that there might be or might once have been other versions, far less any attempt to suggest that *this* version is superior or 'right', while other versions are inferior or 'wrong'. In making this assertion, I am well aware that there are many elements in our Homeric poems, especially the *Odyssey*, which have been argued to be vestiges of different versions of the story. But we have no clear case where, in using such a story for his own purposes, the singer is demonstrably alluding to an earlier version and or insinuating that *his* use of the material is better.

There remain, however, some quite important limits to the poet's autonomy. The world in which his tales are set is one like that of his audience, a Mediterranean world of human beings who speak Greek, most of whom are Greek by descent, and who worship anthropomorphic gods. The few cases in the *Iliad*, and the larger number in the *Odyssey* and the epic Cycle, where the patterns of the real world are abandoned show us that these limits were, to some extent, moveable and that the setting of these limits to some degree reflects the singer's *choice*. But the fact that the world chosen by Homeric poetry as a setting is not a fantastic invention (like science-fiction) but a version of the real world meant that there was a whole range of items in that world of which critics could later say 'It's not like that' and 'Homer gets this wrong'.

One particular constituent that led, and still leads, to problems in gauging the truth-value of the songs was the presence, and in some cases the central role, of heroes who were regarded as, in some sense, historical forebears of some Greeks of the eighth and seventh centuries BC. The consequences are much the same, whether we are dealing with a character who has a fixed place in the collective memory and was then drafted into a role in Homeric epic, or a character who was once the creation of a singer but was then given a role in 'history'. In either case, it becomes meaningful for a member of the audience to say 'Agamemnon never did that' or 'Theseus was not at Troy'.

But there is no sign within the *Iliad*, and only ambiguous evidence within the *Odyssey*, that their poet would have recognized such a criticism as meaningful, and neither the presence of elements of 'the real world' nor that of semi-historical heroes counts against a categorization of the epics as 'fictional', or against the possibility that their poets were aware that they were inventing some of their narrative.

That this *was* their view, or that we should categorize parts of Homeric epic as 'fiction', is not, as far as I know, a thesis that has been argued. Indeed, a quite different position is taken by Wolfgang Rösler in his article 'Die Entdeckung der Fiktionalität', the most recent treatment of the issue known to me.[12] Moving from the implicit assumption of early critics of poetry, Heraclitus and Xenophanes, that poetry should tell the truth, Rösler argues that this is also the conception of early poets themselves, and that, indeed, any other conception is improbable in an oral culture where the role of poetry is primarily to transmit traditions needed to give a social group identity and stability. As custodians of *la mémoire collective* poets are necessarily *maîtres de verité*; they do not invent their *klea andrōn* ('glorious deeds of warriors') but merely give artistic form to predetermined content. In the case of archaic Greek epic, the access to truth was ascribed to divine inspiration by the Muses, and the claim to this inspiration was inseparable from the claim to truth.[13] Only with the advent of writing did this position gradually collapse and the possibility of fictionality arise.

There are several difficulties in this thesis, some of which I shall consider as I follow through the case-studies that Rösler offers to corroborate his argument. But I want to make one preliminary point

---

12. W. Rösler, 'Die Entdeckung der Fiktionalität', *Poetica* 12 (1980), 283–319.

13. Rösler, 285–92; see also M. Detienne, *The Creation of Mythology*, tr. M. Cook (Chicago, 1986), 22ff. A further version of this position is given by C. Gill, pp. 70–2 below, including reference to the present chapter.

about the supposed 'orality' of the epics. Although the *Iliad* and the *Odyssey* may stand nearest, within extant Greek literature, to a purely oral culture, the use of writing had already reached Greece by the mid-eighth century, as Rösler recognizes; and many scholars take the view that these epics could not have their present form and scale if their composition had not been aided by writing. Although the extent and manner of writing's effect on the poems is and will always be debatable, it is incontestable that the actual poems we have would not have survived if they had not moved into a written form at some date. It is, therefore, unwise to impose upon them schemata derived from work on purely oral cultures.

Rösler's first case-study examines the Homeric presentation of the relation of poetry to truth. He sees the presentation of the Muses by the poet or, in the *Odyssey*, by bards, as matching the picture derived from oral cultures: the poet is the mouthpiece of divine knowledge, his themes are the deeds of ancestors, his role is to hand on their *klea*. In doing so, no distinction is drawn between instruction and pleasure. The poet's claim to truth is not limited to historical events but is universal. This interpretation gives maximal value to the poet's overt claims, and I am not alone in wanting to see something less straightforward behind them.[14]

The opening lines of each poem simply request the Muse to sing or tell the poem of the theme: 'Sing, goddess, of the wrath . . .' (*mēnin aeide theā*) and 'Tell me, Muse, of a man of many turns . . .' (*andra moi ennepe Mousa polutropon*). By the time of the composition of these openings, the invocation was clearly conventional, and what the convention signified at that time cannot be deduced from these instances. Thus, although the *Iliad*'s invocation is followed up by a question that is most easily interpreted as addressed to the Muse ('Who, then, of the gods threw these two together to contend in strife?', line 8), the Muse is not again mentioned until the special case of the Catalogue (see below). It is only on one possible understanding of her initial invocation that she is thought of as supplying the totality of the poem that follows, both content and form.

---

14. Svenbro, for example (*Parole*, 29–35), argued that appeals to the Muse are in some way a response of the bard to his sense that his material may not please his audience. Such special appeals as that before the Catalogue in *Iliad* 2 show his awareness that this is a particularly delicate form of 'symbolisation sociale'.

Nor is the idea that the Muse symbolises the community's *mémoire collective*, drawn upon by the poet, supported by the content of the poem. It is not easy to construe the wrath of Achilles or the return of Odysseus as exploits of ancestors of the Ionians and Aeolians of the Eastern (or even Western) Aegean, or of the Aegean coast of Asia Minor, who are the prime candidates for the first audiences of the poems. It is perhaps easier to see Homeric poetry as a crucial bearer of *religious* traditions, as implicitly recognized by Herodotus (2.53.2) when he credited Homer and Hesiod with equipping the Greek pantheon with its traditional roles. But here too there are problems, already a principal cause of criticism of Homer in antiquity, in such scenes as the adulterous union of Ares and Aphrodite. I am not readily persuaded by Rösler's conclusion (p. 293) that the fact that they are 'traditional' *made* these stories true.

The ascription of full knowledge to the Muses who are the source of divine inspiration can indeed be found in the invocation which precedes the Catalogue of Ships.

> Tell me now, Muses that have your home on Olympus—
> for you are goddesses, and are present, and know all things
> but we hear only what is told, and do not know anything—
> who were the leaders of the Danaans and their rulers.
> But the multitude I could not tell, nor could I name,
> Not even were I to have ten tongues, and ten mouths,
> were I to have a voice that did not break, and a heart of bronze,
> unless the Olympian Muses, Zeus the Aegis-bearer's
> daughters, were to call to my mind all who came to Ilion.
>
> (*Il.* 2.484–92)

But should this be taken as applicable to the whole content of both *Iliad* and *Odyssey*? The catalogue is a representative of a different sort of poetry from the rest of the *Iliad*, whether or not it was conceived in its present shape for the place where it now stands, and the special invocation here seems in some way to be related to the special demands of creating and performing such poetry. It could be argued that the poet of the *Iliad* is here alluding to the conventions of oral catalogue poetry, without implying that his whole poem is in the same way derived from the Muses or that this origin guarantees its truth. I am also reluctant to follow Rösler's conclusion from the phrase, 'and you know all things', that the poet's, and Muses', claim to truth is not limited to historical events but is universal. Taken in context, the phrase need do no more than ascribe total knowledge of *this* subject, i.e. the details of the expedition to Troy.

The opening of the *Iliad*, then, does not establish unambiguously that the whole poem is to be taken as a creation not of the poet but of the Muses. The invocation before the Catalogue may make that claim only for the Catalogue itself—a claim that, of course, suggests that the rest of the poem does not depend in the same way upon knowledge imparted by the Muses.

The opening of the *Odyssey* is no more revealing, in this respect, than that of the *Iliad*. Within the poem, however, there are well-known passages where the bards Demodocus and Phemius claim, or are claimed to have, divine inspiration and which may help us to assess the implications of such claims.[15]

First, I examine the sequence in Book 8 of the *Odyssey*. Alcinous orders a feast to entertain Odysseus, and adds:

> And call the divine singer
> Demodocus: for him above others has the god given song
> to give pleasure, in whatever way his heart prompts him to sing.
>
> (*Od.* 8.43–5)

The expressions 'given song' (*dōken aoidēn*) and 'his heart prompts' (*thūmos epotrūnēisin*) draw attention to the capacity to sing rather than to the truth of the song's content. Shortly, a herald brings on the singer

> whom the Muse loved above other men, and gave him good
>   and evil:
> of his sight she deprived him, but gave him sweet song.
>
> (*Od.* 8. 63–4)

Just as 8.45 had picked out the capacity to please, so here the epithet attached to song (*hēdeian*) focuses on pleasure, not knowledge. Of

---

15. Among useful discussion of these passages, see especially S. Goldhill, *The Poet's Voice* (Cambridge, 1991), 49–54.

course, both aspects can coexist, but what is important for this examination is that our poet does not choose to draw attention to any element of truth in the song or of knowledge in the singer. So again at 8.73

> the Muse moved the singer to sing of the glorious deeds of
> > warriors.

As at 45 the heart (*thūmos*) of the singer was said to move him, so here the Muse is said to do so. Of course, the content of the song must come to the singer by some route, but our poet does not draw attention to that here. Likewise, in guiding our response, he depicts the emotional effect of the song on its audience rather than expressing any admiration for the range or detail of his knowledge: Odysseus weeps (83–9), and the Phaeacians experience pleasure (91).

In singing his next song, the lay of Ares and Aphrodite, Demodocus is said simply to 'strike up on his lyre to sing fairly' (265). The Muses are not mentioned, perhaps because the poet of the *Odyssey* perceives this material as different from the rest of his own and of Demodocus' songs.

More emerges when Demodocus sings next. Odysseus asks the herald to take Demodocus a pork steak, in recognition of the honour and respect due to singers from all men, 'since the Muse has taught them ways (*oimas*) and has shown love to the clan of singers' (480–1). This done, Odysseus compliments Demodocus:

> Either a Muse taught you, daughter of Zeus, or Apollo:
> for it is very much as it should be that you sing the fate of
> > the Achaeans,
> all that they did and suffered, and all that the Achaeans toiled,
> as if indeed you were yourself there or had heard from another.
> > (*Od.* 8.488–91)

Odysseus then requests the tale of the Wooden Horse:

> If indeed you tell this tale aright (*kata moiran*)
> then forthwith shall I tell all men
> that the god has readily granted you divine song.
> > (8.496–8)

It would be perverse to deny that here Odysseus suggests that Demodocus has been instructed in the events of the Trojan war by a god, whether Apollo or a Muse. But, of course, in Demodocus' case, the suggestion that he could have heard this from somebody else is not absurd. Within our poet's story, the Phaeacians have contacts with the Greek world; for them, Odysseus is a real man, the Trojan war is a recent and real event. So either a god or a mortal *could* be the source of Demodocus' extraordinarily good knowledge. But that is clearly not what Odysseus wants to suggest. This passage, therefore, offers us more evidence than any other in the *Odyssey* to support the view that the Muse might be seen as the source of a singer's information. It also makes it clear that a significant part of the divine contribution is the poet's ability *to tell well* what he knows ('very much as it should be', *liēn gar kata kosmon*; 'aright', *kata moiran*).

I agree, therefore, that this passage draws upon the convention that the Muse furnishes the singer with knowledge of the details which go to make up his story, and that the context makes it clear that there is no question of these details being anything other than true. But it must be a matter for inference and not deduction that the poet of the *Odyssey* saw himself as standing in the same totally dependent relation to the Muse whom he invokes only in his first line.

The passage in *Odyssey* 8 also shows that the poet can conceive of a singer who sings of something that has not 'actually' happened. There may be an instance of this in *Odyssey* 1. 325–359. The singer Phemius, performing for the suitors in Odysseus' palace under duress, sings of the woeful return (*noston . . . lugron*, 1.326–7) of the Achaeans from Troy. This reduces Penelope to tears, but Telemachus defends Phemius on two accounts: men are more enthusiastic about whatever is the latest song, and it was not Odysseus alone who 'lost his day of return in Troy'. The second defence implies strongly that in Phemius' story Odysseus has perished, something that the suitors would like to hear but that the audience of the *Odyssey* knows to be false (1.11ff.). Phemius is not here represented as drawing on what we might class as *mémoire collective* nor as purveying a song that is true. It is hard not to conclude that the poet wants us to imagine that either Phemius or the singer from whom he got the song 'made up' the portion that killed off Odysseus. In context, of course, Phemius' fabrication amounts to 'lying', since his decision to give a version of events that will please the suitors has a function in the real world. But that is not its only function: Phemius is also creating a work which will entertain, and, viewed in terms of literary history, this example seems to take us some distance towards what we see as 'fiction'.

The final passage illustrating the *Odyssey*'s view of inspiration also conveys the notion that the human imput into a song can be as important as that from the Muses. At 22.347, supplicating Odysseus, Phemius says of his skill:

> I am self-taught, and the god has planted in my mind all
> kinds of paths.

The contradiction here is only apparent: Phemius claims to be self-taught and, by the process of 'dual motivation' found elsewhere in Homer, presents the Muse as the source of his songs. As Penelope Murray has pointed out in her excellent discussion of early Greek views of poetic inspiration,[16] the two ideas are complementary. We should probably not, like Lanata,[17] refer 'self-taught' (*autodidaktos*) only to technical aspects of composition and 'paths' (*oimās*) to subject matter. Both the Muse and his own skill are credited with form and content, and Phemius' claim is 'that he does not simply repeat songs he has learnt from other bards, but composes his songs himself'.[18]

The *Odyssey*'s presentation of songs sung by bards, therefore, seems to allow that some of them may be true accounts of 'historical' events whose composition may leave no room for the creation of subject-matter by the singer. Others, however, may be either false accounts, which necessarily involve the singer's invention, or songs to which the singer contributes a significant part. The comparative evidence of the Serbo-Croat oral tradition makes it tempting to reject immediately the notion that Homer thought of himself or the singers he represents as composing in the sense of inventing material. But, notoriously, the Serbo-Croat singers *were* found to be changing

---

16. P.A. Murray, 'Poetic Inspiration in Early Greece', *JHS* 101 (1981), 87–100 ('Poetic Inspiration'), at 97.

17. G. Lanata, *Poetica pre-platonica* (Florence, 1963) 13–14.

18. Murray 'Poetic Inspiration', 97.

the content of songs while claiming to pass them on unchanged, so the actual phenomenon of invention is paralleled.

It can be objected, of course,[19] that at later stages in an oral tradition a singer may simply be selecting from accumulated variants, and that we can never establish that our 'Homer' is the creator of any one deviation from the tradition that came down to him. I shall not here join those scholars who have thought that they could attribute certain constituents to the last singer in the tradition, though in principle I am happy to do so and to call the last singer 'Homer'. But it does not affect my position that no variant can be demonstrated to have been introduced at this last stage. All that I wish to maintain is that variants were *at some stage* introduced into the tradition. As I have already said, this seems to me self-evident as well as having the support of the Serbo-Croat evidence.

I also claim that the poet whose work at the end of the tradition has survived could conceive of such variants as being generated by bards consciously and not simply under some zombie-like spell of the Muses or in a fit of absence of mind. This latter proposition does not, of course, have the support of the Serbo-Croat evidence. But here I would wish, as many have, to utter a *caveat* on the extent to which that evidence should be treated as strictly comparable. We should also take account of the fact that the poems we have must stand at the end of a tradition of which they themselves and their creator(s) cannot have been entirely typical. In many details of their handling of their story and characters, both the *Iliad* and the *Odyssey* are very self-conscious poems; and some awareness of the processes that created them should not be denied to their poet merely on analogy with other cultures.

Consideration of the various classes of tales told within the *Odyssey* takes us in the same direction. Alongside the songs of Phemius and Demodocus, all but one of which are about events related to the Trojan war, there are three categories of stories not sung by bards but narrated by other characters:

(1) *Prima facie* veracious tales told by characters other than Odysseus—Nestor, Menelaus, Helen and Eumaeus.

---

19. As it has been to me in a very helpful critique of my position by Dr Norman Postlethwaite.

(2) The *prima facie* veracious tale of his adventures told by Odysseus to the Phaeacians.

(3) The sequence of false tales of Odysseus in the second half of the poem. In these, he purports to be from Crete (except in the tale to Laertes), and invents various fictitious relations between himself and his activities and other characters and events of the Trojan war, events which he and other characters in the *Odyssey* treat as 'true'.

Tales in category (3) are formally indistinguishable from the main narrative of the *Odyssey*, and the poet draws our attention to this when he describes the first section of Odysseus' narrative to Penelope as 'like what is true' (*etumoisin homoia*)

> he said [*or* made] many falsehoods in his tale like what is true
>
> (*Od.* 19.203)

Furthermore, the tale of his wanderings told to the Phaeacians, however veracious within the terms of the poem's story, is so presented that we are invited to compare it both to the songs of bards and later to Odysseus' fictions. When it is told, it is to the same audience, and on the same occasion, as the songs of Demodocus—and it turns out to involve the same character, Odysseus. Odysseus' compliment to the bard on his accuracy implicitly claims that he, Odysseus, is getting it right too. But nobody can check Odysseus' story, which moves right out of the world of normal Greek experience. Later, when we have heard a succession of lying tales from Odysseus in which truth and falsehood are cunningly intertwined, it is hard not to develop some doubts about the whole truth of the tale he told the Phaeacians.[20]

The Phaeacian narrative and the false tales have also, I suggest, an effect on the frame in which they are set. If the one is far-fetched and the others utterly plausible but admittedly fictitious, what of the poet's own narrative? The contrast might serve to differentiate this: the true songs of Demodocus and the false tales of Odysseus may combine to indicate that our poet's tale, because told by the Muse,

---

20. For later antiquity's perception of Odysseus' tale as archetypal lying, cf. Juvenal 15. 13–26, noted below by Wiseman, p. 132, n. 33.

is 'really true'. But I suggest rather that the poet offers a range of modes of story-telling *all* of which have some element of fiction, and that he is well aware that an explicit claim of truth for his tale would be problematic.

6. *Hexameter didactic epic.* We might expect that in a poem such as Hesiod's *Theogony* the indissoluble link between poetry and truth postulated for an oral society would be discovered to be alive and well, since the content does indeed fall more obviously into the category of *mémoire collective*. But here too, as Rösler too allows, in a way that he does not for heroic epic, we find a serious modification. The Muses who met Hesiod on Helicon (in an account which even Hesiod's contemporaries can hardly have taken as narrative of a historical event) notoriously claimed to be the purveyors both of truth and of falsehoods (*pseudea*) that are 'like what is real' (*etumoisin homoia*)—just the phrase used by Homer of Odysseus' lies to Penelope at *Odyssey* 19.203:

> Field-dwelling shepherds, evil disgraces, mere bellies,
> we know how to say many falsehoods that are like the truth
> > [*etumoisin*],
> and we know, when we wish, how to voice what is true
> > [*alēthea*].
> > (Hesiod, *Theogony* 26–8)[21]

To me, this rings out as a clear division not simply of Muses' utterances but of poets into two classes: some tell the truth, some do not.[22] Thereafter, any interpretation becomes controversial. What is meant by 'falsehoods that are like the truth' (*pseudea . . . etumoisin homoia*), and to what class of poets or poetry do Hesiod's Muses here refer?

It might be that the 'falsehoods' are no more than either (a) 'lies', in the sense of stories told to mislead by tellers who know them to

---

21. Of the numerous discussions of this passage not explicitly cited in what follows, the most useful are W.W. Minton, 'Invocation and Catalogue in Hesiod and Homer', *Transactions of the American Philological Association* 93 (1962), 190ff.; H. Maehler, *Die Auffassung des Dichterberufs im frühen Griechentum bis zum Zeit Pindars. Hypomnemata* 3 (Göttingen, 1963), 35–48; P. Pucci, *Hesiod and the Language of Poetry* (Baltimore, 1977), 9–16.

22. So W. Stock, 'Hesiod's lügende Musen', in H. Görgemann and E.A. Schmidt, eds, *Studien zum antiken Epos* (Meisenheim am Glan, 1976), 85–112.

be false, or (b) 'erroneous views', i.e. stories mistakenly thought by their tellers to be true. The former category is that into which, of course, the poet of the *Odyssey* invites us to put the false tales of Odysseus. These tales are perceived as 'lies' because their departure from the truth serves a purpose in the world in which the teller is active. There are obviously types of poem whose false content could be chosen in order to mislead.[23] One could doubtless construct a type even of theogonic poetry which fitted this description, for instance, a song attributing to a particular god powers or achievements in which the singer did not believe but which he narrated to enhance a particular cult. But it seems much more likely that Hesiod's Muses might be asserting that they make poets sing what they mistakenly hold to be true, for instance a *Theogony* which offers the wrong genealogies for gods. Neither (a) nor (b) need involve Hesiod in having a concept like that of 'fiction'. But each is, of course, compatible with such a concept, since both the telling of 'lies' and the retailing of 'erroneous views' could involve the elaboration of falsehoods in such a way as to make their telling interesting in itself.

But it seems to me that a third interpretation (c) is at least possible and may be correct. This is that Hesiod's Muses refer to a category of poetry that is truly 'fictional', in the sense that the poet is neither lying nor retailing erroneously held views, but is (or at least is regarded by Hesiod as) telling a story that he has made up to be like reality without claiming that it *is* reality.

If (c) is a correct interpretation of *Theogony* 27–8, then it seems not unlikely, as held for example by Kannicht, that Hesiod is referring to two types of poetry, each in their own terms legitimate. These are heroic narrative epic like Homer's, which offers *etumoisin homoia*, and philosophical poetry like Hesiod's own.[24] That this might have been Hesiod's view of poems such as the *Iliad* and

---

23. Cf. below, categories 8(2) and 10.

24. R. Kannicht, 'Die alte Streit zwischen Poesie und Philosophie', *Altertums-Unterricht* 23.6 (1980), 6–36 (at 13–16, 19–21); now *The Ancient Quarrel between Poetry and Philosophy. Aspects of the Greek Conception of Literature*, Fifth Broadhead Memorial Lecture (Canterbury, NZ, 1988). I agree with Rösler in rejecting the view of W. Neitzel, 'Hesiod und die lügende Musen', *Hermes* 108 (1980), 387–401, that Hesiod is here talking only of non-Hesiodic poetry.

Odyssey does not, of course, show that it was Homer's. But, if my discussion of the Homeric passages has seemed nearer to truth than fiction, then the deployment of this distinction by Hesiod might be seen as lending support to my position.

Whether we choose interpretation (a), (b) or (c), it is probable, and widely held, that Hesiod wants to use the encounter with the Muses to guarantee the truth of the poem he is actually singing, the *Theogony*. The Muses' pronouncement is followed by their gift of a laurel staff and their inspiration of Hesiod with a divine voice, *thespin audēn* (31–2), which he claims to enable him to celebrate both past *and* future (32)—an extravagant claim that surely goes well beyond anything in the *Theogony*.

The move may or may not have persuaded Hesiod's audience to believe him, whether he saw himself as a rival to other theogonic poets whose versions he wishes to dismiss as lies or mistaken views, or to heroic narrative epic. But it does offer us clear evidence of a poet's readiness to question the alleged convention that the poet inspired by the Muses must be taken to tell the truth.

To say this is not to say that, in these lines of the *Theogony*, there is preserved the first break in a poetic cartel: it would be a very remarkable coincidence if the first departure from the postulated traditional view were in fact preserved. Indeed, the very factors which Rösler sees as breaking down the traditional nexus of Muses, singer and truth in the seventh and sixth centuries (the expanding horizons of the Greek world and the increase in recorded knowledge consequential upon the spread of literacy) were surely already operating by the end of the eighth century. Moreover, it hardly requires great alertness in a singer or listener to notice that significantly different versions of the same story are being sung. This must surely have occurred, for example, during performances of the immediate antecedents of our *Odyssey*. Nor is it improbable that, when singers were aware of singing different versions of songs, each should seek some means of making his songs more, and others' songs less, acclaimed. There would, therefore, have been many occasions in the performance of hexameter poetry in the eighth century when a singer might have been tempted to do as Hesiod did in *Theogony* 27–8. In doing so, he must have had to raise the issue of the fictionality of poetry, or at least to make allegations of falsehood which could lead to further questions about the nature of 'falsehood'.

Brief consideration is also needed of Hesiod's other poem to survive intact, *Works and Days*. Didactic epic of a different sort, it offers much biographical information about Hesiod himself, about his brother Perses, and about their quarrel over their father's land. Much of this may be either straightforwardly true or simply a tendentious account.[25] But the apparently conflicting information about Perses and the author's relations with him have raised the question whether a brother (whether called Perses or not) really existed. The arguments are concisely reviewed by Martin West in his commentary, and he concludes 'that he was a real person, but that some of the details of what we are told about him are invented for the purposes of the argument'.[26] To my mind the evidence points just as strongly to the conclusion that Perses is invented. But even the weaker claim is important for my argument. In a poem communicating apparently sincere views on gods, justice and society, as well as practical, if traditional, information on methods of farming, the didactic poet did not think he would weaken the authority he so clearly arrogates by incorporating biographical details about his addressee which members of his audience would detect as fictitious.

7. The next genre I wish to examine is one that is closely related to hexameter narrative epic, namely the dactylic narrative of Stesichorus. This was close to Homeric poetry in choice of theme and details of treatment—and perhaps even in manner of performance, if we accept the recently fashionable view that his songs of up to 2,000 lines were sung not by a chorus but by Stesichorus himself. That controversy need not be pursued here, where our concern is with what, by the fourth century BC, was referred to as the *Palinode*. Some of the facts are relatively clear.[27] In at least one of his songs, almost certainly in that later called *Helen* (frr. 187–191 Page and Davies [= P]), but also perhaps in his *Oresteia* (cf. fr.

---

25. Cf. category 8(2) below.

26. Hesiod *Works and Days*, ed. M.L. West (Oxford, 1978) 33–40 (the quotation is from 40).

27. See the testimonia gathered by D.L. Page, *Poetae Melici Graeci*, frr. 192 and 193 and (more fully, but omitting the Suda text which offers a unique and perhaps important testimony, see below) M. Davies, *Poetarum Melicorum Graecorum Fragmenta* I (1991), 177–180.

223P), Stesichorus represented Helen in the traditional role of the shameless adulteress, implied by the *Iliad* and probably explicit in the *Cypria*. In a later song, Stesichorus recanted, blaming Homer and Hesiod for the way they told the story. In its place, he offered the version which attracted Herodotus and Euripides, that Helen spent the war in the custody of Proteus in Egypt while only a phantom, an *eidōlon*, went to Troy.

Plato's *Phaedrus* preserves for us one of the key lines in the recantation, 'That story is not true'; and an Oxyrhynchus papyrus published almost 40 years ago gave us more details of the opening of the song.[28] Even in saying 'the song', however, I prejudge one issue, for it is widely held that Chamaeleon, whose views are reported in the papyrus, was canvassing the view that Stesichorus wrote two *Palinodes*, not one. This is at variance with most reports of Stesichorus' recantation, from Plato and Isocrates to Dio of Prusa and Aelius Aristides. But some have taken this to be Chamaeleon's view, influenced by a number of sources which refer to Stesichorus' palinode with the plural *humnoi*. Others have argued that Chamaeleon was trying to elevate to the status of a palinode another poem which was not that at all. I think that the correct solution is more radical and at the same time more illuminating for Stesichorus' technique. What Chamaeleon said, I believe, was not that Stesichorus composed two *Palinodes*, but that the *Palinode* had two beginnings (*archai*), or, as Aristides 33.2 puts it,[29] a second prelude (*prooemion*). Why might Stesichorus have given his poem two *prooemia*, and why is this relevant to my enquiry?

Part of the answer to these questions emerges from what he said in these two *prooemia*. According to the papyrus, in one he blamed Homer, in the other Hesiod.[30] But, as far as we know, he did not

---

28. Plato's quotation, at *Phaedrus* 243a, runs: 'That tale is not true, nor did you go in fine-benched ships, nor did you come to the citadel of Troy.' The papyrus is *P.Oxy.* 2506 = Stesichorus fr. 193P.

29. 'But I shall move over to a second preface like Stesichorus': Aristides 33.2 Keil.

30. Stesichorus fr.193P = *P.Oxy.* 2506, 26 col.i: '. . . [bla]mes Homer [because] his poem had [Hele]n in [Troy] and not her phantom, and in the other he blames Hesiod: for there is a pair of Palinod< . . . . >verging, and the one beginning is: "Hither again song-loving goddess", and of the other "Gold-winged maiden", as Chamaeleon recorded.' Others have taken the feminine noun implied by 'other' (*heterāi*) to be *palinode* (*palinodiāi*), whereas on my view it was 'beginning' (*archēi*).

address either. Each opening was addressed, as openings of heroic narrative should be, to a Muse: 'Hither again, song-loving goddess' and 'Gold-winged maiden'. The link between these invocations and criticism of his predecessors surely took the form of blaming Homer and Hesiod for being misled by false utterances of the Muses.

Since Stesichorus, here and elsewhere, demonstrates knowledge of Hesiod's poetry there is no difficulty in supposing that he knew, and may have played on, the Muses' proclamation in *Theogony* 27–8, that they knew how to utter false things that looked true. There may also have been criticism of the Muse that misled each poet; but such criticism would not be necessary, and Stesichorus may have invoked the Muse only to say 'Do not any longer, on this occasion,'—note the 'again' (*aute*)—'mislead me as you misled me before and as you once misled Homer.' I conjecture, but cannot show, that Stesichorus presented Homer's Muse as different from Hesiod's—that would explain why two invocations were needed; and the two invocatory sections would allow Stesichorus to set out briefly, each in turn, the Homeric and Hesiodic stories that he was about to reject.

Did Stesichorus claim any higher authority on which he might feel obliged to reject the version long validated by Homer, Hesiod and their Muses? Here, we must distinguish the ostensible reason offered to his audience and the motive he may in fact have had. We cannot, of course, *know* with what motive Stesichorus rejected the traditional version and offered another. But the explanation most often given, that his Spartan patrons had indicated their displeasure at his earlier poem's defamation of Helen, has always seemed to me very curious. True, we have evidence of Stesichorus composing poetry for a Spartan milieu and can attribute some other changes in myth, such as the location of Agamemnon's palace in Lacedaimon instead of Mycenae (fr. 216P), to a wish to please Spartan patrons. But the portrayal of Helen is surely another matter. Both the general diffusion of Homer and apparent echoes in Tyrtaeus make it likely that Homeric poetry, and hence the traditional portrayal of Helen, was already known in Laconia by the 640s BC. Alcman (21P) had treated a story in the Helen cycle, her abduction by Theseus, which seems also to have been part of the offending *Helen* of Stesichorus (191P). If Homer and Alcman did not offend a Spartan audience, why should Stesichorus have done so when he told the same story?

I suggest that the real motive for change was artistic. Helen was a character of perennial interest in the Trojan cycle, as her involvement in the *Odyssey* does something to show, and a poem that included her had more chance of success than one which did not. But, for a poet such as Stesichorus, who had already composed two substantial poems involving Helen, it would have been hard to introduce Helen yet again without repeating himself. The solution was to change the story, following, it seems, some hint in this direction in Hesiod (cf. fr. 266 Rzach = 358 Merkelbach and West). If this *was* Stesichorus' objective, then by this time, around 575 BC, we have a clear case of a poet who felt free to develop a well-established story on new lines.

A number of other instances of innovation have been ascribed to Stesichorus. Indeed Chamaeleon, in the papyrus already cited, claims (after noting the change in the story of Helen) that Stesichorus was given to mythological innovation and adduces further instances. It is improbable that these changes are the result of some critic saying that the traditional version was either false or disreputable and Stesichorus then scurrying to put it right. Rather they are to be seen as resulting from the attractions of innovation, attractions already registered in Telemachus' remark at *Odyssey* 1.351–2:

> For men give more renown to that song
> which comes newest to their ears.

Of course, the conventions linking Muses, poets and traditional stories, and the hold that was already being acquired by canonised versions, would deter Stesichorus from declaring that reason. It seems that, instead, he was able to offer a compelling reason for departing from the canon—and, indeed, not just one but, in a sense, two reasons. The one that comes across clearest in our sources is the threat of blindness. The story and even phraseology of Plato, *Phaedrus* 243a and Isocrates, *Helen* 64 seem to go back to the *Palinode* itself. Once more, the interpretation is controversial, but in my view the correct reading of these texts is as follows. When beginning to compose the *Palinode*, Stesichorus (he claimed) rose one morning to find himself blind. Recognising his defamation of Helen (*tēn Helenēs kakēgorian*) as the reason for his blindness, he composed the recantation in the form posterity knew it, and his sight was miraculously restored.[31] Of course, once the story had been so told in the *Palinode*, Stesichorus could point to the fact that he was *not* blind as a proof of its veracity.

But how did Stesichorus 'discover' the reason for his blindness? Was it simply by virtue of his professional links with the Muses (*hate mousikos ōn*) as Plato suggests? The Suda preserves a detail which may explain how Stesichorus justified his innovation: he composed the *Palinode* as a result of a dream (*ex oneirou*).[32] Put this together with the term 'he rose' (*anestē*) in Isocrates and we have a plausible sequence of ideas. At some point early in his *Palinode*, after the invocations, Stesichorus explained that he had rejected Homer's and Hesiod's versions because of a dream. In the dream, he had been told he was to be blind until he corrected his defamation; on waking, he had duly done so, and was no longer blind. The most likely individual to have expressed anger at the defamation and to have had the authority to correct the traditional story is, of course, Helen herself, and I conjecture that it was she who appeared to Stesichorus in a dream.

If this is, indeed, how Stesichorus authenticated his new version, we find him playing boldly with Hesiod's own guarantee of truth. Hesiod met the Muses, and was told that they could tell both false tales and true. Stesichorus exploited their capacity to mislead and trumped Hesiod by himself seeing the principal character in the story—in a dream, which was just as respectable a form of communication with gods and heroes as waking visions.

I have spent so much time on this detail because it seems to me to be an important indicator of how far the creator of fiction's autonomy had developed. Stesichorus *purports* to be engaged in the reporting of a tale which is either true or false; if that is so, his own

---

31. 'Rose' (i.e. from sleep) is my interpretation of *anestē* in Isocrates *Helen* 64: 'For when on beginning the song he uttered a slander about her, he got up bereft of sight, but when he recognized the reason for the calamity and composed the *Palinode* she restored him to the same condition.' Cf. Plato *Phaedrus* 243a: 'For bereft of sight for his abuse of Helen he did not fail to recognize the reason, like Homer, but as a man of the Muses he recognized it and at once composed . . . and after composing the whole *Palinode* he immediately regained his sight.'

32. Suda 4. 433 s.v. Stesichoros: 'They say that after writing a defamation of Helen he was blinded and then again got his sight back after writing an encomium of Helen as a result of a dream.'

version can only be true if others are false, and he must declare them to be false. But in order to back up his declaration, he must call a witness. In the terms used by Odysseus in complimenting Demodocus (*Odyssey* 8.491), he must show himself as either having seen the events himself or heard from another. But the way in which he calls his witness surely shows that he is intent on mendacious exploitation of both appeals to the Muse and appeals to witnesses. He had a dream, one of the human experiences which is by its nature uncheckable. Thus, he brazenly backs up one fiction by another. But, while dealing wholly in fiction, Stesichorus pretends to anchor these fictions in the world of real communication by suggesting that representation of a poetic character in a bad light can be counted as defamation (*kakēgoria*).

III

So far, the majority of categories of poetry considered have been narrative, and, as far as we can tell, narrative intended for public performance before substantial audiences. When we turn to sympotic poetry, however, we find a different set of assumptions.[33]

8. *Sympotic elegy.* It is a relevant feature of sympotic elegy that narrative plays a relatively small part in it. The main thrust of this poetry lies in the expression of likes and dislikes, of wishes and fears, and in exhortation.[34] Circumstances are implied which call forth these different reactions; and, in the case of many poems (which I group in a category [1]), it seems reasonable to assume that, on the first occasion of their performance, these were, indeed, the circumstances, and the reactions evinced are more or less sincere reactions. Sometimes, a very tendentious account of circumstances is given, not perhaps strictly false but equally not strictly true (category [2]). But in some poems it can be argued that the circumstances evoked are actually fictions (category [3]).

---

33. In 'sympotic poetry' I include most short, monodic lyric, short elegiac poems, and much of our iambic remains together with the closely related genre of *asynartēta* or epodes.

34. See the characterization in M.L. West, *Studies in Greek Elegy and Iambus* (Berlin, 1974) (West, *Studies*), 14–18; and Bowie, 'Elegy', with further bibliography in n. 1.

Here are some examples of these three types.

(1) In 13W Archilochus urges a stiff-upper-lip in response to the loss of friends at sea. The event, expressed in the sentence (3–4) 'for such men has the much-roaring sea's wave washed away', was most probably real.

(2) When Theognis (54–5) describes those in power in Megara as men 'who previously knew nothing of judgements or of laws, but wore out goat-skins about their flanks', this borders on slander but doubtless has an element of truth.

(3) It is easier to suggest that a poem belongs to this category than to prove it. A strong candidate is Archilochus 4, purporting to be sung during guard-duty on a ship but rather to be taken as a poem for performance in an ordinary symposium where familiar experiences of warfare are evoked:[35]

> but come, with a tankard through the benches of the swift ship
> range, and tear the seals from the bulbous jars,
> and drain the red wine down to its lees: for we too
> cannot stay sober in this guard-duty.
>
> (Archilochus 4.6–9W)

Whereas circumstances of this fragment's performance are controversial, there is little room for doubt in the case of *Theognidea* 257–8:

> I'm a beautiful mare, a winner, but the worst
> of men's my rider, and this gives me very great pain.[36]

In the absence of evidence that the women present at symposia sang elegiac poetry, I take this to be sung by a man who is for the moment 'playing' a woman.

Such evocation of fictional circumstances (if that is what we find here) may have been aided by the singing of some elegiac songs on occasions other than their first performance and by singers other than their composer. For, on any performance other than the first, many particularising circumstances mentioned in a poem will no

---

35. Cf. Bowie, 'Elegy', 16–17 with n. 22.
36. See the other examples I cite in Bowie, 'Elegy', 16–17 with nn. 18–20.

longer be true. Thus Archilochus 13W was surely not sung *only* after a boat went down, nor Theognis 53ff. *only* when a revolution had raised to power an economic class previously excluded from the administration of the *polis*. So too, a not uncommon feature of elegy, address to a named individual—Theognis to Cyrnus, Euenus to Simonides—ceases to operate as a real address. The mismatch between what is sung and the circumstances in which it is sung in later performances of poems in categories (1) and (2) is, indeed, different from what I think is happening in category (3). But the fact that such cases involve a departure from the singing of what is the case may have assisted the creation of poems of category (3).

9. *Sympotic lyric poetry.* Though sympotic lyric is broadly similar to elegy in the relevant respects, there are some significant differences. Alcaeus', Sappho's or Anacreon's naming of the objects of their desire may be analogous to Theognis' addresses to Cyrnus; but the very fact that they are declared as love-objects ties them much closer to the *persona* of the singer, and would have required a different sort of suspension of belief in the literal truth of what was being sung from such simple vocatives. So too, Alcaeus' repeated naming of political enemies links his expression of delight at their fall or outrage at their success much closer to the occasion of his songs' first performance than political comment in Solon or Theognis—therefore here too, on later occasions, the lack of correspondence with reality would be even more marked.

These phenomena bear upon, but do not entail, the creation of fictions. More important is the point that sympotic lyric has more narrative than sympotic elegy, and that this narrative is as likely to be fictional as factual. Thus Alcaeus 6 Lobel-Page (and perhaps 208 Voigt = 326 Lobel-Page) is, in my view, a narrative of a storm which may relate to events that really happened, but which reports them as if they were happening now.[37] Sappho's love-declarations may have been sincere on their first performance;[38] but love-declarations of

---

37. See Bowie, 'Elegy', 17 with n. 21.
38. On Sappho 31, cf. J. Latacz, 'Realität und Imagination. Eine neue Lyrik-Theorie und Sapphos *Phainetai moi kenos* Lied', *Museum Helveticum* 42 (1985), 67–94; W. Rösler, 'Realitätsbezug und Imagination in Sapphos Gedicht *Phainetai moi kenos*' in W. Kullmann and M. Reichel, eds, *Der Übergang von der Mündlichkeit zur Literatur bei den Griechen* (Tübingen, 1990), 271–287.

Anacreon such as 'I love Cleoboulus . . .' (fr.359 Page [=P]) may never have been sincere, and when Anacreon sings (fr.358P) how golden-haired Eros challenges him with a brightly-coloured ball to play with a girl with jazzy sandals, he is blending a mythical fantasy with an ostensibly real-life situation which may itself be imaginary.

10. *Epode.*[39]   Two of Archilochus' epodes have a relevant feature not found elsewhere in extant symotic poetry: the telling of animal fables.[40] In frr. 172–181W, Lycambes is told an *ainos* (animal fable) about the eagle's punishment for his betrayal of his compact with the fox; in frr. 185–7W, the fable of the ape's attempt to be king of the beasts is addressed to Cerycides. Here, with certainty, we can assign fictionality to stories which were probably told to make points in Archilochus' social and political manoeuvring. It is likely enough, of course, that these are not Archilochus' own fictions: he may be telling the audience a version of a fable already well-known, and thus doing something similar to the singers of epic who are argued to be transmitting *mémoire collective*. We are in no position to assess whether Archichus invented these two fables or simply retold them. But we must allow that such stories, involving speaking and rational animals, are unlikely to have been eligible for classification as 'history' by Archilochus' audience. Neither the history nor even, with rare exceptions like Achilles' horses, the mythology of the Greeks was populated by eloquent beasts.

The presence of a class of fiction in these two poems may affect the expectations of an audience in hearing two other epodes where the anecdotes concerned involve human beings. In one of these

---

39. Our remains of sympotic iambic poetry are too scrappy to permit useful conclusions. Although Archilochus 23W seems to describe an erotic encounter between the poet and a woman, and 48W narrates another to Archilochus' friend Glaucus, it cannot be established whether fact or fiction is narrated. Nor can we be sure whether the characters or incidents of Archilochus 19W (Charon the carpenter) or 122W (a father expostulating about a daughter) are real or fictitious.

40. Note, however, the elaborate set of animal comparisons in Semonides' misogynistic fr. 7: our remains of early iambus are so scrappy that we should not exclude the possibility that animal fable did figure in this genre.

(frr. 182–4W), the subject of the story is given a name, Batusiades, and the story opens by specifying the occasion of what happened:

> When the people were gathering for games,
>   and among them Batusiades.
>
> (fr. 182W)

In the other (frr. 168–171W) the story may well have concerned the addressee himself, Charilaus. Archilochus opens with:

> 'Darlingson [*Erasmonidē*] Charilaus,
>   I shall tell you a funny thing,
> dearest by far of my friends,
>   and you'll enjoy hearing it.'
>
> (fr. 168W)

Given that most of our epodes administer stings and not balm, Archilochus may well be tongue in cheek when promising pleasure. We cannot tell whether the 'funny thing' narrated to Charilaus, or the gathering for games in fr. 182W, really happened, but that these play the same role in these poems as animal-fables in others should caution against assuming that they were factual. Stories about humans need be no more bound by truth than stories about animals.

This conclusion may help us in approaching the two other epodes of which much more can be, and has been, said, the very fragmentary remains of the poem which began, 'No longer has your delicate skin the same bloom' (fr. 188–192W), and the epode narrating the seduction of Neoboule's younger sister (frr. 196W and 196A W).[41]

Frr. 188–192W contain two inset narratives: one of the narrator's seduction by the addressee in his foolish youth, one of the rescue from a shipwreck of a man called Coiranos by a dolphin he has saved. The latter borders on animal fable: perhaps the story was

---

41. The most convenient texts and commentaries, referring to much of the voluminous literature on these fragments since their publication in 1974, are to be found in J.M. Bremer, A. Maria van Erp Taalman Kip and S.R. Slings, eds, *Some Recently Found Greek Poems*, *Mnemosyne* Suppl. 99 (Leiden, 1987), 24–69. See also my discussion of frr. 188–192 'One That Got Away', in *Homo Viator. Classical Essays for John Bramble*, eds, L.M. Whitby, P.R. Hardie, J.M. Whitby (Bristol, 1987), 13–23.

widely believed in Paros in Archilochus' time, as it was later, but we are entitled to doubt this. Only two people could check the former story: Archilochus (if we take his narrative to be autobiographical) and the girl with whom he was once, but is no longer, infatuated, and who is not named in our extant lines, and perhaps nowhere was. Archilochus may be telling a version of the truth, but it is likely at best to be a very distorted version (like sympotic elegies in category 8[2] above).

But fiction need not be limited to details of Archilochus' narrative. It very probably extends to the posture of addressing his song to the woman whom he is vilifying. We can be fairly sure that Archilochus performed this poem to a sympotic audience of male friends, *hetairoi*. Neither the victim of fr. 188 nor that of frr. 196 and 196A is presented as a professional entertainer, a *hetaira*, so that we may be confident that the sympotic audience did not include her. Hence, the posture that the poem adopts, of address to the very person being defamed, is a fiction. It is not impossible that the actual person of the addressee is a fiction too, and, if that were so, the emotions expressed would be drawn into the same fictional category, both the hatred of the poem's frame and the passion of its inset. But, as so often, we lack any sort of control on this last stage in the exploration.

More data, or pseudo-data, are available to help us to assess the seduction narrative of frr. 196W and 196A W. This much-discussed fragment, almost a complete poem, also contains a sequence of defamatory statements, deployed by the narrator as a ground for rejecting his young seducee's suggestion that he transfer his attentions to her older sister Neoboule, and by both poet and narrator as a foil to his description of the younger girl's adolescent charms. We may suppose that the former, and even perhaps the latter, are tendentious rather than scrupulously true, and that we are again encountering the phenomenon noted in category 8(2).

But into what social context in the real world of the Greek Aegean in the mid-seventh century can we put a poem in which the performer narrates the seduction of a girl who, though unnamed, is securely identified in the poem as from the same house as Neoboule? This is, unquestionably, the Neoboule whom tradition names as the daughter of Lycambes, enemy of Archilochus and, along with his daughter(s), victim of Archilochus' vituperative *iamboi* after the arrangements for his marriage to Neoboule had been annulled.

Given all we know of Ionian attitudes to the role of young girls before marriage, the poet's narrative of his sexual conquest of the younger sister in the flowery meadow would have been just as destructive to the reputation of Lycambes and his household as the overtly defamatory statements about the older sister Neoboule. We may surely also judge that a report of Archilochus' poetic performance[42] must have destroyed any chance of his repeating his success or even maintaining an affectionate relationship with that younger sister. Yet the starting-point of the poem is the poet's assertion (again fr. 196W) that he is overcome by longing (*pothos*) for the girl, an assertion that some see as corroborated by a presentation of the actual seduction that is tender and allusive rather than harsh and explicit.

At present I only see two satisfactory explanations, although at times I have been tempted by others.

(1) We may hold that the whole story of Archilochus' quarrel with the family of Lycambes is a fiction: a broken engagement with Neoboule, in frr. 196 and 196A a seduction of Neoboule's younger sister, and finally *iamboi* leading to the girls' suicide. The fiction may have been developed more or less coherently in a number of poems in different metres, but presumably with the same audience, Archilochus' male friends (*hetairoi*). None of the characters in this fiction existed, none of the 'events' happened. This is different from the view that they were stock characters in a drama, a view once advanced by Martin West and demolished effectively by Chris Carey.[43] It does not presuppose dramatic performance, nor that Lycambes and Neoboule existed in any literary or sub-literary works other than those of Archilochus.

(2) Lycambes and his family were historical figures, but he was an enemy of Archilochus, and, in pursuing his feud, Archilochus blended truth with fiction. Sometimes he may have referred to events

---

42. Addressed to a male friend, as is shown by fr. 196W: 'but longing, the looser of limbs, my friend, conquers me'.

43. West, *Studies* 27; C. Carey, 'Archilochus and Lycambes', *Classical Quarterly* 36 (1986), 60–67. Of discussions since 1986, note especially that of S.R. Slings in *Greek Poems*, 24–61, and in S.R. Slings, *The I in Personal Archaic Lyric* (Amsterdam, 1990), 23–6 (Slings, *The I*). Slings, *The I* also rejects West's theory of stock characters (23–4), and is, unfortunately, unaware (see esp. 7 n. 18) of Carey's article.

which had in some form taken place.[44] In other poems he *invented* incidents which were calculated to bring shame and disrepute on Lycambes' household; the kiss-and-tell story has not lost its power in modern politics.

On both these views, the claim to feeling longing and the incident narrated to explain it are alike fictions. On hypothesis (1), the point of the fiction is simply to entertain, on hypothesis (2), entertainment is allied to political ends. The effectiveness of such poetry in the prosecution of a feud will have been all the greater if the genre used by Archilochus was one in which both factual accounts (perhaps frr. 168W and 182W) and fictions (like the animal fables) were equally at home.

In this context it is relevant to draw attention to a phenomenon that has emerged from time to time in a number of genres and that requires at least brief discussion: the poet's creation of a *persona* for himself (or herself) that we would be unwise to identify with his or her historical identity.[45] There has been more systematic discussion of this 'lyric I' in relation to modern than to ancient literature, but a recent volume brings together four useful essays.[46] In the first, S.R. Slings offers a very helpful analysis of first-person statements in early elegiac, iambic and lyric poetry and draws an important and necessary distinction between a 'fictional I' and a 'biographical I with untrue statements'. The former he sees, for example, in Anacreon 'the entertainer' of fr. 360P, 'Boy with the girlish looks . . .' or Alcaeus fr. 10 Voigt (in which the feminine adjectives show that it was to be sung in the person of a girl). To the latter he assigns the Archilochus epode (frr. 196W and 196A W) that I have just discussed. Although I might disagree on some details, there is much in his account with which I agree. I certainly welcome his

---

44. Perhaps, for example, the breach of hospitality alleged in the frame of the fox and eagle fable, fr. 173W: that fable is not an obvious choice to illustrate the broken engagement of the tradition.

45. This is also apparent in the poetry of Hipponax, but I do not attempt a close examination of this. First, he is composing significantly later than Archilochus (?540/530 BC), and by then awareness of fiction in poetry is already apparent and conceded by Rösler. Second, there are even fewer controls on our interpretation of Hipponax's scenarios than on those of Archilochus.

46. Slings, *The I*.

conclusion[47] (against Rösler 1985) that the orality of early Greek personal poetry is no obstacle to supposing it to be trading in fictions, and endorse his observation that, even on our limited material, we can see different genres of that early Greek poetry behaving in different ways.

I am naturally less ready to accept Slings' acceptance of the common view that the epic poet 'is a guardian of history and therefore his songs are true by definition' (13)[48] and his insistence that, in the purveying of fiction, the 'lyric poet' has a role that is to be sharply distinguished from that of the epic poet. Part of the purpose of my separate treatment of different genres of early Greek poetry earlier, distinguished not only by the broad criterion of metre but also by length and stance of poem, is to show how, even within the same genre, different expectations seem to pertain, and how certain stances seem to be found running across different genres.

Thus, the metrical criterion of iambic trimeters and trochaic tetrameters, or of elegiac couplets, cannot alone guide the audience to expect either truth or fiction. Trimeters may clothe political autobiography; tetrameters may narrate a military campaign; elegiac couplets may record a city's history in a sweep of mythical past to recent history. Length, content and, above all, context of performance may have led audiences of these types of poem to expect a preponderance of truth, whereas the same men hearing the same metres used for shorter poems about wine, women and (self-referentially) song would readily take incidents to be invented and the 'I' to stray from the biographical to the fictional. The presence of animal fables in epodes may have helped to tip the scales of their judgement towards fiction, even if we (unlike the contemporary audiences) cannot readily tell whether epodes involve total fiction or simply the ascription of fictional acts to historical characters. We also find the animal fable used by a hexameter didactic poet, Hesiod, in a set of admonitions addressed to his brother Perses. Here too, details of the biography that Hesiod offers of himself and of Perses can be questioned, as can even the existence of the vital addressee.

---

47. Against W. Rösler, 'Persona reale o persona poetica? L'interpretazione dell'io nella lirica greca arcaica', *Quaderni Urbinati di Cultura Classica* 19 (1985), 131–144.

48. See also his arguments in S.R. Slings, 'Poet's Call and Poet's Status in Archaic Greece and Other Oral Cultures', *Listy Filologické* 112 (1989), 72–80.

The range of expectations found in these types of poetry may have had no effect on the expectations of an audience of an *Iliad*, an *Odyssey* or a *Theogony*. But I think that the burden of proof lies with those who insist that such performances carry with them quite different expectations. I am confident that Stesichorus already views the corpus of myths that he shares with hexameter epic not as an immutable *mémoire collective* but as stories where his own invented fictions may be substituted for what earlier poets have sung. That Hesiod himself should both raise the issue of truth and fiction at *Theogony* 27–8 and perhaps create a fictional addressee for his *Works and Days* cannot, of course, show that he regards either Homeric epic or his own *Theogony* as fictions, but it should make us hesitate before insisting that he must be a prisoner of the attitudes to *la mémoire collective* found in traditional oral societies. My reading of the *Odyssey* suggests to me that its poet too is aware that stories can be created, or creatively adapted, and that his own role is not wholly different from that of his fictionalizing character Odysseus. But I concede that this cannot be demonstrated, and will not be surprised if some scholars are reluctant to follow me.

Chapter Two

Plato on Falsehood—not Fiction

CHRISTOPHER GILL

Hesiod and Homer and the other poets . . . composed false stories which they told people and are still telling them.

(*Republic* [*R.*], 377d4–6)

Well then, shall we take it that all the poets, beginning from Homer, are imitators of images of virtue and the other things about which they make poems, but have no grasp of the truth . . . ? (*R.* 600e4–6)

Real falsehood is hated by human beings as well as gods . . . But falsehood in words—when and for whom is it useful so that it doesn't deserve to be hated? (*R.* 382c3–7)

How could we contrive one of those necessary falsehoods . . . some noble lie with which to convince the rulers themselves if possible, or, if not, the rest of the city? (*R.* 414b8–c)

'. . . form a picture of our state of education—and its absence— as being something like this. Imagine human beings as though in an underground house like a cave, with a long entrance extended towards the light . . .' 'A strange picture,' he said, 'and strange prisoners.' 'Like us,' I said. (*R.* 514a1–4, 515a4–5)

Dividing the subject between us, we shall all try, as far as possible, to provide what is fitting for your specifications. But you must consider, Socrates, whether this account of ours meets the case or if we should look for some other instead.

SOCRATES: Critias, what could we find better than this? . . . and it is a great advantage that it is not a made-up story but a true account.   (*Timaeus* [*Ti.*] 26d5–e5)[1]

I

I begin by drawing three types of distinction between kinds of discourse. The first relates to the speaker's intended form of communication with a listener. This distinction involves two aspects: that between factual and fictional discourse, and that between forms of factual discourse. Factual discourse is intended either to convey to the listener what the speaker takes to be true ('veracious'), or to convey what the speaker takes to be false ('lying'). Fictional discourse is different in kind from factual: its statements (and other forms of expression) do not constitute truth-telling or lying, and in this sense fiction has no truth-status.

The second type of distinction differs from the first in that it characterizes discourse by reference to whether it is *in fact* true or false rather than whether the speaker intends to convey what he or she takes to be true or false.

The third type of distinction relates to the mode of expression. I have in mind such distinctions as that between analytic discourse and non-analytic (representative or narrative); between prosaic discourse (historical, philosophical) and poetic (epic, dramatic, lyric); between literal discourse and figurative (imagistic, musical); and between general and specific discourse. This type of distinction differs from the first two in several ways, notably in not designating truth-status in either of the senses involved in those distinctions. But I include this distinction here because the question of the truth-status of a given discourse is often connected closely with that of the mode of expression involved. Thus, for example, a given statement may be false (in intention or fact) on the literal level but true (in intention or fact) on the figurative level; or it may be false in a specific case but true in general. This is only the most obvious way in which the distinctions drawn in the first two types may be connected with those in the third type.

---

1. All translations in this chapter are mine.

My claim is that these distinctions, while broadly intelligible to modern readers, do not correspond in one crucial respect to the conceptual framework presupposed by Plato. The distinction between factual and fictional discourse, which is familiar to us, has no obvious equivalent in Plato's framework. I support this claim, and pursue its implications, by reference to two aspects of Platonic writing in which we might expect to find the distinction drawn between fictional and factual discourse.

One, treated in Section II, is the discussion of poetry in the *Republic*. Although the discussion involves emphatic, and partly innovative, uses of the notion of 'falsity' in connection with poetry, the purpose of these uses is not, I argue, to define what we understand as the 'fictional' quality of epic and dramatic poetry.[2] The other aspect, treated in Section III, consists of the myths or images (such as that of the cave in *R.* 514aff.) which Plato insets into his arguments. These myths are presented with various indications about their truth-status. But although these myths are clearly, in *our* terms, 'fictional', and Plato's indications help *us* to recognize their fictional status, I do not think that this is the purpose of Plato's indications.[3] These are only two of the features of Plato's work on which one might focus in order to establish this claim; another, considered more briefly in Section IV, is the question of the status of the Platonic dialogues as records of conversations between historical individuals, a status which we should see as being at least partly fictional. But these aspects provide the clearest indications of Plato's conceptual framework in this respect, and enable us best to situate this framework in relation to the others treated in this volume.

If my claims about Plato's conceptual framework are valid, this raises questions about the extent to which Plato is typical of his culture, or exceptional, in this respect; and I discuss these questions in Section V. I consider, but discount, the idea that the distinction between factual and fictional discourse was already well-articulated

---

2. I speak of 'poetry' here instead of 'literature' because at this date the literary genres which we might consider plausible candidates for 'fictional' status are poetic ones, i.e. epic, tragedy, comedy; the prose novel or romance only emerges in the later Hellenistic and Roman periods.

3. This part of the chapter represents a partial modification of an earlier discussion: 'Plato's Atlantis Story and the Birth of Fiction', *Philosophy and Literature* 3 (1979), 64–78.

by Plato's day in the Greek conceptual framework and in the communicative practices presupposed by this framework. Although Plato's ideas on this topic are clearly innovative and controversial, I do not see them as revising a well-established distinction between factual and fictional discourse. Indeed, I suggest that some of the pre-Platonic passages which are sometimes interpreted as expressing such a distinction may be interpreted better in terms of the other types of distinction outlined earlier. That is to say, the passages presuppose a conceptual framework of the same general type as we find in Plato.

This raises the larger issue of whether we posit, or discover, change over time in the understanding of fiction (and of the fact–fiction distinction) within Greek culture, and, if so, whether we regard such change as constituting progress or development. I do not pursue the full implications of this issue here, although I mark its significance. What I emphasize rather is the extent to which the features of Plato's conceptual framework noted here persist in later Greek theoretical texts. I suggest that we find in Aristotle a framework of the same general kind as in Plato (that is, one that does not incorporate the distinction between factual and fictional discourse). It is also striking, and potentially significant, that the emergence of the Greek novel or romance (which we see as being the first unequivocally fictional narrative genre in Greek literature) is not accompanied by the emergence of any equivalent terminology, or system of classification, in which the novel is characterized *as fiction*.[4] This fact can be explained in various ways; but one possibility which should not be overlooked is that these novels were not actually read as fiction in our sense.

My suggestion, in short, is that the absence of a clear distinction between factual and fictional discourse in Plato, far from being idiosyncratic, may reflect a larger feature of Greek (or ancient) thinking and cultural assumptions in general. This prompts my final question, in Section VI, whether our own inclination to regard the fact-fiction distinction as one which carries substantial theoretical weight derives from certain specifically modern concerns; and I conclude by offering some suggestions about what these may be.

---

4. This point is discussed by J.R. Morgan, pp. 176–8 below, and forms the starting point of B.P. Reardon's study of the problem; see text to n. 107 below.

II

To support my general claim about Plato's conceptual framework, let us examine his arguments about the falsehood of most Greek poetry in *Republic* Two–Three (376e–392b) and about the deceptiveness of poetry in *Republic* Ten (595a–608b). My thesis is that, although these arguments involve the innovative and controversial deployment of the notions of falsehood and deceptiveness, the innovativeness is not to be explained as an attempt to define the fictional quality of existing Greek poetry or of representative poetry in general.[5] Before looking in detail at the relevant passages, it will be helpful to outline the overall pattern of thinking about ethical education and development in which the two discussions of poetry are designed to fit and to make sense.

Central to the argument of the *Republic* is the presentation of an ideal programme of ethical education, which consists of two coordinated and interdependent stages.[6] The first stage consists of the implanting of sound dispositions and a good way of life, through the management of the kind of cultural practices in which the young are brought up. This stage of education takes the form, primarily, of the shaping of patterns of aspiration and desire (the elements of *thumos* and *epithumia* in Plato's tripartite model of the psyche). It also includes the development of *some* rational functions, notably those involved in the formation of the beliefs which are correlated with the shaping of sound patterns of aspiration and desire, and which serve to maintain the 'harmonisation' of the psyche which such shaping brings about.[7] But is is the second stage of education

---

5. G.R.F. Ferrari, 'Plato and Poetry', in G. Kennedy, ed., *Cambridge History of Literary Criticism* (Cambridge, 1989), 92–148, gives a thoughtful and illuminating treatment of all Plato's discussions of poetry, and one which also argues that 'Plato never in fact works with [the] concept [of fictionality]', 98; see also 108–9, 136–41.

6. The account offered here summarizes the view I give in *The Self in Dialogue: Personality in Greek Epic, Tragedy, and Philosophy* (Oxford, 1994), ch. 7. My 'Plato and the Education of Character', *Archiv für Geschichte der Philosophie* 67 (1985), 1–26, discusses the relevant texts (though I now think it understates the coherence of Plato's programme). See also C.D. Reeve, *Philosopher-Kings: The Argument of Plato's Republic* (Princeton, 1988), chs 2–3, J. Lear, 'Inside and Outside the *Republic*', *Phronesis* 37 (1992), 184–215.

7. See *R.* 441a–444e (also 429b–432a), taken with Gill, 'Education of Character', 8–15.

which provides the full development of rationality, in which the exercise of the capacity for abstract reasoning and dialectical analysis may lead ultimately to knowledge of objective ethical truth.

The two stages of the educational programme are interdependent in the following ways. The first stage, the formation of sound patterns of aspiration and desire and correlated beliefs, is presented as a prerequisite, if the second stage, the development of analytic rationality, is to lead to the acquisition of ethical knowledge.[8] But it does not follow from this that the second stage consists only in the rationalisation of the dispositions and beliefs implanted in the first stage; it is crucial to the theory that the second stage, if carried to its conclusion, yields objective knowledge and not simply the theorization of social practices and attitudes.[9] The two stages are also interdependent in that the first stage of education can only yield the right kind of patterning of dispositions and beliefs if it is directed by those who have objective ethical knowledge and can apply this in their exercise of political authority.

The two discussions of poetry in the *Republic* relate to this larger programme of ethical development in this way. The first discussion forms the central part of the account of the first stage of this programme,[10] while the second part follows, and presupposes, the account of the second stage (in *Republic* Six–Seven). The context of the two discussions bears crucially on the question of the kind of falsehood, and deceptiveness, attributed to poetry. In essence, the claim that most Greek poetry is false (in *Republic* Two–Three) consists in the claim that it fails to represent the kind of behaviour, psychological states, and beliefs which would be represented by poetry directed with those with knowledge of ethical truth, and

---

8. See *R.* 497b–502e (esp. 498a–c) and 537d–539d, on the dangers of engaging in dialectic *without* the formation of sound patterns of aspiration and desire, and true beliefs; and 401e–402a, on the way in which the arrival of reason enables the educatee to recognize with understanding the value of the kind of cultural practices in which he or she was initiated as a child.

9. This is one of the main points of the myth of the cave (*R.* 514aff.), the form of which is discussed in III below.

10. The discussion of poetry forms part of the account of *mousikē* (broadly 'the arts'), which, together with *gumnastikē* (physical education), makes up the first phase of education (*R.* 376c–412a), whose function is to provide the basis for (pre-theoretical) justice in state and psyche (427d–434d, 441c–444e).

which would implant sound dispositions and a sound way of life. The claim that representative poetry is 'three degrees removed from the truth' and 'deceptive' (in *Republic* Ten) consists in the claim that poetry deceives people into thinking that it can convey knowledge of ethical truth, when it cannot, and when (by the nature of its form) it serves rather to propagate certain kinds of psychological and ethical falsehood.

In the first discussion, the complaint about the falseness of most Greek poetry seems, initially, to take a form which, while controversial, is not unprecedented in Greek culture. This is the complaint that poets misrepresent gods and heroes by making statements about them and attributing actions to them which are out of line with what is claimed to be their true nature.[11] But, as the discussion proceeds, it becomes clear that Plato's complaint forms part of a distinctive, and innovative, line of thought, and that, in this context, the 'falseness' involved has an extended meaning. What Plato has most in view is the way in which poetry, especially dramatic poetry, invites identification with the figures represented. As Plato presents the matter, poetic figures are like real human beings in that they constitute (representations of) integrated patterns of behaviour, psychological states, and beliefs. Identification with such figures over time brings about the patterning of the psyche (the complex of aspiration, desire and reasoning) in imitation of the figures represented.[12] Part of this process is the shaping of beliefs in line with those of the figures represented, and of the poets themselves, whose beliefs inform their representations. In Plato's view, the beliefs embodied in Greek poetry are, for the most part, false; they are wrong, for instance, about the extent to which death is an evil, or about whether

---

11. See *R.* 377eff., also Xenophanes frr. B1, B11, B12 (Diels-Kranz), and Pindar, *Olympian* (Pind. *Ol.*) 1.27–36. The relative familiarity of the point explains the readiness of the interlocutor to accept Socrates' complaints in 377e–378e.

12. See *R.* 386a–392a, 394d–398b; also 399a–c and 400d–402a. See also Ferrari, 'Plato on Poetry', 92–3, 108–11; a relevant fact is the extent to which, in the still predominantly oral culture of 5–4th-c. Greece, reading of poetry (esp. epic and tragedy) involved 'performance' and 'acting' on the part of the reader, a point brought out well by E.A. Havelock in *Preface to Plato* (Oxford, 1963), ch. 9.

justice brings happiness.[13] Therefore, identification with such figures involves the absorption of false beliefs (and of the correlated patterns of aspiration and desire) into the personality, thus making up what Plato, in a pointed and surprising phrase, calls 'falsehood in the psyche' or the 'lie in the soul' (*en tē(i) psuchē(i)... pseudos*, 382b9–11).

The idea of 'falsehood in the psyche' is introduced in the course of what is, in a way, a digression in the argument, justifying the claim that a god never changes his form or nature or deceives others (*R.* 380d–383c). But it is an idea which is significant for the discussion as a whole, and helps us to understand the full implications of the claim of the 'falseness' of most Greek poetry. Falsehood in the psyche is explained as 'being deceived', or ignorant, in one's mind 'about the most important things' (382a6–7, b1–3). While such a state consists, in part, in having false ethical beliefs,[14] it is clear from the larger context that such 'falsehood' is a property of the personality as a whole, and one which derives from the implanting of the wrong patterns of aspiration and desire.[15] Correspondingly, 'truth' (at least, 'truth in the psyche') must also be a state of the whole personality and not just a property of statements or beliefs; and it is consistent with this that it is claimed that 'a god is something simple and true (*alēthes*) in action and word' (382e8).

In the same context, we also find the suggestive comment that 'there is nothing of the false (or 'lying') poet in a god' (*poiētes... pseudēs*, 382d). The idea of the 'false' poet seems to allude to the earlier claim that poets, characteristically, utter falsehoods (377dff.). The comment takes on added significance, coming as it does just after the introduction of the idea of 'falsehood in the psyche' (382a–e). Poets are, typically, 'false', it would seem, because their representations, produced by people who are ignorant in their psyche 'about

---

13. See *R.* 387d–e, 392a–c (the latter point is qualified by the acknowledgement that Plato's claim that justice brings happiness is yet to be provided by the argument). See further S. Halliwell, 'Plato and Aristotle on the Denial of Tragedy', *Proceedings of the Cambridge Philological Society* n.s. 30 (1984), 49–71, at 54–5.

14. E.g. such life-shaping beliefs as those specified in *R.* 387d–e, 392a–c (see preceding note) might well count as beliefs 'about the most important things' (*kuriōtata*).

15. In a similar extension of usage, 'true' and 'false' are later applied to types of pleasure, *R.* 585d–586e.

the most important things', instil falsehoods in the psyche of their audience.[16] This comment also suggests the idea, developed a little later, that poets are 'false' in that, by encouraging us to identify ourselves with emotionally complex figures (whose responses are based on false beliefs), they invite us to be false to the self-consistency and coherence that constitutes human nature at its best and 'truest'.[17] Thus, Plato's initial complaints about the falsehood of most Greek poetry involves certain special and extended senses of 'falsehood', which are related to his conception of the first stage of ethical education.

Although Plato's argument in *Republic* Two–Three is innovative in its use of the notion of falsehood in poetry, I think it is clear that the innovativeness is not directed at defining (what we should see as) the 'fictional' character of existing Greek poetry. The true–false distinction is not used to distinguish factual from fictional discourse. Indeed, the reiterated claim that what Homer says about Achilles and others is 'false' seems to presuppose that Homer's account is in some sense a factual one, recording the deeds of real people, although, as we have seen, the sense of 'falsehood' involved goes beyond that of factual incorrectness.[18] Plato's failure to deploy the true–false distinction in this way is the more striking because his discussion brings out much of what *we* should regard as the fictional character of poetry (or literature, or film).

It is clear from his account that he envisages the poet engaging in what we might call 'the construction of character', through the

---

16. See discussion above, and references in nn. 12–14.

17. See references in n. 12 above, esp. 394e–395d (the guardians here represent human nature at its best). See further J. Annas, *An Introduction to Plato's Republic* (Oxford, 1981), 96–8; Ferrari, 'Plato on Poetry', 112–13, 115–19; Lear, 'Inside and Outside', 191–2 and 208–15. For further development of this idea in *R.* 10, see below.

18. See e.g. *R.* 391a–d; the argument is that, *if* the figures involved were sons of gods/goddesses (and therefore, on the Platonic view, necessarily good), the attribution of bad actions *must* be 'false' (see 391d3–e2 and 377e1–3). Thus, the criterion of falsehood is not that of factual incorrectness; but the argument seems to presuppose that the Homeric poems present what are, in principle, facts, whose truth or falsehood can be ascertained on the basis of this criterion. Cf. Thucydides' use of Homer as, in principle, a source of evidence for the past, though one marred by the poetic tendency to 'exaggerate' (*epi to meizon ... kosmēsai*, 1.10.3, 1.21.1), a comment which, in itself, implies the basically factual status of the Homeric poems; see further J.L. Moles, pp. 100–1 below.

matching of beliefs with psychological states and actions in the figures represented.[19] It is clear too that he accepts that our involvement with represented figures, although intense, is accompanied by an awareness that these figures and events do not form part of real life.[20] But his innovative use of the notion of falsehood is not designed to characterize (what we should conceive as) the 'fictional' dimension of poetic creativity and of audience-response. At least, this is true only in the paradoxical sense that much of what Plato criticizes as the 'falseness' of poetry corresponds to something that we prize in fiction: that is, the imaginative extension of our personal experience, attitudes, and values, a point I shall pursue later.[21]

Plato's discussion of poetry in *Republic* Ten (597a–608b) also involves innovative uses of language; but these centre on the ideas of 'deceptiveness' and 'degrees of distance from the truth' rather than falsehood. In seeking to understand the meaning of these ideas, it is helpful again to place the discussion in relation to the *Republic*'s two-stage programme of ethical education. Whereas the core of the first discussion is that most Greek poetry fails to provide the implanting of sound dispositions and beliefs that the programme requires, the core of the second discussion is that poetry is, by its nature, incapable of providing the analytic education towards ethical knowledge produced by the second stage. Indeed (by its nature), it tends to subvert the kind of rational structure of personality that the educational programme as a whole is designed to create.[22]

---

19. See discussion above, esp. references in n. 12. Aristotle too envisages the matching of words, attitudes, and actions as part of a poet's inclusion of 'character' (*ēthos*) in his work, *Po.* chs 6 and 15, although, as suggested below (V), his framework also lacks a clear distinction between fictional and factual discourse.

20. See *R.* 388d, 391e, 395d, 396c–e; also 605c–e, discussed below.

21. See Annas and Ferrari references in n. 17 above, and VI below.

22. I am presupposing that Plato's two discussions of poetry in *R.*, while differing because they are correlated with the two stages of his educational programme, are broadly consistent. See also Ferrari, 'Plato and Poetry', 120–5, and, for a powerful statement of the opposite view, J. Annas, 'Plato on the Triviality of Literature', in J. Moravcsik and P. Temko, eds, *Plato on Beauty, Wisdom, and the Arts* (Totowa, N.J., 1982), 1–28.

Thus, a prominent theme in the first phase of the argument (595a–602b) is that poetry deceives its audiences into thinking that it is an effective way of conveying knowledge of ethical truth, when it is not. Poetry, because it is, by its nature, effective in conveying the surface 'look' and emotional 'feel' of human life, convinces people into thinking that they are thereby gaining access to ethical truth. But this is not so. It is, at its best, only effective in giving the *impression* that, by conveying the look and feel of human life, it is also communicating knowledge. In fact, even if a given poet had such knowledge, he would not be able to communicate it by this means. In making sense of this argument, we need to bear in mind how Plato thinks that knowledge of ethical truth is, in fact, acquired: namely by a programme of dialectical education which is preceded by, and grounded in, the right kind of training of dispositions and practices. As we have seen, in Plato's view, poetry (if appropriately directed) can play a role in the first, habituative, stage of education. But the very feature that makes it, in principle, effective in this stage of education (the fact that it is correlated with a psychological state that falls short of full rationality) makes it ineffective as a replacement for the dialectical programme sketched in Books Six and Seven.

That this is the type of 'deceptiveness' that Plato has in view in the first stage of his argument comes out in two passages whose significance is not always appreciated. Plato gives the example of a painter depicting 'a shoemaker or carpenter or other craftsmen, although he knows about none of these skills'. But, despite his ignorance in this respect, if he is 'a good painter, by making a painting of a carpenter and showing it from a distance, he would deceive at least children and foolish people into thinking that it really is a carpenter' (598b9–c4). Shortly afterwards, he draws an analogy between this process and that by which a poet 'uses words and phrases to give some of the colour of the different skills, though he himself knows nothing except how to represent them, so that, as a result . . . what is said in this way seems absolutely right, whether about generalship or anything else' (601a5–b1).

It is worth noting the apparent oddity of these claims. Plato is not talking about the skill of the painter in painting (the surface appearance of) *beds*, as the opening stage of the argument might lead one to expect (596bff.). He is talking about the painter painting, improbably, a *carpenter* or other craftsmen. This is an indication that his centre of concern is not, primarily, with the ontological status of the art-work, or with the capacity of art for illusionistic realism.[23] His centre of concern is rather with disputing the claim of representative artists, above all poets, to convey knowledge. In particular, he disputes the idea that, because Homer, for example, can seem to give a convincing representation of a general (Achilles, for instance) that he is, as he is widely taken to be in Greek culture, communicating knowledge 'about all human matters, as regards virtue and vice, and about divine matters too' (598e1–2).[24]

This line of argument is developed in the following stage (602c–605c). Here the claim is not only that poetry, like the other arts, is defective as a medium of communicating knowledge (in spite of the impression of knowledge given by the poet), but also that poetry, like painting, is positively inimical to the maintenance of a rational state of mind and sound beliefs. The claim here is that poetry, like painting, produces its effects by inducing certain kinds of deception or error. The success of visual representations depends on their deceiving us into seeing a flat surface as raised or lowered (thus making us see a canvas, for instance, as a temple). Analogously, the success of poetry is said to depend on our responding to another kind of deceit or error, namely the ethical misjudgments built into successful poetic representations. Plato cites here, as in Book Three, the example of the misjudgements communicated by our involvement in a powerful representation of grief (such as Homer's portrayal of Achilles in *Iliad* Eighteen), including the overstatement of the extent to which death is an evil. By creating the 'feel' of what such grief is like, the poet invites us to experience the 'irrationality' of a person in

---

23. See further Ferrari, 'Plato and Poetry', 127–8, and A. Nehamas, 'Plato on Imitation and Poetry in *Republic* 10', in Moravcsik and Temko, eds, *Plato on Beauty*, 47–78, at 61–4.

24. Plato's argument that Homer's lack of recorded achievement in politics or education is proof of lack of ethical knowledge (598e–600c) seems wholly perverse. But Plato's point is that, since the ability to write good poetry is not in itself evidence of such knowledge, we need some *additional* form of evidence to justify the claim that Homer does have such knowledge. Also, the argument underlines the point that Homeric and other Greek poetry is judged here as being in competition to the educational scheme Plato offers, esp. to the dialectical second stage, which purports to offer the kind of ethical knowledge (effective in politics and education) Homer is alleged to have lacked.

such a state of grief; and so to make such irrationality part of our character.[25]

The general form of the argument is similar to that discussed earlier, according to which 'false' representations of gods and heroes produces 'falsehood in the psyche'. But the psychology of the 'deception', and of the 'irrationality' it produces, are more fully analysed here.[26] It is suggested that these effects are inherent in the character of poetry as a mode of communication, and are not just the effects of some (albeit most) falsehood-inducing poetry. This strengthening of the position probably reflects, in part, the implications of the introduction of the second phase of the educational programme. Whereas poetry, as a type of discourse, is functionally adapted to the psychological processes involved in the first phase, it is far from adapted to that of the second phase. Indeed, its characteristic result, that of inducing, by the representation of the 'look' and 'feel' of irrational states of the human psyche, identification with these states, tends to subvert the condition of overall rationality (combining sound disposition and ethical knowledge) that the programme is designed to produce.[27]

It is clear from this analysis that the second discussion of poetry, while innovative in its deployment of the notion of deception, is not designed to be innovative in defining (what we should understand as) the 'fictional' character of poetry. This point is the more striking since the ideas deployed *could*, with appropriate modifications, serve this function. Thus, the first part of the argument (596b–598d) could be modified easily into the claim that the poet's job is to create a world of life-like 'appearances' (*phantasmata*), which gains the audience's complicity but which has, avowedly, no

---

25. See 602d and 603e–605c, esp. 603e3–5, and 604b9–c3; also 387d–388d, referred to in 603e4–5. See further Ferrari, 'Plato and Poetry', 132–4.

26. In the earlier discussion, the linkage between 'false' representation of gods and heroes and 'falsehood in the psyche' is an implication of the argument rather than an explicit part of it. Here, the linkage between the 'deceptive' power of poetry and the 'irrationality' it produces is explicit (603c–605c).

27. See also 605c10 and 606a7, where poetry is said to have this destructive effect even in the case of 'the best of us', and to have a bad effect on 'the best part of us' (i.e. reason).

truth-status.[28] Again, the idea that the poet's art of 'deception' lies in promoting engagement with (representations of) intense and complex states of mind, thus widening our range of emotional response (603c–605c), is one that we could easily accommodate in a theory of fiction.[29] Indeed, Plato's concluding argument against poetry in Book Ten (that it makes 'even the best of us' let ourselves be carried away by such representations, 605d–606d) does, in a way, presuppose the 'fictionality' of the experience involved.

His key point is that we should not suppose that, because our involvement in such cases is with what is not real life, the process of involvement has no long-term effect on our real-life character (606a–d); and this point does, by implication, presuppose that our involvement is with what is, and is recognized as being, fictional. But this aspect of the process is not at the forefront of Plato's attention, and there is no attempt to find innovative vocabulary to mark this fact (indeed, there is no verbal signal that the involvement is with a *fictional* person).[30] This is a powerful indication that the centre of his interest lies elsewhere, and that to rewrite his argument in terms of 'fiction' is to superimpose a different conceptual framework.

III

I move now to the status of the myths and images inset into the dialogues. The thesis I maintain is broadly the same as in the case of Plato's discussions of poetry: that, although these myths are clearly, in our terms, 'fictional', and Plato's indications help us to recognize their fictionality, their status is best understood in terms of the distinctions tabulated at the start of this chapter (apart from the distinction between factual and fictional discourse).

---

28. Indeed, Plato's argument *has* sometimes been so interpreted, e.g. by R. Collingwood, summarized by Nehamas, 'Plato on Imitation', 60–1, Gulley, 'Plato on Poetry', *Greece and Rome* 24 (1977), 154–69, at 155–9, and, to some extent, Gill, 'Plato's Atlantis Story', 68–9; but I do not now think that this interpretation can be sustained.

29. See the Annas and Ferrari references in n. 17 above, and VI below.

30. After the initial statement that one becomes involved with, for instance, Homer's representation of 'one of the heroes' (605c11–d1), Plato talks simply of 'one's own' and 'another's' experiences, without explicit acknowledgement that the 'other' is a fictional other: see 605d7, e5, 606b1–2.

However, the difference in the character of the material means that different issues are raised. In particular, the myths raise the question of the kind of falsehood (or fiction) involved in an attempt to put into words (in mythical or imagistic form) an understanding of the truth which is necessarily incomplete, because it reflects an uncompleted search for truth. This question is, in one way, a peculiarly Platonic concern, and one deriving from his philosophical framework and his characteristic mode of writing. But, in another way, this widening of the issues prepares us for the more general questions about Plato's relationship to his culture and about the concepts of falsehood and fiction, which I raise in Sections V and VI.

As a way of making the transition between Plato's discussion of poetry in the *Republic* and the question of the status of Platonic myths, I want to take account of two passages in the *Republic* which, taken together, shed some light on Plato's thinking about his myth-making. The first passage is one that has already been noted. The idea of the 'falsehood in the psyche' is introduced by way of a contrast with the 'falsehood in words' (*R.* 382a–c). The first is characterized, in paradoxical language, as what is 'truly falsehood' (*alēthōs pseudos*) or 'really falsehood' (*tō(i) onti pseudos*), while the second is presented as a 'copy' or 'image' in words (*mimēma* or *eidōlon*) of falsehood in the psyche (382a4, b9–c1). What is 'truly falsehood' is 'to be deceived . . . and ignorant in one's mind [psyche] about the way things are' (*ta onta*); and, in particular, to be deceived 'about the most important things' (*ta kuriōtata*); and this is a type of falsehood nobody would want to have (382a7–b5). The falsehood in words, by contrast, is sometimes useful as a 'preventative medicine' against enemies or, indeed, friends (under special circumstances, 382c6–10, 331c–d). Also, in story-telling (*muthologia*), 'because of not knowing the truth [*t'alēthes*] about the distant past, we make the false as like the true as possible, so as to make it useful [*chrēsimon*, 382d1–3]'. Later in the argument this latter idea is picked up, in the suggestion that the maintenance of the organisational structure of the ideal state could be helped by the propagation of one of these 'necessary falsehoods' (*tōn pseudōn . . . en deonti*), namely the 'noble lie' (*gennaion . . . pseudomenous*) of the myth of the metals (414b8ff.).

In analysing the line of thought of these passages, it is useful to draw on the distinctions made at the start of this chapter. Crucial here is the difference between the type of falsehood specified in the first distinction (deliberate lying) and in the second (saying or believing what is *in fact* false). Plato's contrast between 'falsehood in words' and 'falsehood in the psyche' (382a–c) corresponds with this difference. The status of the 'noble lie' can also be specified in terms of this difference. The noble lie is properly described as a 'lie' because what is involved is deliberate non-veracity (414b8ff.); but the lie is clearly designed to propagate an idea which the argument presents as true, namely that each member of the ideal state should be placed in the class for which he or she is naturally suited.[31]

However, to specify further the kinds of 'lie' and 'truth' involved, we need also to refer to the different modes of expression exemplified in my third type of distinction. The noble lie is false *as narrative*: more specifically, it is false as a narrative of a certain kind, namely a factual narrative about the past (that is, a *historical* narrative). It is factually untrue that the population of the ideal state were 'in truth' (*en alētheia(i)*) moulded in the earth and that the education just described constituted simply their 'dreams' (*oneirata*, 414d5–6). On the other hand, it seems clear that Plato would regard the noble lie as conveying what is true as analysis or interpretation. The relationship between the citizens in the ideal state can properly be understood as the kind of 'brotherhood' (being offspring of the same motherland) which the story presents, a relationship which carries the obligation to protect the motherland by ensuring that social organisation corresponds to natural ability. Correspondingly, Plato seeks to assimilate his 'lie' to the status of traditional legends, in which, as he puts it earlier, 'because of not knowing the truth about the distant past, we make the false as like the true as possible, so as to make it useful'.[32] In the case of the noble lie, at least, the kind of 'usefulness' he has in mind is the way in which the factually false

---

31. See 415b3–c6, taken with 412c–e, 413c5–d2 (also 375a–376c and 427d–434a).

32. 382d1–2, 414b8ff. See also 415d1–2, where the interlocutor envisages the noble lie achieving, *eventually*, the status of a traditional myth. Plato's comments do not, I think, imply that the factually false status of *muthologia* about the distant past is *generally* recognized; indeed, his remarks in 414c1–7 seem to imply that traditional myths are treated as factually true narratives, and the critique of 'false' poetry in 377eff. seems to make the same assumption (see n. 18 above). However, 382d1–2 makes it plain that, for analytic purposes, the factual falseness of myths should be acknowledged.

narrative (if accepted in the way that traditional myths are) can serve to propagate a general idea Plato regards as true.[33]

Applying these distinctions can take us some way towards understanding Plato's line of thought. But, to go further, we need to make reference to the conceptual framework involved, so as to see the significance of, for instance, Plato's differentiation between deliberate non-veracity (lying) and falsehood in the psyche. Part of what is being assumed is an 'objectivist' model of truth, according to which it makes sense to distinguish between what is supposed to be true and what is in fact true. The distinction drawn in 382a–c presupposes that there are objective truths as regards 'the most important things' (*ta kuriōtata*),[34] and that, by the same token, certain beliefs constitute what are (by objective standards) 'truly' or 'really' falsehoods. A related assumption is that, at a fundamental level, human beings are naturally disposed to look for, and live by, these truths. This assumption is expressed here in the idea that 'nobody willingly wants [*oudeis hekōn ethelei*] to be deceived about the most important things'; and, elsewhere in Plato, in the recurrent idea that 'nobody goes wrong willingly' (*oudeis hekōn hamartanei*).[35] The theme is taken up again in the passage preceding the introduction of the noble lie. Here it is argued that 'to be deceived about the truth' is something that nobody wants, and, hence, that loss of true beliefs also happens against the will of those concerned (*akontes*, 412e10–413a10). Thus, the processes by which people (unknowingly) lose true beliefs, namely through argument, painful experience, or strong emotion, are appropriately redescribed as 'theft, witchcraft, and force' (413b–c).[36]

The conceptual framework indicated here serves to explain the thinking about truth and communication underlying the two

---

33. For the use of myths to propagate such general truths in the community, see also *Laws* 663c–664b.

34. This phrase probably signifies the kind of life-shaping, ethical truths about which the poets are said to propagate falsehoods: see e.g. 387d–e and 392a–c (also n. 14 above).

35. 382a8, b1–5, c3–4; for the latter idea as a recurrent Platonic theme, see M.M. Mackenzie, *Plato on Punishment* (Berkeley, 1981), ch. 9.

36. Plato seems to have in mind, and to be revising, the line of thought in Gorgias, *Helen*, esp. 10, 12–14. On Gorgias and the 'bewitchment' of language, see A. Laird, pp. 170–3 below.

passages under discussion (382a–d and 414b8ff.), as well as in the adjacent treatment of poetry (376eff.). It is clear why, against this background, Plato regards lying as less ethically worrying than 'falsehood in the psyche' or ethical ignorance.[37] As Plato underlines, with paradoxical relish, lying, as in the case of the noble lie, may be the most effective way to propagate truth.[38] Indeed, given what is said in 382d about the (factual) truth-status of *muthologia*, the whole process of (revised) story-telling envisaged in the first phase of Plato's educational programme consists of lies, though they are lies which are functionally adapted to implant the kind of dispositions and practices that are the basis of 'truth in the psyche'.[39]

What is worth underlining is that close analysis of these passages, in the light of Plato's conceptual framework, does not require us to make reference at any point to the idea of 'fiction', as we understand it. In saying this, I am not denying that the status which is ascribed to the 'falsehood in words' (as regards *muthologia*, for instance), and to the noble lie, is, in our terms, 'fictional', at least in the sense that the relevant type of narrative is consciously made-up or fabricated (though not in the sense that the audience is meant to be aware of this status).[40] It is, therefore, understandable that translators of the *Republic* tend, at these points, to slide from translating *pseudos* as 'falsehood' to translating it as 'fiction'.[41] But, as I have suggested, the conceptual structure of the passages can be analysed effectively in terms of truth and falsehood; and it is quite unclear how any of the ideas we associate with 'fiction' are relevant to this structure.

---

37. Contrast Kant's assumption that the (unqualified) prohibition 'do not lie' can be taken as a prime example of a moral law, *Groundwork of the Metaphysic of Morals*, tr. H.J. Paton in *The Moral Law* (London, 1986), 67–8.

38. In fact, in *R.* 414b8ff., as in *Laws* 663c–664b, the 'lie' is innocuous or transparent; and the purpose of the stress on the 'lie' involved is, presumably, to underline the framework of thinking about truth and communication involved; see also *Hippias Minor* 372a–373a.

39. See discussion above (text to nn. 11–17), and Ferrari, 'Plato and Poetry', 112–13.

40. See 32 above, and for a case where the status of the myth *is* meant to be recognized (the Atlantis story), see discussion below.

41. See e.g. D. Lee, Penguin Classics (Harmondsworth, 1976), at 382d; G.M.A. Grube, Pan Classics (London, 1981), at 382d and 414c; P. Shorey, in the Bollingen *Collected Dialogues of Plato* (New York, 1964), at 414c.

These passages in the *Republic* provide a—partial—framework for understanding the status of the Platonic myths, that is, the status of what we might regard as being Plato's 'fictions'. The most suggestive pointer is the comment about *muthologia*, that, 'because of not knowing the truth about the distant past, we make the false as like the true as possible' (382d1–3), taken together with the status of the noble lie. It is characteristic of what we call Plato's 'myths' that they present, usually in narrative or descriptive form, accounts of subjects of which we do not, and indeed cannot, know the truth (not, at least, in the form in which this is presented in the myths).

The reasons why the truth is not available vary. In the case of the Atlantis and *Statesman* myths, it is because the events described, like those of the type of story-telling noted in *R.* 382d, belong to the distant past, from which we are separated by various kinds of cultural and natural discontinuity.[42] In other cases, we are offered a detailed narrative or description of human life after death; or, in a related mode, accounts of human life and the physical world from a divine or quasi-divine perspective.[43] Other such cases, the status of which is to be discussed shortly, include the 'prophetic' account of human aspirations given by Diotima in the *Symposium* (*Smp.* 201d–212b); the 'myth of the cave' (*R.* 514aff.), picturing our human condition as regards the attainment of objective knowledge; and the creation-myth of the *Timaeus* (27c–92c). In all these cases, for a variety of reasons, we do not know the truth about the subjects described—at least not in the specific, quasi-factual form presented in the myths—and the myths are, to this extent, 'noble lies', false in the form which they are presented, though ones which are made, presumably, 'as like the true as possible' (*R.* 382d2–3).

However, there are two significant differences between the noble lie and the Platonic myths. One is that, in the case of the noble lie, it would seem that the audience is intended to accept the story as factually true in the form in which it is presented; at least, the

---

42. See *Timaeus* (*Ti.*) 17–27 and *Critias* (*Criti.*), and see further below, and *Politicus* (*Plt.*) 268d–274e.
43. That is, the eschatological myths of *Gorgias* (*Grg.*) 523a–527e, *Phaedo* (*Phd.*) 107d–114c (including the quasi-divine picture of the physical world as we know this in 108c–113c), *R.* 614b–621d, *Phaedrus* (*Phdr.*) 246a–257a (an account of the nature of psyche from a quasi-divine perspective).

audience is not intended to be alerted to its status as falsehood.[44] In the case of the Platonic myths, by contrast, the truth-status—or falsehood-status—of the myths is made explicit within the dialogue between the myth-teller and the interlocutor. Secondly, as regards the noble lie, the truth of the general idea conveyed by the noble lie seems to be presumed; at least, it is not called into question.[45] In the dialogues, by contrast, it is, typically, made clear that the myth-teller is not fully in possession of knowledge of the truth of the idea conveyed by the myth; sometimes, indeed, no human being can be. To this extent, the myths, unlike the noble lie, cannot be characterized as factually false narratives conveying general truths; their status is rather that of factually false narratives (and descriptions), conveying the results of the myth-teller's *search* for truth. The 'falsehood' involved in the myth is, thus, not simply that inherent in the mode of expression, as used as a vehicle for the material involved; it also inheres in the fact that the myth-teller is not fully in possession of the truth of the idea conveyed through this vehicle.

The difference can be characterized, to some extent, in terms of the two-stage educational programme of the *Republic*. In the case of the noble lie (and the revised myth-telling in the first phase of education), the truth of the ideas conveyed in, or underlying, the stories is presumed; at least, it is presumed that *there can be* a human authority with knowledge of the truth in question. Attention is focused rather on the kinds of story (and, more generally, the kinds of communicative vehicle) which can convey (true) beliefs and the correlated psychological states (the patterns of aspiration and desire).[46] In the dialogues themselves, we are—up to a point—rather in the realm of the second stage of education. At least, the mode of discourse is, typically, dialectical, conducted by figures of whom some are dispositionally and intellectually capable of engaging in

---

44. See *R.* 414b8ff. and n. 32 above. One might restate the point as being that Plato is assimilating his story to the *class* of stories (*muthoi* about the distant past) the factual truth of which is not, typically, called into question. See also *Laws* 663e–664a.

45. See above, text to n. 31. In the parallel passage in *Laws* (660eff.) the truth of the idea *is* argued for, although it is added that, even if it were not true, no idea could more beneficially be propagated among the population of the state (663c–664a).

46. See discussion in II above, esp. text to nn. 6–9, and *R.* 400d–402c, 414b–415d.

dialectic. Correspondingly, it is appropriate for them to raise questions about the extent to which they have achieved, or could achieve in principle, the kind of knowledge of truth that the discussion takes as its goal. And the extent to which this is the case has implications for the truth-status of the myths told in the dialogues, as well as that of the arguments.[47]

In illustrating these features of Plato's myth-making, I focus first on indications about the truth-status of the myth considered as a factual narrative or description, and then as the vehicle of a general idea. A clear-cut example of the former comes in the *Phaedrus*. When Phaedrus points out that Socrates has made up the 'Egyptian' legend he tells, Socrates replies, tartly, that what matters is not the source of such a story, but the truth or falsity of the idea it conveys (275b–c). This is, in effect, to concede the falsity of the story as historical narrative, a point also signalled at the start of the story.[48]

A much more complex case is the presentation of the creation-story in *Timaeus* (29b–c).[49] It is argued that the degree of truth attainable by a given form of discourse (*logos*) is necessarily limited by the subject-matter of the discourse. *Logoi* whose subject-matter is 'being' (*ousia*) are, in principle, capable of achieving 'truth' (*alētheia*), while those whose subject-matter is 'becoming' (*genesis*), can only be 'likely' (*eikōs*) and merit 'trust' or 'credibility' (*pistis*). Hence, as regards the *genesis* ('coming to be' or 'becoming') of the universe, we must be content if we can achieve 'likelihood', and so

---

47. To say this is not to deny that the myths (like the revised myths in the first phase of Plato's educational programme) can have a non-cognitive function, in affecting aspirations and desires. But the question of what this function involves cannot be separated wholly from the question of the truth-status of the idea conveyed in the myth. See further n. 55 below.

48. 'I can tell you what I have heard [*akoēn*] from our ancestors, but, as regards its truth [*t'alēthes*], only they know. If we were able to find this out for ourselves, would we still concern ourselves with human conjectures [*doxasmatōn*]?' (274c1–3). I take it that the 'truth' involved here is that of the story as factual narrative (about the actions and words of the gods concerned); but Socrates may also have in view the difficulty of discovering the truth of the general ideas conveyed in such stories, a difficulty which forces us to rely on 'human conjectures' (about divine words and actions) of the type represented in this story.

49. I am grateful to Rosemary Wright for underlining the relevance of this passage for my topic. See further her 'How Credible are Plato's Myths?', in G.W. Bowersock, W. Burkert, M.C.J. Putnam, eds, *Arktouros: Hellenic Studies presented to B.M.W. Knox* (Berlin, 1979), 364–71.

the status of the account is presented as being, at best, a 'likely story' (*eikōs muthos*, 29d2).

Part of what is suggested in this passage is that, in such a topic, the aspect on which we can, in principle, reach the 'truth' is that of the intelligible principles underlying the nature and creation of the universe. As regards the aspect of the topic that falls into the category of 'becoming', the character of the universe as a physical object (and as a physical object which has 'come to be' in its present form), we can achieve only likelihood or credibility. Also, the extent to which even this is possible is limited by the extent to which we, as human beings, can understand the supra-human, or 'divine', scale of what is involved; thus, the resulting account is to be characterized as a 'likely story' (*eikōs muthos*), rather than a 'likely account' (*eikōs logos*).[50]

In the *Timaeus*, the limited truth-status attached to the myth derives from the limited extent to which the myth, with its specific kind of subject matter, can serve as a vehicle for the truth about intelligible beings.[51] The additional problem of reaching knowledge of such truth at all is not emphasized here, although it is acknowledged.[52] When this problem is emphasized, it is also recognized as carrying implications for the truth-status of the relevant myth. Thus, for instance, at the end of the arguments for the immortality of the psyche in the *Phaedo*, both Socrates and his interlocutor underline the fundamental difficulty, for human beings, in reaching the truth on such matters; and Socrates emphasizes the need to investigate further the assumptions made in the argument (107a9–b9).

The provisional character of the conclusion reached bears on the truth-status of the account of the after-life of the psyche, an account which only merits attention 'if', as Socrates acknowledges, 'the psyche is immortal'.[53] This point should be borne in mind in gauging

---

50. *Ti.* 27c4–d3, also, on types of *logoi*, 27b3–c3. The *muthos–logos* contrast is common elsewhere: see e.g. *Grg.* 523a1–3, *Ti.* 26e4–5, discussed below.

51. The myth serves as a vehicle for such truth in the sense that it conveys (inadequately) the role of the universe as an expression of intelligible being.

52. The problems acknowledged, unemphatically, in *Ti.* 29b7–8 and 29c4–d3, are given more emphatic statement in the *Seventh Letter*, attributed to Plato, 340b–345c, esp. 342–3 and 344b.

53. *Phd.* 107c2; the connection is made in less qualified terms in 114d4: 'given at least that [*epeiper . . . ge*] the psyche has been shown to be immortal'.

the significance of the comments made by Socrates at the end of the myth:

> No sensible person would claim that the facts of the case are just as I have presented them; but to suppose that this or such-like is the case . . . seems to be a risk worth taking . . . and we should use such stories to enchant ourselves . . .
>
> (114d1–7)

These comments acknowledge that it is inappropriate to claim truth for the specific details of the description of the life of the psyche after death; on the surface level, the description is a 'noble lie', albeit one that has been made as 'like' the truth as possible.[54] But also, given the (provisional) status of the conclusion of the argument, on which the validity of the story depends, its truth-status is yet more qualified. Thus, the 'risk' involved is a two-fold one, including both the acceptance of the conclusion of the argument and of the specific details of the story; and the comments made underline the two-fold character of the risk.[55]

A similar point applies, in varying ways, to three notable myths, or myth-like passages: the 'palinode' in the *Phaedrus* (244a–257b), Diotima's speech in the *Symposium* ([*Smp.*] 210d–212b), and the myth of the cave in the *Republic* (514a–517a). These three passages all offer a visionary picture or image of what is involved in gaining objective knowledge of ethical truth, and of the kind of life that goes with such knowledge. But all three passages give indications that the one who presents the visionary picture (Socrates) does not present himself as being in possession of the relevant kind of knowledge. Therefore, the truth-claims of the myths are qualified not just by the mode of expression involved (its being 'poetic' rather than dialectical, or a quasi-religious prophecy, or simply an 'image' of the truth)[56] but also by the status of the speaker in relation to the kind

---

54. See *R.* 414b8ff., and 382d1–3, discussed above; and, for the idea of such stories as yielding, at best, 'likelihood', *Ti.* 29b–d.

55. Thus, it is not quite right to claim that Plato resorts to myth here in an attempt to bring reassurance (or 'enchantment', *epa(i)dein*, *Phd.* 114d7) when argument fails, as Ferrari suggests, 'Plato and Poetry', 143–4. The kind of 'enchantment' offered depends on the validity of the conclusions which give point to the story (n. 53 above).

56. See *Phdr.* 257a, also 243a–b and 244a; *Smp.* 201d and 210a; *R.* 514a1, 515a4; see further below.

of truth conveyed in these modes of expression. Indeed, the connection between these two points is underlined in each case.

Thus, in the *Phaedrus*, the nature of the psyche (on which the rest of the account depends) is said to need a god's power to describe; what is offered, instead, is a human picture of what 'it is like' (*hō(i) . . . eoiken*).[57] In the *Symposium*, the gap between Diotima's quasi-divine understanding of the nature of desire (*erōs*) and Socrates', merely human, understanding is underlined repeatedly. Thus, Socrates' restatement of her vision of the 'mysteries' is, as he himself indicates, a matter of 'conviction' not knowledge.[58]

In the *Republic*, before the three images which are used to convey a conception of the kind of objective ethical knowledge that the argument requires, Socrates makes it plain that he speaks as one who has 'opinions without knowledge' about the nature of this kind of knowledge. Hence, he can only offer his opinion about what is 'most like' (*homoiotatos*) this knowledge; and the subsequent 'image' of the cave is an appropriate medium for someone to offer a vision of something he does not claim to understand fully.[59] Only someone who had passed through the cognitive stages pictured in the myth would be able to substantiate the truth of what is pictured (and, thus, to offer an account which does not need to resort to images). As Socrates indicates in the comments following the myth, it is hard—if not, perhaps, quite impossible—to see how anyone could do this, without completing an educational programme designed by someone who already had such knowledge.[60] Thus, the qualified truth-status of the myth or image in these cases does not derive

---

57. *Phdr.* 246a4–6; see also the acknowledgement that the idea of an immortal being (which is again central to the account) is something which we (mortals) 'construct' (*plattomen*) without having seen or understood adequately (246c6–7).

58. See *Smp.* 206b, 207c, 210a, 211e–212a; also 212b2, in which he claims to have been 'convinced' or 'persuaded' (*pepeismai*) by what he reports. Even if we take it that Socrates *has* completed the 'mysteries' described, and hence achieved the kind of 'immortality' available to a human being (211e4–212a7), this will not give him Diotima's quasi-divine perspective on the nature and scope of such human 'immortality'.

59. See *R.* 506c–e, esp. e3–4; also 514a1, 515a4.

60. See 517b–521b, esp. 519bff.; the type of person envisaged in 496b–497a might be an exception. Hence, the comment that those pictured in the image are 'like us' (515a5) is appropriate enough, although the image also offers 'us' a picture of the procedure by which to improve our state.

simply from the mode of expression deployed, considered as a vehicle for the type of content conveyed. The selection of mode is itself correlated with the degree of knowledge claimed by the speaker, and the combination of the two serves to determine the status of the myth.

There is still one important myth to be considered, that of Atlantis; but let me sum up the implications of Plato's presentation of his myth-making, as discussed so far. I think it is clear that we can see Plato's myths as being 'fictional' in two senses. They are fictional in the sense that the specific details conveyed (the 'facts of the case', so to speak) are made-up; and the mode of expression chosen (myth or image) reflects this character. Also, unlike the noble lie (which is also made-up, in this sense), the fabrication is explicit; so the audience involved is made a party to the 'fiction'. Further, the fact that the myths are presented, typically, as being made-up by someone who does not claim to be in full possession of knowledge of the subjects so pictured (or of the kind of knowledge pictured) is an index of 'fictionality' of another type. In the absence of this knowledge, the picture so provided is a product of (what we should see as) invention or construction at the level of idea as well as of specific 'facts' and mode of expression.[61] But, although it is clear that Plato's myth-making can be so described, and that this description makes sense in relation to *our* thinking about fiction, it is also clear that this description does not interlock with Plato's concerns and conceptual framework. The features I have noted do not derive from a concern with story-telling for its own sake, or with authorial and narrative 'truth-games'. They derive, for the most part, from acknowledgement on the part of Plato's speakers of the difficulties, and incompleteness, in gaining the kind of knowledge of objective truth that is standardly taken as the goal of enquiry in the dialogues.[62]

There is, however, one apparent counter-instance to this generalization. A striking feature of the presentation of the Atlantis story is that, although we are prepared to expect a functional fable (designed

---

61. For 'fiction' and 'fictionality' in this sense, see VI below.
62. See also Ferrari, 'Plato and Poetry', 113: 'Whereas fiction for us has positive and autonomous value, a speculation, while useful . . . remains a second-best, a stab at truth'; see further below on the implications of this point for understanding the form of the Platonic dialogue in general.

to illustrate the excellence of the ideal state of the *Republic*), we are told, repeatedly, that the story is 'not a made-up story' (*plastheis muthos*) but a true account (*alēthinos logos*).[63] The kind of 'truth' involved seems clearly to be that of the account as a historical record of factual events, since great detail is given about the transmission of the account and the historical context of the events described.[64] However, given the contrasting indications that the story is, rather, the illustration of a philosophical thesis, and given certain other 'mythical' features of the story,[65] we are also encouraged to suspect that the story is *not* true in this sense. Correspondingly, it may seem that, here at least, Plato is engaging in a narrative or authorial truth-game, inviting his audience to treat as 'true' what he also implies is not 'true' in the relevant sense.

This is a suggestion I have made elsewhere; and I supported it by reference to apparent allusions in the presentation of the Atlantis story to the discussions of poetry in the *Republic*. Since I took the *Republic*'s analysis of the truth and falsehood of poetry as constituting, in effect if not in aim, an exploration of the fictional quality of poetry, I took these allusions to support the interpretation of the Atlantis story as, in part at any rate, an experiment in fiction.[66] A

---

63. See *Ti.* 26e4–5 and 20d7–8, 21a4–5; also 17c–20c.

64. See *Ti.* 20e–25e, also *Criti.* 109d–112d. In *Grg.*, by contrast, the eschatological story which is also claimed to be an account (*logos*), not a myth (*muthos*), and a true one (*alēthes*), 523a1–3, is rather to be understood as 'true' in respect of the ideas it conveys. The uncharacteristic assertiveness with which this kind of 'truth' is claimed in *Grg.* reflects the combative, rhetorical mode of discourse Socrates adopts in the dialogue, esp. after the breakdown of the normal procedure of dialectic as a shared search for the truth (505c–506c).

65. These include the positioning of the story in the remote past and (in the case of Atlantis) in a remote, and now lost, location, and the involvement of gods and 'godlike' figures in the embellishment of the communities involved: see e.g. *Ti.* 23e–24a, 24e–25d, *Criti.* 109b–e, 113c–114c. In the light of these 'mythic' touches, the quasi-historical presentation of the story seems like historiographic *pastiche* (see esp. *Ti.* 21dff., *Criti.* 109eff.) rather than actual history. See further C. Gill, ed., *Plato: The Atlantis Story* (Bristol, 1980), xii–xiv, xx–xxi.

66. In *Criti.* 107b–108a, Critias' concern with artistic verisimilitude seems to align him with poets, as analysed (and criticized) in *R.* 598bff., although Critias, like the other interlocutors, is also presented as a philosopher-politician, capable of engaging in the kind of philosophically directed creation most poets are *not* equal to (*Ti.* 19d–20a, *R.* 401b–402c, 598e–601b). See further, Gill, 'Plato's Atlantis Story', 65–74, and 'The Genre of the Atlantis Story', *Classical Philology* 72 (1977), 287–304, at 288–91.

crucial part of this suggestion was the idea that Plato, by his allusions to the *Republic*'s discussions of poetry, and by his puzzling
combination of indications about the status of the story, alerted the
audience to the fictionality of the story. Thus, in advance of the
creation of a recognized *genre* of fictional writing, Plato (on this
view) invited his audience to play 'the game of fiction', that is, the
game of pretending to treat as 'true' what is known to be 'false'.[67]
This presentation has a special appropriateness in the case of a story
which, by comparison with other Platonic myths, is rich in its profu-
sion of graphic detail and sparing in its indications of the underlying
philosophical message.[68] Plato seems to be enjoying story-telling for
its own sake as well as initiating his audience in the special kind of
truth-game that constitutes fiction.

Although I do not wish to disown this view entirely, or to deny
the suggestive role of the Atlantis story in the history of Greek
forms of narrative, I would like to mark some reservations from the
line of thought just summarized. I think that an interpretation of this
kind needs to offer a more positive explanation than I provided as to
why Plato should want to explore the game of fiction. I tended to
assume too readily that there is present in Greek culture (or any
culture) an inbuilt disposition to distinguish factual from fictional
discourse (in the way that we do) and to evolve (what we see as) the
practice of fiction.[69] I was over-inclined to read the *Republic*'s
discussions of poetry as involving, at least by implication, a distinction between factual and fictional discourse, whereas those discussions now seem to me to be directed by different conceptual
concerns, of a kind analysed earlier.[70]

Also, I now think that the features of the Atlantis story which I
associated with Plato's experimentation with fiction can be
explained, more credibly and economically, by pursuing the implications of Socrates' request for a narrative celebration of the ideal
political state of the *Republic* (17c–20b). It is helpful here to recall
the status of the noble lie of *R*. 414bff., which is, in effect, an

---

67. 'Plato's Atlantis Story', 76.
68. See esp. *Criti.* 113c–120d, followed by the hasty moralizing and abrupt aban-
    doning of the story in 120e–121c.
69. See further on this point V below.
70. See 'Plato's Atlantis Story', 64–5 and II above.

invented version of the type of 'charter' or 'foundation' myths which give the validation of tradition to the character of a given society.[71] What Socrates requests in the *Timaeus* is simply a narrative exemplification of the merits of the ideal state; but what he is offered is something closer to the noble lie, a traditional story which validates a primaeval version of Athens (here taken as a historical equivalent of the ideal state), by celebrating its foundation and greatest achievement (*Ti.* 20d–26d). Part of the validation offered for the noble lie (and, by inference, for the collective myths on which it is modelled) is that the events presented are taken to be true, although it is not normally expected that the myth will include historical corroboration of this factual truth.[72] Critias' emphasis on the factual truth of his celebratory account of primaeval Athens may be taken as signalling the genre of the story, a charter-myth presented (like other charter-myths) as being (factually) true, and in this way substantiating the character of the *polis* thus celebrated.[73]

The acceptance of such myths as true did not normally depend on the kind of historical corroboration that is offered in this case. The fact that this is provided here may reflect Plato's own thinking about what *would* be required to make such a charter-myth appear true after the development of historiographical techniques and criteria.[74] The provision of such corroboration also reflects a feature of Plato's later thought (and one which is also, and more straightforwardly, evident in *Laws* Three), namely an interest in the process of historical, and pre-historical, verification, and in the analysis of past events as a mode of political

71. On such 'charter' myths, see e.g. G.S. Kirk, *Myth: Its Meaning and Function in Ancient and Other Cultures* (Berkeley, 1970), 254–7.

72. See discussion of *R.* 414b8ff. above, esp. n. 32.

73. The references to the 'truth' of the story occur in connection with its charter-myth function, i.e. the celebration of primaeval Athens, taken as the historical equivalent of the ideal state: see 20d–21a, 26d–e.

74. In *Laws* Three (esp. 701d–702e), the (imagined) foundation of an ideal *polis* in Crete is preceded by political theorizing grounded on a study of prehistorical evidence for the growth of the *polis* and of recent political history; the Atlantis-story prefigures this procedure, providing a quasi-historical charter myth to validate the ideal *polis*.

theorizing.[75] The claim of historical truth may, therefore, reflect an interest in that kind of 'truth', and in the idea that the combination of truth-seeking historical enquiry and truth-seeking political theory is a valid one.

Of course, the Atlantis story is not itself a traditional charter-myth, nor is the account of its transmission and of the supporting cultural and physical evidence meant to be taken as, literally, establishing its factual truth. But the story enacts what would be involved in such a procedure. It also signals an interest in the thought that charter-myths, historiographical accounts, and political theorizing, can all be understood as modes of collective reflection on what constitutes a 'great' achievement or a worthwhile community;[76] and that establishing the truth in this matter partly depends on establishing the truth of the 'facts' involved. This line of thought now seems to me to provide an explanation for Plato's truth-claim for his story which is, on the whole, more credible that that which associates this with the evolution of the concept of fiction.

IV

I now consider the implications of the discussion so far for the understanding of the status of what are, in a larger sense, Plato's 'fictions', namely the dialogues in which the myths are placed. (The question is both complex and intensely controversial; and my remarks here can only be generalized and dogmatic.) As in the case of Plato's myths, there are two distinct senses in which we can see Plato's dialogues as fictional. One is that they represent versions of

---

75. See esp. *Ti.* 22a–23b (problems posed for transmission of evidence by cultural and natural discontinuity), 24a–c (a form of comparative sociology), *Criti.* 109e–110b (investigation of the past and the problem of evidence), 110c–111d (physical evidence of changes in landscape; note esp. the vocabulary for verification or 'truth' in this connection, 110d5, e6, 111a3–4, c3–4, d7–8). See *Laws* 3, esp. 682a4, 683e10–684a1; see further Gill, 'The Genre of the Atlantis Story', 301–2, 'Plato and Politics: the *Critias* and the *Politicus*', *Phronesis* 24 (1979), 148–67, at 161–2.

76. Relevant here are the apparent allusions in *Ti.* 24d–e, to the proems of Herodotus (Hdt.) (see also 7.20), and Thucydides (1.1, 1.23), also in *Ti.* 256b–c to Hdt. 7.139; and the allusions in those historical writers (also, perhaps, *Ti.* 21c–d) to epic prototypes, esp. the *Iliad*, on which see J.L. Moles, pp. 93–4, 96, 101–3 below. On the use of allusions to the Persian and Peloponnesian Wars to construct the Atlantis story, and to frame its political message, see Gill, 'The Genre of the Atlantis Story', 294–8, *Plato: The Atlantis Story*, xvii–xx.

conversations between (mostly) historical individuals, which express, in a more or less fully fictionalized form, the ideas, modes of discourse, and character of those individuals. The other is that they represent a search for knowledge of objective truth of a kind that is, for the most part, presented as not fully achieved in the dialogues.[77] Accordingly, the arguments in the dialogues constitute a species of speculation or 'construction', rather than a set of doctrines presented as based on knowledge or objective truth; and they can be seen as being, in this extended sense, 'fictional'.

Leaving aside, for the moment, the question whether Plato would recognize or accept the ideas of 'fictionality' involved here, I want to draw attention to a marked disparity in the extent to which Plato signals the existence of these two types of fictionality. Although it is possible for us to make plausible guesses about the extent to which dialogues are 'fictional' in the first sense (and, occasionally, to detect the process of fictionalizing at work),[78] there are no formal indications of the degree of fictionality involved. Although the later dialogues are, for the most part, plausibly seen as more fictional than the earlier ones, there are no formal indications of this difference, for instance, in the presentation of the transmission of the dialogues.[79] As regards the second type of fictionality, by contrast, Plato gives a wide range of indications, some of which have been noted already, about the extent to which the arguments represented fall short of achieving the kind of conclusion sought, and the kind of knowledge taken as the goal of enquiry. Although there is no general agreement about the proper way to understand either of these features of Plato's writing, or the disparity between them, I think it is possible to offer a line of explanation which bears on both points.

Plato may well have accepted that 'fictionality' in the first sense was inherent in the project of writing, as he and others did, 'Socratic dialogues' (sōkratikoi logoi), which both celebrated and perpetuated

---

77. See discussion above, esp. text to nn. 52–60.
78. E.g. in the idealizing account of Socrates' death by hemlock poisoning, which I discuss in 'The Death of Socrates', *Classical Quarterly* n.s. 23 (1973), 25–8.
79. Thus, e.g., the accounts of the transmission of the *Theaetetus* (142c–143c) or *Parmenides* (126b–127a) are as detailed and circumstantial as that of *Smp.* 172a–174a), but most scholars would regard the former as more 'fictional' in the relevant sense than the latter.

the Socratic method of philosophical enquiry through dialogue. Indeed, fictionality of this type is especially a part of the Platonic version of this practice, since, as a major philosophical intellect, he uses the form to pursue the questions which Socrates raised in ways in which Socrates almost certainly did not. Part of Plato's mode of perpetuating the Socratic project seems to have been to use the form of written dialogue as a way of illustrating, and promoting, the Socratic conception of philosophy as shared enquiry, through organised discussion, with the ultimate goal of defining, and achieving, systematic knowledge of objective truth. A crucial part of the project seems also to have been to underline the obstacles to achieving that goal, obstacles constituted by the defective understanding and character of the enquirers, the conceptual difficulty of the project, and the inadequacy of the methodologies and forms of discourse involved. It is understandable, then, that Plato's perpetuation of the Socratic project should contain clear indications about the nature and extent of these obstacles.[80]

It is much less clear why the perpetuation of the Socratic project should require Plato to signal the degree of fictionality involved in the creative extension of Socrates' work. Even Thucydides, writing in a straightforwardly historical mode, does not, after his famous programmatic comments (allowing himself to compose speeches in the light of his analysis of the events and their significance), offer localized signals about the degree of fictionality involved in each case.[81] For Plato, writing in a mode whose generic status (in so far as it can be placed precisely in relation to other practices of the day) is not straightforwardly historical, there is even less reason to do so.[82]

The question remains, whether Plato would recognize or accept the characterization of these features of his writing as involving

---

80. See further C. Gill, 'Dogmatic Dialogue in *Phaedrus* 276–7?', in L. Rossetti, ed., *Understanding the Phaedrus, Proceedings of Symposium Platonicum* II (St Augustin, 1992), 156–72; and C.L. Griswold, ed., *Platonic Writings, Platonic Readings* (New York, 1988), esp. chs 6 (K.M. Sayre), 9 (Griswold), 15 (N.P. White and H.-G. Gadamer).

81. See Thuc. 1. 22, discussed by J.L. Moles at pp. 104–6 below.

82. For an attempt to place the Platonic, and other Socratic, dialogues in this context, see A. Momigliano, *The Development of Greek Biography* (Cambridge, Mass., 1971), 46–62.

'fictionality', in either of these senses. I think the drift of the preceding discussion makes plain what our answer should be to this question: namely, that the procedures involved would be conceived in terms of truth and falsehood, and of the role of the modes of expression deployed in conveying truth and falsehood. Although the fictionality involved in the fictionalizing of Socrates' conversations is distinct from that in the Platonic myths, it is clear that this fictionality could also be analysed in terms drawn from the *Republic*, such as that of the noble lie, the verbal falsehood designed to propagate the process of acquiring 'truth in the psyche', or of 'making the false as like the true as possible so as to make it useful'.

As regards the second type of fictionality, little argument is needed, I think, to show that the manifestations of this could be analysed, Platonically, in terms of the representation and promotion of the search for truth, and of the forms of 'falsehood' (and the attempt at 'likelihood') thus involved. I think it is also clear that Plato would not be very happy with the idea that such procedures can properly be described as the 'construction' or 'invention' of truth, for reasons which I elaborate in Section VI.

V

My thesis has been that Plato's conceptual framework, and the procedures informed by that framework, can be analysed effectively in terms of the types of distinction presented at the start of this chapter, with the exception of that between factual and fictional discourse. If this thesis is accepted, it remains to ask whether Plato is exceptional or typical in this respect within his culture. Clearly, Plato's theorizing about truth and falsehood involves innovations. But the important question is whether his innovations involve the ignoring or erasure of a distinction which was already explicit (or, at least, strongly implied) in his culture, and which persisted in later Greek culture.

Before broaching the question in this form, some methodological distinctions need to be drawn, and possible positions defined. We need to distinguish between:

(1) the assumption that fiction is a universal human practice, carried out in different forms and under different descriptions in all actual or conceivable societies; and

(2) the assumption that 'fiction' signifies a determinate practice (that it is, more or less, what *we* mean by 'fiction') performed in some societies, under some explicit or implicit description which we can recognize as being that of 'fiction'.

Either position is intellectually tenable; but it is clearly the latter assumption which has informed my discussion so far, and, I think, that of the other contributors to this volume. The question then arises: by what criteria do we determine whether a given practice is presented under a description (implicit or explicit) which we can recognize as being that of 'fiction'? As I understand this question, it is one which involves considering social or institutional roles as well as the conceptual framework associated with these roles.

In E.L. Bowie's essay (ch. 1 above), if I understand him correctly, the key criterion is whether or not a poet sees himself as exercising individual choice in selecting between (or making up) the version of the stories he presents, as distinct from acting purely as the mouthpiece of a collective tradition. If he does the former, he is described appropriately as an 'author', in roughly our sense, that is, as a source or inventor of fiction. By this criterion, Stesichorus, and later Pindar, are clearly fictional authors, since they reject some stories about the gods and prefer others (which they have, in some sense, 'made up').[83] Their role in this regard is anticipated, to some degree, by the figure of Odysseus in Homer's *Odyssey*, who tells stories which the audience knows are lies (that is, who selects or makes up the versions of events he narrates). The fact that Homer's poem contains a figure of this type has implications for the status of Homer's poem: if Odysseus can create 'fictions', so, by implication, can Homer. The 'fictionality' involved in these cases is implicit (though signalled in the ways described). But one way to interpret Hesiod's enigmatic distinction between 'false things which resemble true' and 'true things' is as a distinction between Homeric fictional poetry and Hesiodic factual poetry, thus arti-

---

83. See Bowie's discussion of the evidence for Stesichorus' palinode (pp. 23–8 above); also Pind. *Ol.* 1.27–36.

culating the conceptual differentiation embodied in these poetic practices.[84]

The main problem with this kind of approach, as it seems to me, inheres in the assumption that, if a poet sees himself as selecting a given version of a story (or indeed, in some sense, 'making it up'), his role is, therefore, to be understood as being that of an individual author of fictions. The role of Hesiod, Stesichorus and Pindar, in the relevant passages, may be understood better as a social or ethical one, in so far as they present themselves as using the persuasive power of poetry to proclaim, and to convince their audiences, of what is 'true' about the gods. The distinction drawn in the prologue of Hesiod's *Theogony* (27–8) may be taken rather as expressing the claim to state what is 'true' about the gods instead of false things which 'resemble' (and purport to be) true, as (by implication) some other poets do. As for the representation of Odysseus as one who is capable of telling 'false things which resemble the true' (*Od.* 19.203), this does not seem to me necessarily to carry the implication that the *Odyssey* is to be understood as fictional. Odysseus' role as someone capable of lying is simply part of the character of the traditional figure which Homer presents. To put the point in terms suggested by these poets themselves, part of Homer's job, as a Muse-inspired poet, is to use the persuasive and pleasing power of poetry to propagate what is 'true' of the hero Odysseus.

The issue can be put in a larger intellectual context. I think that we should take account of the views of Eric Havelock and others, who have argued that we should understand poetic self-descriptions in archaic Greek poetry in the light of the primary function of the poet in a predominantly oral culture. This function, as they see it, is to serve as a medium for the transmission of the collective 'wisdom' of the society, embodied in the pleasurable and memorable form of narrative and other verse forms.[85] Although this function is fulfilled by (what we should conceive as) creative selection, adaptation, and

---

84. See esp. Homer (Hom.), *Odyssey* (*Od.*) 19.203, and Hesiod, *Theogony* (Hes. *Theog.*) 27–8; the fact that the latter passage echoes the phrasing of the former is taken by Bowie to support the claim that Hesiod is alluding to Homeric narrative epic and distinguishing it from his didactic type of poetry.

85. See e.g. Havelock, *Preface to Plato*, chs 3-5, and *The Greek Concept of Justice* (Cambridge, Mass., 1978), chs 2–6; also J. Svenbro, *La parole et le marbre: aux origines de la poétique grecque* (Lund, 1976), esp. 16ff., 29ff., 46ff.

invention of versions of narrative, theme, and idea, this is not a process which is understood in those terms by the poets themselves.[86] As the passages of Hesiod, Stesichorus, and Pindar indicate, it is seen rather as a process of using the inspirational power of poetry to communicate 'truths' about matters of common concern (such as the nature of the gods) which hold good for the society as a whole, even though the poets play a special role in defining and articulating them.

Havelock has also pointed out that this conception of the poet's role was still sufficiently current at the time of Plato's composition of the *Republic* for him to take it as a target for attack, in ways to be discussed shortly.[87] It is also worth noting that, in the debate in Aristophanes' *Frogs* (405 BC), a good deal of the argument presupposes a not dissimilar conception of the poet's function. The poet is conceived as someone who 'teaches' his society by the ethical patterns embodied in his representations of the heroes of Greek tradition, representations which are regarded as influencing the audience's beliefs and practices. The processes of selecting versions of myths and presenting them in verbal, musical, and theatrical style—processes which *we* might see as being aspects of the poet's creativity or 'fictionality'—are considered as part of this process of communal education.[88]

There is a specific reason why this feature of the debate is the more striking. One of what *we* see as the most innovative aspects of Euripides' later drama, in plays such as the *Orestes* and *Helen*, is the way in which, by drawing on unusual and unexpected versions of myths and by modifying the tragic style so as to bring it closer to satyr-play or comedy, Euripides seems to advertise the 'fictionality' of his work.[89] Some of the features of Euripides' dramaturgy which

---

86. The point has often been made that oral poets typically see themselves as mouthpieces of a tradition ('singing *the same song* as they learned'), even when investigators see them as engaging in creative invention, and being in competition with their fellow poets, see e.g. A. Lord, *The Singer of Tales*, 2nd edn (New York, 1974), 23–9.

87. See Havelock, *Preface to Plato*, ch. 1. The composition of *R.* is usually dated to the mid 370s.

88. See *Frogs* 1008–98; also 939–91.

89. See further e.g. F.I. Zeitlin, 'The Closet of Masks: Role-playing and Myth-making in the *Orestes* of Euripides', *Ramus* 9 (1980), 51–77, and C. Segal, 'The Two Worlds of Euripides' *Helen*', *Proceedings of the American Philological Association* 102 (1971), 553–614, at 610–12.

we interpret in this way are noted in the *Frogs* and elsewhere in Aristophanes.[90] But the question of fictionality does not enter into the debate in the *Frogs*, or into the criticisms (explicit or implicit) of Euripides elsewhere in Aristophanes. In the *Frogs*, for instance, 'Euripides' is not presented as rejecting the ethical conception of the poet's role, or as arguing that (as we might put it) the plays are only 'fictions', and that artistic rather than ethical criteria should be paramount.[91] Also, the criticism made by 'Aeschylus' of Euripidean tragedy is not that it replaces the ethical function of poetry by that of creative invention but that it fulfils the ethical function in the wrong way (by using versions of myths and dramatic styles which propagate the wrong ethical norms). In this respect, what we might see as the development towards fictionality in tragedy in this period is *not* reflected in a major contemporary text on the topic.

Against the background of these characterizations of the poet's role in archaic Greek poetry, and in the late fifth century, the grounds of Plato's attack on the poets (for propagating 'falsehoods' in their representations of gods and heroes, and for 'deceiving' people with the claims to wisdom) are more intelligible than they would be otherwise. Although Plato's uses of the notions of falsehood and deception are—and are marked as being—innovative and distinctive in some respects, we can see them as constituting a response to a way of thinking about the functions of the poet (as a spokesperson for the ethical 'truths' of the society) which is implicit in the passages of Archaic poetry considered and in the *Frogs*.

In these respects, Plato's discussions, far from ignoring or blurring a recognized distinction between factual and fictional discourse, seem to develop, and to give a theoretical framework for, a well-established practice of understanding poetry in terms of the truth or falsehood of its ethical content. Indeed, there are other grounds for doubting that the distinction was widely recognized in Plato's time. Thucydides' famous programmatic remarks, defining the (desiderated) truth-status of the results of his historical enquiry, do not treat

---

90. See, e.g., on the non-tragic realism, *Frogs* 1058–66, also 1039–57; and, on the sensational romance-and-adventure style, *Thesmophoriazusae* 1008ff.

91. On the contrary, 'Euripides' characterizes the poet's role as an ethical educator, in *Frogs* 1009–10 (cf. the similar characterization of the poet's function by 'Aeschylus' in 1053–5).

poetic sources as different *in kind* from factual ones.[92] Even one of
the most suggestive of all comments made in this period, Gorgias'
reported claim that, in the case of poetry, 'the deceiver [i.e. the
successful poet] is more just than the non-deceiver and the deceived
[audience or reader] is wiser than the undeceived', even if it constitutes a characterization of the 'deception' involved in fiction, still
uses the language of truth and falsehood to express this idea.[93]

The question whether 'fiction' figures in the conceptual framework
of Greece (and Rome) after Plato is clearly too large to discuss in
general here. But I want to add some remarks about Aristotle's
thinking, and also about the relationship between the Greek
romantic novel and its conceptual and critical context, so as to give
a larger perspective to this discussion.

In Aristotle's *Poetics*, we find some comments which seem to
indicate an acknowledgement of, and interest in, the fictionality of
literature, of a kind that is rather different from the material
discussed so far. Aristotle discusses, for instance, the extent to which
a tragic poet must stick to traditional stories or is free to make up
stories; he also discusses what is involved in the process of plot-
composition and in the emotional realization of what is being
portrayed.[94] Also, in connection with Homer (ch. 25), he suggests
that poetry, *qua* poetry, has requirements, in its representation of
events and people, which are different from those involved in the
presentation of real life events and people. Thus, for instance, he says
that in poetry 'one should prefer plausible impossibilities [*adunata*

---

92. Poets are treated simply as sources but as unreliable ones, because they 'exaggerate' the scale of what they treat; see Thuc. 1. 10, 1. 21, J.L. Moles (p. 101
below), and n. 18 above.

93. See Plutarch, *Moralia* 348d, cited in Russell and Winterbottom, *Ancient
Literary Criticism*, 6. The drift seems to be that the successful poet 'deceives' in
so far as he involves the audience in the emotional power of his represented
world, and the audient who has 'sensibility' lets himself be 'deceived'; for a
slightly different reading of this passage, see J.R. Morgan, pp. 180–1 below. See
also Gorgias' *Helen*, on the power of poetic *logos* to induce emotional identification, and on *logos* as a 'deceiver', Russell and Winterbottom, 7–8; the Plutarch
passage seems to unite these ideas, and to present (fictional) emotional identification as deception/being deceived. See also n. 36 above.

94. See esp. *Po.* ch. 9, 1451b11–32, ch. 17, 1455a22–1455b16; also ch. 14,
1453b22–6.

eikota] to implausible possibilities'; and that 'there is not the same kind of correctness in ethics [or politics, *hē politikē*] or any other art, as in poetry'.[95] He also suggests that for a poet to present things 'as they should be' (*hoia dei*) is as valid as for him to present things 'as they are' (*hoia . . . estin*).[96]

If we give weight to these comments in interpreting Aristotle's general way of analysing poetry (that is, as a mode of *mimēsis* or representation) we may well reach some conclusion such as the following. For Aristotle, poetic *mimēsis* involves the making of 'likenesses' which, while they represent the world, are not to be judged simply by the standards of non-mimetic accuracy but also by standards appropriate to poetry itself. To this extent, Aristotle may seem to be defining something that is essential to the idea of fiction, namely that it should not be judged by the same standards of correctness, and of truth and falsehood, as factual discourse. This may lend support to the general claim that Aristotle's conception of poetry as a mode of *mimēsis* is one which partly presupposes and partly explores the fictional status of poetry.

However, to reach these conclusions would be premature and in some ways misleading, in the light of Aristotle's argument as a whole. The comments cited from ch. 25 need to be placed against Aristotle's general view (which is also expressed in that chapter) that poetic representations should conform to the same standards of possibility and rationality as other accounts of human life. What Aristotle singles out are permissible exceptions to this general view, exemplified in the use by poets such as Homer of techniques inherent to the poetic art.[97] This reflects a more general feature of Aristotle's approach, which is to treat poetry as subject to analysis

---

95. See *Po.* ch. 25, 1460a26–7, also 1461b9–15; 1460b13–15. A related comment is that 'Homer most of all taught other poets the right way to lie' (*pseudē legein hōs dei*), i.e. by inducing the audience to draw false inferences from what is presented (1460a18–26).

96. *Po.* 1460b10–11 (the third possibility is to present them as they are said or thought to be), and 1460b32–5.

97. See e.g. 'For the most part, [poetic stories] should contain nothing irrational' (1460a28–9), and 'if the poet's compositions contain impossibilities, they are faults' (1460b23). Also, Aristotle thinks that the poet should, in general, 'get things right', i.e. achieve 'correctness' by the standards of other arts; but he distinguishes a failure in this respect (an 'incidental' failure) from one which is 'essential' to the poet's art, the latter being more a serious one (see 1460b15–32).

and evaluation in similar ways to other (fact-based) forms of discourse. Thus, for instance, he describes the poet's function as being to present 'the sort of thing that can happen' (*hoia an genoito*), that is, 'what is possible in terms of probability or necessity' (1451a37–8).

It is clear that the relevant standards of probability and necessity are those of reality as expressed in other forms of discourse. Thus, poetry is compared with philosophy in this respect; and, while it is also contrasted with history, this is not because history is factual and poetry is not, but because 'poetry [like philosophy] makes general statements [*ta katholou . . . legei*] and history particular ones [*ta kath' hekaston*]'. Poetry is here treated as a mode of bringing out general features of reality (the necessary or probable connections between events in human life), though a mode which does so through the representation of poetic particulars.[98] It is in connection with this project (adding names and episodes to plot-structures, conceived as analyses of connections between events) that Aristotle, for the most part, considers the question of the poet's scope for inventiveness in stories and figures.[99] That is to say, he comes to this topic by way of the conception of the poet as an analyst of the general structures found in reality rather than by way of the conception of the poet as an inventor of 'fiction', if this is taken to signify a form of discourse which is different in kind from factual discourse.

These two aspects of Aristotle's thinking may be reconciled, perhaps, in the following general characterization of his approach. Aristotle conceives tragedy and other poetic genres (unlike history or philosophy, say) as forms of *mimēsis*, 'representation'. Each poetic form is characterized by certain generic features: it has its own specific objects of *mimēsis*, and its own specific means and

---

98. See *Po.* ch. 9, 1451b6–7 and context, also 1452a1–29 (explaining the connection between the intelligible and the unexpected in poetry), 1455a16–21, 1459a17–30; and, for this interpretation of Aristotle's view, see also J.R. Morgan, p. 182 below. Aristotle's contrast between poetry and history seems to ignore the possibility of the kind of analysis of the intelligible structure of reality through historical particulars (and speeches) which is taken as Thucydides' goal (1. 22), as noted by J.L. Moles, pp. 104–10 below. But see further G.E.M. de Ste Croix, 'Aristotle on History and Poetry', in B. Levick, ed., *The Ancient Historian and his Materials* (Farnborough, Hants, 1975), 45–58.

99. See *Po.* 1451b11–39, 1455a16–21, 1455a34–1455b23, 1460a11–1460b5.

mode of *mimēsis*.[100] It is also characterized as having as its goal a specific type of effect on the audience (in the case of tragedy, the *katharsis* of pity and fear, 1449b21–8). To this extent, Aristotle conceives poetry as a mode of fictional discourse which is distinct in kind from factual discourse, and which is to be evaluated by reference to this status.

On the other hand, Aristotle also conceives poetry as fulfilling (within the mimetic mode) similar kinds of function to those fulfilled by non-mimetic modes of discourse such as philosophy. Poetic representation embodies, in poetic particulars, an analysis of the intelligible structures of human action and life; and it is, accordingly, *also* judged by reference to (real-life) standards of rationality and possibility.[101] Further, Aristotle believes that we respond to the objects of poetic *mimēsis* (human actions and life) with much the same kind of ethical and emotional responses as we would to their real-life equivalents.[102] The fact that the figures and events involved are—and are recognized as being—'fictional' does not mean that we respond to them differently from the way in which we would respond to similar figures and events presented in non-mimetic modes of discourse. In both these ways, then, mimetic modes of discourse are seen as comparable to, rather than distinct from, non-mimetic modes.

If this general characterization of Aristotle's position is accepted, it enables the following comparison of his position with Plato's. The difference between their views of poetry is not that Aristotle acknowledges the fictionality of poetry, whereas Plato does not. Both of them do so, and in not dissimilar forms, although Aristotle does so in a way that is more central to the structure of his account.[103] The difference lies in the fact that Aristotle accepts (what

---

100. See *Po.* chs 1–6. Although *mimesis* is seen as having its roots in general human desires (principally, the desire to know, to recognize *x* as *y*, ch. 4, 1448b4–24), desires which are also manifested in philosophy, for instance, Aristotle does not, in *Po.*, situate poetic *mimesis* within a larger scheme of types of *mimesis*, and does not in ch. 9 seem to regard philosophy and poetry as being also modes of *mimesis*.

101. See n. 97 above.

102. See e.g. *Po.* 1452b30–1453a17, 1453b11–1454a15. (On the contrast with Plato, see n. 104 below.)

103. Aristotle's analysis of types of *mimesis* in *Po.* chs 1–5 is clearly an elaboration of Plato's in *R.* 392c–400c.

Plato denies) that poetry can constitute, in mimetic form, a valid means of analysing the intelligible structure of human action and life, and one that (in the case of tragedy, especially) can stimulate deep ethico-emotional responses to the structure thus analysed.

Indeed, Aristotle's account is often, and plausibly, taken as a defence of poetry against Plato's criticisms. In particular, Aristotle seems to aim to meet the claims of *Republic* 10, that poetry, as imitation, is *ipso facto* incapable of doing more than conveying the 'look' and 'feel' of human life. He also denies that responding to the power of poetry involves ethico-emotional responses which are out of line with those which are appropriate to real-life situations.[104] But, if this is so, then Aristotle accepts the validity of the general criteria Plato uses to criticize poetry. He accepts that it is appropriate to judge poetry not just as 'fiction', but also as a mode of analysis or interpretation of reality (at least as a mode of discourse which embodies such analysis), and comparable in this respect with non-mimetic modes. Aristotle does not couch his account in terms of 'truth' and 'falsehood';[105] but it would seem to follow from his account that poetry in general has certain truth-claims, and that certain poems are 'truer' than others, in so far as their structures, and the responses invited, answer to the structures of human life analysed by other (true) non-mimetic modes of discourse. (Indeed, such ideas are perhaps implied in his comments on the 'philosophical' character of poetry, by contrast with history, and in his concern that poetry should, in general, meet certain standards of rationality and probability.)[106]

But, in other respects, Aristotle's account may be taken as a more theorized statement of the conception of the poet presupposed in the archaic and Aristophanic material discussed and attacked by Plato, namely as someone whose work expresses the deep 'truths' recognized by his or her society in a form that communicates these

---

104. Contrast *Po.* 1452b30–1453a17 with *R.* 605c–606d, discussed in II above. See further Halliwell, *Aristotle's Poetics*, 158–9, 229–30.

105. These notions figure in ch. 25, 1460a18–26, 1460b32–1461a9, but as subordinate aspects of the larger discussion of the standards of rationality and probability required in epic, as in tragic, poetry.

106. See nn. 97–8 above. Also, some of Aristotle's qualitative judgements of tragic plot-construction and characterization reflect his concern that the play should embody a connected and intelligible structure: see e.g. 1451b33–1452a1, 1455a16–21.

effectively to the audience. The 'fictional' status of the exercise is acknowledged by the account, as forming a crucial part of what makes the communication effective, but the poet's function is conceived as being that of communicating truth-bearing content in this form.

I want to make one further observation about the ancient conceptual and critical framework, in order to place Plato's thinking in a still larger context. Although we do find in later Greco–Roman rhetorical writing some relevant distinctions, these are not sufficient to justify the claim that there is a clear articulation of the distinction between factual and fictional discourse, and a secure understanding of 'fiction' as a form of literature. This point is reflected in—and helps to explain—a feature of the ancient literary landscape which has been much discussed in recent years. Although it is clear that there emerges in the late Hellenistic and Roman periods a genre (as we see it) of narrative fiction, a form of novel or romance, this form of writing is ignored almost totally by ancient critics and writers. This seems to reflect, in part, the relatively unambitious character and objectives of this form of writing. In particular, it may reflect the fact that the romances cannot be readily interpreted (unlike epic, tragedy, history, rhetoric, and even comedy) as conveying the ethical or political 'truths' of communal life. But it seems also to reflect the conceptual difficulty of placing in the ancient critical map a form of narrative that is (as we see it) purely fictional.[107]

The very few, and often very late, ancient comments that we have on this form of writing present it either as a—derivative or low-grade—type of history (*historia*) or as being, in some sense, 'dramatic' (*dramatikon*).[108] The first point reflects in part the typical form of the romances: a narrative account of the events of human lives in the past. The second point presumably also relates to the central role of dialogue (dramatic) form in the romance. But it may also reflect the fact that, in the ancient world, drama, in its various forms, was

---

107. See further B.P. Reardon, *The Form of Greek Romance* (Princeton, 1991), esp. chs 3 and 4.

108. See further B.E. Perry, *The Ancient Romances* (Berkeley, 1967), 78–9; E. Rohde, *Der Griechische Roman*, 4th edn (Wiesbaden, 1960), 375–6; also J.R. Morgan, pp. 178, 189, n. 21, 194–5 below.

the standard medium for (what we call) fictionalizing or fictional writing.[109] Thus, to call a narrative form 'dramatic' was to go as far as one could in this type of critical language to signify its fictional character.

The fact that there was no determinate category of 'fiction' in ancient criticism is part of what underlies the suggestion made earlier (Section I above) that ancient narrative fiction may not have been read *as fiction*, in our sense. The basis of this suggestion is partly that, where there is no recognized *genre* of narrative fiction, this fact makes a qualitative difference to the experience of reading such works. Also, the absence of the genre is correlated with other features of the critical framework, which bear on the contemporaneous reception of such works, in so far as we are able to reconstruct this.

B.E. Perry argues that the ancient romance, at least in its non-comic forms, would have been understood as an extended version of the fictionalizing (or 'dramatic' elaboration) that figured as a standard feature of ancient historiography and rhetorical writing.[110] Some of the romances present themselves as accounts of the private lives of historical or legendary figures, and are placed in actual or imaginable historical contexts. They are placed—like much of Xenophon's *Education of Cyrus*—as 'dramatic' elaboration in the interstices of historical or quasi-historical accounts.[111] Others are framed as expanded versions of rhetorical exercises (the *ekphrasis*, or description of a picture, for instance).[112] In both types, especially the latter, 'dramatic' narrative and dialogue are interleaved with learned information and general reflection, that is, with 'facts' and general 'truths'. In all these ways, the ancient romances present themselves

---

109. Hence (what we should conceive as) styles of 'fictionality' are sometimes defined by reference to different dramatic genres. The relevant distinctions are drawn by ancient writers in connection with theorizing about rhetorical and historical writing and not the romance or novel. See Perry, *Ancient Romances*, 74–5, 144, and Rohde, *Griechische Roman*, 376–9; also J.R. Morgan, pp. 189–91 below, and T.P. Wiseman, pp. 129–30 below.

110. See Perry, *Ancient Romances*, 72–9, 108–24, 173–8, and Reardon, *The Form of Greek Romance*, ch. 6; also J.R. Morgan, pp. 184–7 below.

111. In this respect, even Thucydides' speeches (1. 22) are examples of 'fictionalizing' interstices in a factual account.

112. On this feature, see S. Bartsch, *Decoding the Ancient Novel: The Reader and the Role of Description in Heliodorus and Achilles Tatius* (Princeton, 1989).

not so much as pure 'fiction' but as a more heavily fictionalized version of other genres which were conceived as having some kind of veridical content. Indeed, given the indeterminate boundaries of this type of writing, and the close links with other narrative and rhetorical forms, it is not wholly clear that we can really demarcate a *genre* here at all.

This topic obviously raises important issues in its own right, and is, correspondingly, discussed elsewhere in this volume.[113] But these brief comments may be enough to bring out my main point here. This is that the absence in Plato of a clear sense of, or interest in, the distinction between factual and fictional discourse is not a purely idiosyncratic feature of his conceptual framework (though it is developed in special ways within that framework), but one that reflects deeper and more lasting aspects of the ancient conceptual and literary map. The inclination to view literature (even literature which is acknowledged to be in some sense, 'fictional') in veridical terms, as conveying certain types of truth, persists, in an attenuated form, in the framing of the romance.[114] The fact that the romance is such an unsuitable vehicle for truth-bearing, as traditionally understood, probably goes some way towards explaining the ancient critical neglect of this form of writing.

VI

I want to conclude this chapter by raising, briefly, two questions about *our*, contemporary, thinking about fiction. I want to ask why we place value on 'fiction', as a literary form; and why we regard the question of the 'fictionality' of a given form of discourse as an important and interesting one. I think that, by offering suggestions on both these topics, I can throw into relief the claims made here about Plato's conceptual framework, and that of his culture, as regards the idea of fiction.

---

113. See A. Laird, ch. 5 below, J.R. Morgan, ch. 6 below, and D.C. Feeney, Epilogue below. They all claim that we can find more or less what *we* regard as 'fiction' in the ancient romances or novels and in other areas of Hellenistic and Roman literature, despite the absence of any systematic theory of fiction or fictionality; but see also text to n. 114 below.

114. See J.R. Morgan, pp. 197–202 below.

Modern Platonic scholars, in identifying—and challenging—Plato's views on literature, offer, by implication, an answer of a certain type to my first question, that of the reason why we place positive value on fiction as a literary form.

> . . . by imaginatively participating in the represented situation we become familiar with it, through a 'sympathy' that implies no necessary approval of the actions or attitudes portrayed and therefore needs no censor, and so we come to understand it perhaps better than had we kept our analytic distance.

> In putting oneself in the place of another character, one comes to see things from their point of view . . . In the process I will come to understand why Achilles [for instance] thought it all right, indeed required by honour, to do things which I would find cruel and senseless . . . We tend to think that this phenomenon is valuable because it extends our moral horizons and makes us more open-minded and flexible than we would be purely on the basis of our own experience. Reading novels is taken to be a source of moral growth.[115]

These comments are, of course, intended as exegesis and not theoretical statement; but they imply two interconnected ideas which form a recurrent strand in modern thinking about fiction.[116] One is the idea that, in fiction, one can engage imaginatively with figures of whom one would not necessarily approve in real life, and that such imaginative engagement does not necessarily carry with it moral approval. The other is the idea that this kind of imaginative self-extension has a positive moral value in itself. There is a moral value in coming to 'understand' Achilles, through imaginative engagement with his point of view, even if we do not, as a result, adopt in real life the moral values which form an essential part of his point of view. There is a positive moral value simply in becoming 'more

---

115. Ferrari, 'Plato and Poetry', 120; Annas, *Introduction to Plato's Republic*, 96–7; see also n. 17 above.

116. I do not wish to suggest that Ferrari and Annas, as individuals, necessarily hold as beliefs the ideas explored below, but simply that the intelligibility of their comments about Plato rests on the fact that they express familiar modern ideas which carry these larger implications.

open-minded and flexible'; and fiction has value in fostering this special type of imaginative and moral self-extension.

These ideas are so integral to modern thinking about fiction that it is easy for us to see their absence from Plato as evidence of a kind of defectiveness or perversity in his thought. But it is worth registering the fact that, if we can set our own preconceptions aside for a moment, it is not self-evident that these ideas must form part of any human conceptual framework. Indeed, these ideas can, if queried, seem rather puzzling. How can there be a type of imaginative engagement with a fictional figure which does *not* involve moral engagement (approval or disapproval) with his or her represented actions and standpoint? Why is this non-judgemental type of imaginative engagement, which is taken to yield 'understanding' of the figure's standpoint, thought to be a means of 'moral growth' *without* involving moral response to this standpoint in a way that bears on one's own real-life standpoint?[117]

I think it is possible to frame answers to these questions; but to do so informatively one needs to refer to certain prevalent features of modern Western cultural life. One is the way of conceiving the creation of works of art, and the response to them, in private and subjective terms. Art is conceived, on this model, as a mode of communication between one private consciousness (say, 'the author') and another (say, 'the reader'), a mode of communication mediated, in some forms, by the creation of fictional figures, who express their own (fictive) centres of consciousness and point of view. The imaginative extension of one's private, subjective standpoint, by engagement with *another* private, subjective standpoint (that of the author or his or her figures, or both), is conceived as having value in its own right and constituting what counts, in this model, as moral growth or learning. One needs also to bring into the picture certain prevalent features of modern Western ethico–political thinking, such as the liberal-individualism that leads us to give positive value to recognizing the point of view of another person (or culture) even if we do not, as a result, modify our own (except in so far as the act of recognition involves an extension of our point of view).

---

117. See further on this puzzle P.F. Strawson, *Freedom and Resentment* (London, 1974), ch. 2, esp. 27–8.

Clearly, one would need to elaborate these points in order to give full explanation of the ideas which, I suggest, underlie these modern scholarly responses to Plato.[118] But enough has been said already, perhaps, to bring out the radical difference between the modern conceptual framework and that which, as I have suggested, is present in Plato and in Greek culture in general. In Greek culture, art is conceived in terms of communal participation in a public event (an epic recitation, a tragic performance, a display of 'epideictic' oratory). The idea that artistic experience should normally be analysed in terms of the relationship between an individual author and an individual reader emerges, if at all, only late and intermittently. At the same time, as indicated already, the role of the poet, like the historian, orator, or philosopher, is conceived as expressing the communal 'truths' of the society. This is accompanied by a prevalent tendency to conceive ethical and political issues in forms which I have characterized elsewhere as 'objective-participant' rather than 'subjective-individualist' (the latter form being exemplified in the kind of modern ideas noted earlier).[119]

In the light of this larger difference between ancient and modern conceptual frameworks, it is easier to see why the ideas noted above do not appear in Plato, or, I think, in other ancient writers. There is lacking the set of special cultural and intellectual preconditions that would lead them to give a positive value to non-judgemental imaginative identification with fictional figures as a means of extending one's subjective world-view. Even in cases where we find something seemingly like these ideas (in Plato or elsewhere), the formulation, and the surrounding framework, of the ideas is quite different, and for explicable reasons.[120]

The second strand of modern thinking I want to note here centres on the idea that 'fiction' and 'fictionality' serve to identify a problematic zone rather than a determinate and familar mode of writing or discourse. Talk of 'fictionality' often occurs in connection with the claim that certain types of discourse usually regarded as factual,

---

118. C. Taylor, *Sources of the Self: The Making of the Modern Identity* (Cambridge, 1989) gives us much of the material which we could use to do so.

119. See *The Self in Dialogue*, Introduction.

120. See discussion above, esp. text to nn. 17, 19–21, 29–30.

or, more broadly, veridical in status, are really fictional. Thus, for instance, Hayden White has claimed that histories are 'fictions', or, more precisely, 'fictions of factual representation';[121] and other such claims are sometimes made about forms of discourse usually regarded as factual. What is involved in such claims is not only the idea that the writing of history, for instance, inevitably consists of selective inclusion and omission and interpretative presentation. What is also, and more importantly, involved is the idea that no interpretation of the past can achieve objective truth. Correspondingly, any interpretative analysis has only the status of a (subjective) construction or fabrication; and in this sense it is no different from fiction.

What gives plausibility to such claims is the prevalence in contemporary intellectual life of a number of types of relativism, subjectivism, or scepticism. These theories lend support, from different directions, to the idea that all forms of discourse express the social, or individual, attitudes generated by a particular set of historical circumstances; and that there is no way of reaching outside those attitudes so as to gain access to independently grounded objective truth. A related strand, which is sometimes taken to support this line of thought, is constituted by theories which explain the significance of discourse by reference to shared social conventions ('language games', in one model) rather than by the correspondence between forms of discourse and objectively existing truths.[122] The implications of these theories are sometimes expressed in the claim that all forms of discourse, including those usually thought to be factual, or, more broadly, veridical, are, in fact, 'fictions'.[123]

---

121. This is the title of one of the essays in *Tropics of Discourse* (Baltimore, 1978). I am grateful to Charles Martindale for this reference, and for underlining, in a paper he sent me, this strand in modern thinking.

122. The 'language games' theory is that of the later Wittgenstein. Derrida's idea of discourse as a 'play of signifiers' represents a more extreme version of this theory. For a helpful discussion, bringing together contemporary debate in philosophy and literary theory, see C. Norris, *The Contest of Faculties: Philosophy and Theory after Deconstruction* (London, 1985).

123. In terms of the distinctions given at the start of this chapter, the claim is that the second type of distinction, relating to the (objective) veridical content of discourse, i.e. whether it is, *in fact*, true or false, is not significant. Also, the first distinction is nullified, on this view, since even supposedly factual discourse is claimed to be fictional.

How far does the line of thought just summarized relate to anything to be found in Plato, as discussed earlier? It is true, of course, that Plato is an objectivist in so far as he consistently presents knowledge of objective truth as the proper goal of intellectual enquiry; and, to this extent, he holds a different position from the modern theorists noted. On the other hand, as has been emphasized recently, there are aspects of Plato's thought which prefigure the scepticism about the achievement of knowledge which is an important strand in Hellenistic philosophical debate.[124] These include the recurrent Platonic theme, noted earlier, that, while knowledge of objective truth is properly taken as the goal of intellectual enquiry, there are huge obstacles, intellectual, psychological, and social, to the achievement of such knowledge, and its communication, once achieved. As we saw, Plato's resort to 'mythical' modes of discourse is sometimes designed to acknowledge the fact that his speakers are trying to characterize a type of knowledge (principally, knowledge of objective moral truth) which they do not possess, and which is immensely difficult for human beings to acquire.[125] I suggested earlier that, in so doing, Plato was signalling—what we should see as—the 'fictionality' of such myths. In such cases, the fictionality does not inhere in the falsehood of the myth as factual narrative but rather in the (explicitly) incomplete or provisional truth of the myth as the vehicle of an idea. Such 'fictionality' applies to the arguments in which the myths, or descriptive images, occur as well as to the myths themselves. It might seem, then, that Plato, like the modern thinkers noted earlier, acknowledges the 'fictionality' of types of discourse which one might otherwise suppose to be directed at discovering and communicating truth.

However, this last conclusion goes rather beyond what can reasonably be claimed. Although acknowledging that *some* forms of discourse (including some of his own myths) express the failure to achieve knowledge of objective truth, Plato does not go on to claim that *all* discourse must necessarily do so;[126] or that such knowledge is, in principle, unavailable and is not a proper goal of enquiry. His

---

124. See references in n. 80 above.
125. See discussion in II above, esp. text to nn. 47, 51–60, 78–80.
126. An apparent exception is *Seventh Letter* 342–4; but see further references in n. 80 above.

position thus remains distinct from that of the modern thinkers noted. Also, even in Plato's acknowledgements of the incomplete truth of his myths or arguments, there is no equivalent for the modern claim that the status of such discourse is 'fictional'. The modern claim presupposes the familiarity of the idea of fiction as a determinate type of discourse. It also presupposes that it is philosophically defensible to maintain that some (or all) discourse has, in reality, no truth-status, no veridical content, despite what is usually supposed. Given all that has been said so far in this chapter, it seems clear that these conditions are not fulfilled in Plato's conceptual framework, or perhaps that of antiquity generally. Indeed, the fact that these conditions are not fulfilled seems to constitute a significant difference between ancient and modern thinking in this area.

Chapter Three

Truth and Untruth in Herodotus and Thucydides

J.L. MOLES

I

THERE was considerable debate in the Classical world about the nature of historiography, a debate which took several forms; there were major theoretical discussions, of which the most important surviving are those interspersed throughout his work by the Greek historian Polybius; those of Cicero, a historian among many other things; of Dionysius of Halicarnassus, historian, critic and rhetorician; of Plutarch, biographer and historian among many other things; and Lucian, who though not a historian was a highly educated and intelligent man and shrewd literary critic.[1] We hear of many other such discussions—by rhetoricians, philosophers

This chapter is based on a paper given at Florida State University, Tallahassee, on March 2nd 1989 and (in revised form) at the Crossmead Conference.

1. Polybius 1.14.1–9, 2.56.1–16, 8.8.3–11, 12.1.2–28a.10, 16.14.1–20.9, 29.12.1–12; K. Sacks, *Polybius on the Writing of History* (*Polybius*) (Berkeley, 1981); Cicero, *Letters to his Friends* (*Fam.*) 5.12 (the letter to Lucceius), *On the Orator* (*De oratore*) 2.51–64; A.J. Woodman, *Rhetoric in Classical Historiography* (*RICH*) (London, 1988), 70–116; Dionysius, *Letter to Pompeius* (*Pomp.*) and *On Thucydides*; W.K. Pritchett, *Dionysius of Halicarnassus: On Thucydides* (Berkeley, 1975); Plutarch, *On the Malice of Herodotus* (*De Herodoti malignitate*), ed. and tr. L. Pearson and F.H. Sandbach in *Plutarch's Moralia* 11 (Loeb edn, Cambridge, Mass., 1965), 2–129; Lucian, *How History should be Written* (*Hist. conscr.*); G. Avenarius, *Lukians Schrift zur Geschichtsschreibung* (Meisenheim am Glan, 1956).

and practising historians. There is also much debate within ancient historiography itself and some material in the writings of rhetoricians and literary critics. There is a correspondingly lively modern debate, which is fuelled by several different factors: historians' need to use ancient historiographical works as sources, the difficulty of interpreting ancient views on historiography, modern theories of historiography, and, to an ever-increasing extent, modern literary theory.[2]

The debate raises fundamental questions. What, if any, is the relationship between literature and life? Is literature self-sufficient, self-contained and purely fictional? Or does it reflect, and is it governed by, external reality? In the case of historiography, the answer appears simple: history, in ancient terminology, relates things that were done or things that happened (*erga/res gestae*), and so the historian's job is to reproduce these things. In the words of Lucian, *Hist. conscr.* 51: 'Above all, let him bring a mind like a mirror, clear, gleaming-bright, accurately centred, displaying the shape of things just as he receives them, free from distortion, false colouring, and misrepresentation.' Surely *mimesis* through the medium of a mirror is as close to reality as one can get? So simple a notion, however, is soon dispelled by exposure to the ancient historiographical texts and the ancient and modern debates about them.

I postpone discussion about the details of these debates until the end, and for the moment merely say that, at least until very recently, when it became much more sophisticated, the modern debate has tended to polarise between historians and literary critics. For the former, ancient historiography aims, or should aim, to tell the truth, by which is meant: to relate things that actually happened and establish their causes. Accordingly, if an ancient historiographer does not

---

2. T.P. Wiseman, *Clio's Cosmetics* (Leicester, 1979) and 'Practice and Theory in Roman Historiography', *History* 66 (1981), 375–93; C.W. Fornara, *The Nature of History in Ancient Greece and Rome* (Berkeley, 1983); I.S. Moxon, J.D. Smart and A.J. Woodman, eds, *Past Perspectives: Studies in Greek and Roman Historical Writing* (Cambridge, 1986); Woodman *RICH*; A. Cameron, ed., *History as Text* (London, 1989); useful reviews of Woodman's controversial but indispensable book by J. Moles, *History of the Human Sciences* 3.2 (1990), 317–21, and R. Brock, *Liverpool Classical Monthly* 16.7 (1991), 97–102; sustained practical application of Woodman's theory in R.H. Martin and A.J. Woodman, eds, *Tacitus: Annals 4 (Tacitus)* (Cambridge, 1989).

tell the truth in that sense, there can be only three explanations: error, dishonesty, or misconception of history's true function.[3]

For the literary critics, by contrast, ancient historiography may aim to tell the truth, but there are many sorts of truth; or it may not aim to tell the truth: it can, quite legitimately, approach the status of fiction, hence accusations of 'lying' are fundamentally misconceived. To quote A.J. Woodman (whose arguments I shall be debating, implicitly or explicitly, throughout this paper): 'Our primary response to the texts of the ancient historians should be literary rather than historical since the nature of the texts themselves is literary. Only when literary analysis has been carried out can we begin to use these texts as evidence for history; and by that time . . . such analysis will have revealed that there is precious little historical evidence left.'[4]

Modern historians naturally dislike such views, because they challenge the very basis of ancient history as an intellectual discipline, since the 'evidence', at almost all periods, consists overwhelmingly of literary texts. While most historians concede that ancient historiographical texts are in some senses 'literary', they nevertheless insist that this 'literary' aspect is detachable and there is solid fact underneath. On this view, ancient works of historiography are like Christmas cakes: if you don't like almond icing, you slice it off, and you've still got a cake—a substantial object uncontaminated by icing. The traditional terminology of this debate—'historical' and 'literary'—and the implied polarisation between the two are crude and, in important ways, question-begging, but they obviously have some substance, so I shall employ them provisionally.

In this discussion, I want to mediate between 'literary' and 'historical' approaches to the question, primarily through a close reading of the prefaces of Herodotus and Thucydides (presented in my own very literal, and sometimes controversial, translations). What emerges, I think, from the content and form of these programmatic

---

3. Thus e.g. K.J. Dover, 'Thucydides "as History" and "as Literature"', *History and Theory* 22 (1983), 54–63, at 55: 'if Thucydides tried to achieve something incompatible with the factual record, he would be a liar' (quotation slightly adapted).

4. 'From Hannibal to Hitler: The Literature of War', *University of Leeds Review* 26 (1983), 107–24, at 20.

statements is the way in which 'literary' and 'historical' objectives are alike present and deeply interfused.

On the one hand, both writers see themselves as inheritors of the tradition of epic narrative, especially as expressed in Homer's commemoration of a great war in the *Iliad*. Both writers also see themselves as developing the project built into Homer's poem (a project itself not without a certain 'historical' concern), namely that of analysing the causation and process of war and conflict, and of doing so by the invention of significant speeches and by the selection and presentation of concrete events. On the other hand, both writers also see themselves as engaged in a project which is distinctive from that of the poetic tradition in its attempt to establish factual truth and to distinguish this from factual 'untruth' or 'falsehood'.[5]

Thucydides is more explicit about the nature and methodology of this project than Herodotus, and also about the kind of history (that is, primarily, recent history) in which this project can be pursued effectively. Indeed, in this respect especially, he presents himself as a critic, and rival, of Herodotus as well as a successor. But, in the prefaces of both historians, as in their full-scale narratives, we can recognize the combination of objectives (the perpetuation of epic narrative and interpretation and the innovative search for factual truth) that makes it so difficult to characterize their writings either in terms of 'literature' or 'history'. This combination also makes it difficult to characterize their work in terms of 'truth', 'falsehood' or

---

5. Herodotus' concern for truth has recently come under renewed attack at the most basic level: did he really see the things he said he had seen? See e.g. D. Fehling, *Die Quellengaben bei Herodot* (Berlin, 1971), now in English (with additions and corrections) as *Herodotus and his 'Sources'* (J.G. Howie, ARCA 21, Leeds, 1989); O.K. Armayor, 'Did Herodotus ever go to the Black Sea?', *Harvard Studies in Classical Philology (HSCP)* 82 (1978), 45–62, 'Did Herodotus ever go to Egypt?', *Journal of the American Research Center in Egypt* 15 (1978), 59–73, *Herodotus' Autopsy of the Fayoum: Lake Moeris and the Labyrinth of Egypt* (Amsterdam, 1985); a related, though less radical, position in S. West, 'Herodotus' epigraphical interests', *Classical Quarterly (CQ)* 35 (1985), 278–305, and 'Herodotus' portrait of Hecataeus', *Journal of Hellenic Studies (JHS)* 111 (1991), 144–60. I do not accept all Armayor and Fehling's claims, which are rejected by S. Hornblower, *Thucydides* (London, 1987), 13–25 and J. Gould, *Herodotus* (London, 1989), 136–37, 151–52, and soberly assessed by J. Marincola, *Arethusa* 20 (1987), 26–33. In fact, Herodotus' concern for truth is complex and ambivalent (pp. 93–5 below). For a particular 'test case' see pp. 118–20 below.

'fiction', though if we examine their own descriptions of their project, we have a better chance of seeing how these concepts match with theirs.

II

Herodotus' *History* has two formal prefaces, the first (1.1–5) introducing the work as a whole, the second (7.20.2–21.1), over two-thirds the way through the work, introducing Xerxes' Persian expedition against Greece. The first preface falls into three parts and is constructed like a sandwich: initial preface, narrative about the remote past, resumed preface. The initial preface (traditionally dated to the early 420s BC) reads as follows:[6]

> This is a demonstration [*apodexis*] of the enquiry [*historiē*] of Herodotus of Halicarnassus, in order that neither should the things done by men fade away through time, nor should great and wonderful achievements [*erga*], some performed/demonstrated [*apodechthenta*] by Greeks, some by barbarians, become without glory, both in other respects and for what cause they waged war on each other.

Herodotus begins by emphasizing his theme's greatness, and this became standard practice in ancient historiography. The enormously wide scope of the theme, however, is quite untypical: 'things done by men' (any men), 'great and wonderful achievements' (the word 'achievements' covering both deeds and buildings, works of art and the like, done by Greeks and barbarians, not just Persians). Only at the end does he state a specific theme: war between Greeks and Persians, though even then he says 'barbarians' to keep it nice and broad. The theme is so widely defined—in fact it is hardly defined at all—as to pre-empt accusations of irrelevance: hence such later protestations as, 'My account has sought additions from the beginning' (4.30.1).

---

6. H. Erbse, *Festschrift Bruno Snell* (Munich, 1956), 209–22; T. Krischer, 'Herodots Prooimion', *Hermes* 93 (1965), 159–67; H.R. Immerwahr, *Form and Thought in Herodotus* (Cleveland, 1966), 17–19, 43–44, 80–81; P.A. Stadter, 'Arrian's Extended Preface', *Illinois Classical Studies* 6.1 (1981), 157–71 at 158–59; G. Nagy, 'Herodotus the *Logios*', *Arethusa* 20 (1987), 175–84; Woodman, *RICH*, 2–3; D. Lateiner, *The Historical Method of Herodotus* (Toronto, 1989), 8–15.

There is a general implication that he is concerned with truth—the things have been done, the great achievements demonstrated, his work is the product of 'enquiry',[7] causation is stressed—but he certainly does not emphasize truth, which makes a striking contrast to his immediate predecessor Hecataeus, who had prefaced his *Historia* with the iconoclastic claim (fragment 1):

> Hecataeus of Miletus gives the following account. I write these things, as they seem to me to be true. For the stories of the Greeks are many and ludicrous, as they appear to me.

Herodotus promises to record 'wonderful' achievements. He will appeal to his readers' emotions, their sense of wonder—much of his material is indeed mind-boggling—and appeal perhaps also to their moral sense, since 'wonderful' can include 'admirable' and, as we shall see, Herodotus is an overt moralist. There may also be a veiled implication that some of the material will be untrue (fabulous monsters and peoples, the sort of material one finds in the *Odyssey*)—as indeed some of it is. 'The wonderful' becomes the normal classification for such material.[8]

Herodotus' work has commemorative value (a standard historiographical claim) but the wording 'to avoid great achievements becoming without glory' echoes a famous passage in the *Iliad* (9.189), where the great hero Achilles is described as 'singing of the glorious deeds of men'. Thus, Herodotus' theme is of epic greatness, and his own role is, perhaps, correspondingly heroic (as will certainly be implied soon). The analogy with Homeric epic is reinforced by the wording of the last clause, which reflects Homer's search for the 'first cause' both of the disastrous quarrel of Agamemnon and Achilles in the *Iliad* (*Il.* 1.8 'Which of the gods, then, set them together to fight in strife?') and of the whole dispute between Achaeans and Trojans (cf. *Il.* 22.116, 24.27–28, *Od.* 8.81–82). So the father of history aligns his theme, war—and war between two great racial groupings—and by extension, himself, with Homeric epic and Homer the poet, as ancient critics recognized by

---

7. On the complex implications of Herodotean 'enquiry' see e.g. C. Dewald, 'Narrative Surface and Authorial Voice in Herodotus' *Histories*', *Arethusa* 20 (1987), 147–70; Gould, *Herodotus*, 8–12.

8. E.g. Aristotle, *Poetics* 24.1460a12ff.; Dionysius, *Roman Antiquities* (*Ant. Rom.*) 1.77.2–3, 2.60.4–5; Tacitus, *Annals* (*Ann.*) 4.11.3, 4.66.2, 11.27.

describing Herodotus as 'most Homeric' (e.g. Dionysius, *Letter to Pompeius* [*Pomp.*] 3; 'Longinus', *On Sublimity* 13.3).

Given that the achievements are wonderful, given the general tone and associations of Homeric epic, it is implied that his work will have an encomiastic slant, as ancient critics also recognized (e.g. Dionysius, *Pomp.* 3; Plutarch, *On the Malice of Herodotus* 826A, 867C). It became a normal expectation that historiography would have this slant (e.g. Polybius 16.14.6; Dionysius, *Pomp.* 3, *Ant. Rom.* 1.1.2–3, 2.1; Lucian, *Hist. conscr.* 45, 7–14). Both the Homeric and the encomiastic aspects must affect the truthfulness of Herodotus' representation of history. Quite unhomeric, however, is the proud obtrusion of the historian's identity in the first two words—a pattern already set by Hecataeus and followed by Thucydides and many later historians. The effect is double: the naming suggests that Herodotus himself will be an important figure in his *History* (as indeed he is); the use of the third person suggests objectivity and detachment.

The logic of the 'in-order-that-not' clauses is that the great deeds of history actually depend on Herodotus' own work for their continued existence, and this proud claim is emphasized by word play: his theme is deeds 'demonstrated' (great deeds are only great if publicly acknowledged), his work a 'demonstration'. Theme and work are parallel and interdependent: if the deeds are great and immortal, so too is Herodotus' history. It is a common ancient assumption, usually implying no criticism, that the ancient historian seeks personal glory from his work.[9] The 'demonstration'/ 'demonstrated' play opens the possibility that Herodotus is not just commemorating history: he is creating it. Finally, we have Herodotus' stress on historical causation: a Homeric formulation, of course, but one that is fundamental to Herodotus' historical concerns. Again and again, his narrative pinpoints, and explains, key moments of change. Here at least, the 'literary' and the 'historical' are indissoluble.

Then follows the 'sandwiched material', summarizing previous accounts of the causes of Greek–barbarian enmity, allegedly given

---

9. Cf., e.g., Thucydides 1.22.4 (below); Sallust, *The War with Catiline* (*BC*) 1.1–4, 3.1–2, *The War with Jugurtha* (*BJ*) 1.3, 2.4, 4.1; Livy, *Preface* (*Praef.*) 1, 3; Pliny, *Letters* 5.8.1–2; Lucian, *Hist. conscr.* 5.

by learned Persians and Phoenicians, which is followed, in turn, by the resumed preface (1.5.3–4):

> This, then, is what the Persians and Phoenicians say. But I am not going to say that these things happened this way or otherwise, rather I shall indicate the man whom I myself know to have begun unjust deeds towards the Greeks, and I shall then advance forwards into my account, going through small and great cities of men alike. (4) For of the cities that were great in the past, the majority have become small, and the cities that were great in my day were small formerly. Knowing, therefore, that human prosperity never remains in the same place I shall make mention of both alike.

Herodotus ostentatiously refuses to pass judgement on the truth or falsity of the previous accounts of the causes of enmity between Greeks and barbarians: he himself will start with the man whom he knows to have begun unjust deeds towards the Greeks. The ambiguity is typical. Throughout his work he claims the right to retail material without judging its historicity—'My duty is to say what is said, but it is not at all my duty to believe it, and let this statement hold for my entire account' (7.152.3). This non-committal stance takes several forms—genuinely non-committal, or implying the untruth of the material, or implying, if not its untruth, at least its relative insignificance. But the formal stance allows him to retail all sorts of material without exposing himself to the charge of untruth. On the other hand, there are countless passages which do reveal a concern for establishing the truth, or where he does proclaim things as true. But he chooses his ground. In general, no ancient historian is more alive to the problem of truth, or (on the whole) more dextrous at protecting his own position, than Herodotus.

The sandwiched material is an intriguing mixture—a long series of mythical 'snatchings' of women (including that of Helen by Paris), which is risqué, entertaining, and further enlivened by snide Herodotean asides. Although billed as 'Persian' and 'Phoenician', as if Herodotus had meticulously consulted oriental sources, its content is solidly Greek. 'The invented source' will become commonplace in ancient historiography and related genres of literature.[10] Yet the section has serious undertones; it suggests a concern with causation, with recurrent patterns in events, especially the reciprocal pattern of crime and counter-crime and punishment, with what is constant in history and what changes, with historical method, especially the weighing of sources. In all respects it is utterly typical of much of Herodotus' own material. Herodotus has it all possible ways: he uses the sandwiched material to begin his work in great style, to maintain the association between that work and Homer's *Iliad*, to entertain his readers, to suggest ideas dear to himself—yet he also distances himself from it and makes a distinction between myth and solid, verifiable history. Such ambiguity of attitude both to myth and 'things that are said' is characteristic of the ancient historian, yet rarely articulated with such flair.

So Herodotus will start his narrative with 'the man whom I myself know to have begun unjust deeds towards the Greeks'. As the sandwiched material anticipated, concern with historical causation now expands to include allocation of blame. History is not only about the documentation of events and analysis of causes: it has overt moral concern, which must inevitably affect the presentation of fact. History may have an encomiastic slant, but this still permits negative moral judgements. This is the same combination of concerns as in epic, an analogy again suggested by the allusion to the Homeric 'beginning-of-evils' motif (cf. *Il.* 1.6, 8; 5.62–63, 11.604, 22.116, 24.27–28; *Od.* 8.81–82), and in tragedy, as we shall see shortly.

'I shall then advance forwards in my account, going through small and great cities of men alike': note again the close nexus between theme and work: Herodotus' work is like the journeys he undertook in his research to produce it. There is another pointed Homeric reminiscence, to *Od.* 1.3 ('he saw the cities of many men and knew their minds'): Herodotus the historian is an *alter ego* of the great Odysseus, intrepid traveller, spinner of tales, dispassionate observer and judge of men in all their various manifestations; theme, work, writer form an indissoluble union. Herodotus will go through small cities as well as great, because of the instability of human prosperity. This serious moral and theological note sounds constantly

---

10. Fehling (English translation) 51–59, 154–74.

throughout his work, but also justifies a further extension to his already vast original edifice: he will treat not just great things, but small too.

Finally, the second preface in book 7 (7.20.2–7.21.1) argues for the supreme greatness of Xerxes' expedition, as compared with previous ones:

> Of the expeditions which we know of, this was much the greatest, so that neither Darius' against the Scythians seems an expedition by comparison with this one . . . nor the Scythian one . . . nor the one (according to what is said) of the Atreidae against Troy . . . All these campaigns and others which happened like them are not worthy of this single one.

Here, the Trojan expedition gets particularly short shrift; this emphasis, together with the distinction in the resumed preface between the myths that are 'said' and what 'we can know' (a distinction Herodotus upholds throughout his history) suggests a critical attitude to Homeric material, and critical in both senses, depreciatory and discriminating.

Let us briefly explore the implications of Herodotus' extensive imitation of, but apparent rivalry with, Homer and Homeric epic. The question is important both for Herodotus and for many ancient historians. The imitation reveals itself in such things as the choice of theme: war; the characterization of the theme; the mask or *persona* of the historian (a complex amalgam of epic poet, epic hero in general and Odysseus in particular, hence both 'outside' and 'inside' the narrative); the size of the work; the expansiveness and digressiveness of treatment; language, vocabulary, rhythms; introduction into the narrative of dramatized conferences and conversations; epic representation of battle scenes; formal 'catalogues' of opposing forces; direct divine input into human affairs; general moral and theological stance.

If a historian imitates not history itself but another historian, even if only in abstracting data from him, factual distortion is likely. His work at that point is an imitation not of external reality but of another work, which is itself an imitation. If a historian imitates a non-historian (as, in one sense, Herodotus regards Homer), whether for purposes of homage, rivalry, evocative effect, or supplementation of deficient material according to received stereotypes, factual distortion is certain, though it may vary greatly according to circumstances. This tendency, however, is to some extent counterbalanced by Herodotus' rationalist detachment from, sometimes amounting almost to rejection of, Homeric material.

Herodotus' prefatory discussions, then, written with marvellous subtlety and ambiguity, show us that his work, so far from being a mere mirror of history, is a glorious mixture: partly history, partly literature, partly prose, partly 'verse'; an immortal prose epic which will immortalize its (in some ways) epic theme; embracing true things, false things, things of indeterminate status, great things and small things, things both of the remote past and of historical times, things both Greek and barbarian; vast in scope yet with an ever narrowing focus, concerned with both the documentation of a great mass of specifics and the tracing of universals, its tone Homerically objective, intensely personal, dispassionate, involved, uncritical, rigorous, serious, entertaining. Who said Herodotus was simple?

III

Thucydides' *History* contains two formal prefaces, the first introducing the work as a whole (1.1–23), the second, about two-thirds the way through the work (5.26), introducing the second phase of the war. The first preface has a 'sandwich' structure, consisting of initial preface, narrative of past events, resumed preface. Thus, the architecture of Thucydides' prefaces is exactly the same as Herodotus', which is no accident, as becomes clear from the initial preface[11] (written some twenty-five years after Herodotus'):

---

11. A.W. Gomme, *A Historical Commentary on Thucydides* (Oxford, 1945), 89–157; N.G.L. Hammond, 'The Arrangement of the Thought in the Proem and in other Parts of Thucydides I', *CQ* 2 (1952), 127–41; H. Erbse, 'Über das Prooimion (1.1–23) des thukydideischen Geschichtswerkes', *Rheinisches Museum* 113 (1970), 43–69; W.R. Connor, *Thucydides* (Princeton, 1984), 20–32; N. Loraux, 'Thucydide a écrit la guerre du Péloponnèse', *Metis: Revue d'anthropologie du monde grec ancien* 1 (1986), 139–61; Woodman, *RICH*, 5–32; S. Hornblower, *A Commentary on Thucydides* I (Oxford, 1991), 3–66; A.M. Bowie, 'Exordia in Thucydides: Homer and Herodotus', in H.D. Jocelyn and H. Hurt, eds, *Tria Lustra: Classical Essays Presented to John Pinsent* (Liverpool, 1993), 152–62.

Thucydides the Athenian wrote up the war between the Peloponnesians and Athenians, how they waged war on each other, beginning immediately it started and expecting that it would be great and more worthy of record than those which had happened before it, going on the indication [*tekmairomenos*] that both sides went to it with their whole preparation in their prime and seeing the rest of the Greeks joining one side or the other, some immediately, others having it in mind to do so. [1.1.2] For this was the greatest upheaval to occur among the Greeks and some part of the barbarians, and extending virtually over the majority of mankind. [1.1.3] For to discover clearly the things before it and the things still more ancient was impossible because of the quantity of time intervening, but from indications which I trust as I look back [*skopounti*] over as long a period as possible, I consider them not to have been great either in wars or in other respects.

The echoes of Herodotus' preface and second preface are unmistakable:

Herodotus of Halicarnassus	Thucydides the Athenian
through time	quantity of time intervening
great / greatest	great / greatest
Greeks . . . barbarians	Peloponnesians . . . Athenians Greeks . . . barbarians
they waged war on each other	war . . . they waged war on each other
this [expedition] was much the greatest	this was the greatest upheaval
worthy	worthy of record

It is immediately apparent that while Thucydides is certainly engaged in the imitation of external reality, he is at least equally engaged in the imitation of another text. The verbal echoes make it plain that he is (in some ways) following in Herodotus' footsteps, just as Herodotus (in some ways) followed in Homer's. But Thucydides insists on the supreme greatness of his theme—his superlatives assault the ear—implicitly confuting Herodotus, just as Herodotus had confuted Homer. There is the same pattern of imitation-plus-rebuttal, but this time it poses even acuter interpretative problems, because this is historian vs historian. Is this an example of literary rivalry for its own sake or serious intellectual disagreement?

Disagreement, explicit or implicit, with one's predecessors is standard in ancient historiography.[12] Of course serious issues are often at stake (the nature of history, problems of historical method and so on), but the ancient historian's characteristic stance towards his predecessors is one of disparagement (the stance of Herodotus towards Hecataeus, cf. 2.143.1).[13] The exaggeration and tetchiness of many such attacks often indicate literary rivalry for its own sake, which Livy indeed takes for granted as a sufficient motive for writing history (*Praef.* 2).

Thucydides' imitation of Herodotus is so extensive and so detailed (as subsequent analysis will show even more clearly) that it must partly convey homage to an acknowledged master, yet it is obvious that rivalry is also important: his stress on his theme's supreme greatness is exaggerated. The Peloponnesian war was not the greatest upheaval and certainly did not extend virtually over the majority of mankind; this is a crude attempt to attain Herodotean universality. Literary rivalry can distort historical fact. But at the same time Thucydides, unlike Herodotus, has an overt concern with the establishment of fact; he wants to prove his case (dubious though it is) to the hilt. His war is also not just a war: it is an 'upheaval' (*kinēsis*). War is the great catalyst of change, creating all sorts of other changes—social, economic, political, physical, moral: Thucydides is concerned with all of these.

There follows a long historical retrospect designed to prove a historical fact: that earlier periods were not great. Thucydides' reconstruction of these very murky periods may or may not be historically brilliant, but it certainly is a further imitation of Herodotus: it too is a narrative of earlier periods, sandwiched between initial and resumed prefaces. Like Herodotus also, Thucydides is concerned to depreciate Homeric subject matter and the historical accuracy of Homer (1.9.3, 10.1, 10.3–5, 11.1–2).

Thucydides precedes this historical retrospect with the observation that you cannot 'discover the past clearly'—you can only reconstruct it through 'indications' (1.1.3). At the end of the retrospect in 1.20, he re-emphasizes this difficulty, but then (1.21.1) asserts the

---

12. Cf. e.g. Woodman, *RICH*, 131 on Livy's preface as a debate with his predecessor Sallust.

13. See S. West, 'Herodotus' Portrait of Hecataeus', *JHS* 101 (1991), 144–60.

superiority of his account of the past and his methods to those of two groups, poets and prose writers or logographers:

> [1.20.1] I have discovered ancient things to be like this ['ancient things' picks up the wording 'the things before it and the things *still more ancient*' in 1.1.3], though it is difficult to trust every single indication [*tekmērion*].

People's uncritical attitudes to facts are then illustrated in two areas: (a) hearsay material about the traditions of one's native land (Athenian example); (b) 'things that still are now and are not forgotten through time' (two examples, both Spartan and both of which Herodotus had got wrong).[14]

> [1.20.3] So unpainstaking for most people is the search for the truth; they turn rather to what lies ready to hand.   [1.21.1] But anyone who considered from the aforesaid indications [*tekmēria*] that things were more or less what I have described would not go wrong, neither trusting what the poets have eulogised about them, embellishing them for the purpose of exaggeration, nor what the prose writers [*logographoi*] have put together for the purpose of enticement to the audience rather than the truth, things that cannot be checked and the majority of them having prevailed owing to time untrustworthily to the point of myth, but believing that they have been discovered from the clearest signs sufficiently in so far as they are ancient things. [1.21.2] And this war, even though people always judge the present war when they are fighting it to be the greatest, but when they have ceased fighting wonder rather at the old, will nevertheless from the deeds themselves reveal itself to those who look at it [*skopousi*] to have been greater than them.

The apparent vagueness of reference in 1.21.1 masks polemic against Homer and Herodotus: the criticism of poets recalls the earlier criticism of Homer within the 'sandwiched material' (1.10.3: Homer 'as a poet embellishes for the purpose of exaggeration'); that of prose writers recalls the refutation of Herodotus' views in 1.20.

---

14. I.e. Herodotus says the opposite of what Thucydides says; in both cases historians dispute which of the two is really right (see Hornblower, *Commentary*, 57–58).

But people's uncritical attitudes are partly illustrated in relation to contemporary facts; and the things which distort their perception of truth—laziness, myth content—apply to both past and contemporary history. (The categories of chapters 20–21 recur in chapter 22, where Thucydides discusses his historical method regarding the Peloponnesian war.) Thus although on one level Thucydides rejects his 'sandwiched material' as not properly historical, he also links it with his treatment of the contemporary war. To some extent, the material functions as a demonstration of correct critical method and suggests ideas that will become important in the main narrative: the ceaseless struggle for dominance, competition between sea and land powers, the contrast between Athenian and Spartan ways of life, the rule of the stronger over the weaker, and so on.

Serious discussion of the nature of history and of correct historical method goes hand in hand with further extensive imitation of Herodotus, in whom we have seen the same ambiguity. But different from Herodotus is the renewed insistence that history seeks the truth, 'truth' here clearly implying factual truth. Yet the very emphasis discloses the existence of an alternative view: that the aim of history was rather to give pleasure—and pleasure not of any refined, cognitive, Aristotelian kind, but pleasure in exciting events, great dramas, bizarre exotica, and so on, material particularly found in, though not restricted to, myths. That alternative view of the aim of historiography is widely attested—for example, in Polybius, Cicero, Livy and Lucian[15]—and widely exemplified in practice, and, as we shall see, even Thucydides hints that his readers can obtain something of that sort of thing from him. But the pleasure principle in this form must, as Thucydides implies, militate against factual accuracy.

By contrast with the 'indications' or 'signs' (*tekmēria*) one must use to recover the past, the supreme greatness of the present war can be established from the deeds themselves, though one must allow for two contrary sources of distortion: people's lack of perspective about the size of whatever war they are currently fighting and their tendency to 'wonder rather at the old' (surely another criticism of Herodotus' 'wonderful' 'old' history). We note Thucydides' concern with history both as a continuum and as something divisible into

---

15. Woodman, *RICH*, 72–73, 183–85; *Tacitus*, 1–5.

present and past. This seems to sound a solidly historical note; but, even as it sounds, another note is heard, that of the dactylic rhythm of epic poetry. The Greek of 'will nevertheless reveal itself to have been greater than them', the last words of this section [*dēlōseĭ hŏmōs mēizōn gĕgĕnēmĕnŏs aŭtōn*], sounds like a line of an epic hexameter, the aural effect being all the greater for the contrast with Thucydides' usual inspissated and unlovely style. On the one hand, Thucydides distances himself from Homeric material, on the other, he implicitly aligns himself with it.

We have seen the same ambiguity in Herodotus and it is widespread in ancient historiography. Both Appian (*Praef.* 15.62) and Arrian (*Anabasis* 1.12.5)[16] strike recognisably heroic poses in their prefaces. Livy begins his *History* with a dactylic reminiscence of epic, but then distinguishes the uncertain truth status of epic from the solid truth of history, yet then in turn ambiguously reiterates the link (*Praef.* 1, 6, 13). Even Sallust and Tacitus begin their works with similar dactylic flourishes (Sallust, *BJ* 1.1, 5.1; Tacitus, *Annals* [*Ann.*] 1.1.1). Generally speaking, the more ancient their material, the more classical historians avail themselves of the epic tradition; but there are obvious exceptions. All ancient treatments of Alexander use quasi-epic treatment, and, even in Thucydides, the technique of contrasting the characters of Pericles and Cleon by means of precise verbal echoes is based on, and seems designed to evoke, Homer's contrast between Achilles and Thersites.[17] Such a technique illuminates, but may also distort; the distortive potential in the mere act of comparison is increased by the Homeric reminiscence.

A final point in 1.21.2 is the bold personification, 'this war will reveal itself', which sets the scene for chapter 23, where the historian's ability to circumscribe the war and its attendant calamities through language and reason seems to be put in doubt. But that is later.

In chapter 22 Thucydides discusses his historical method regarding the war, the rhetorical point being that if the supreme greatness of the Peloponnesian war is revealed by 'the deeds themselves' (1.21.2),

---

16. J.L. Moles, 'The Interpretation of the "Second Preface" in Arrian's *Anabasis*', *JHS* 105 (1985), 162–68.

17. F. Cairns, 'Cleon and Pericles: a Suggestion', *JHS* 102 (1982), 203–204; also Bowie (n. 11).

he needs to demonstrate that his account of 'the deeds' is soundly based. No passage in Greek literature has generated greater interpretative controversy, yet none is so important for our understanding of ancient historiography.

> [1.22.1] As for all the things that each side said in speech [*logos*], either when they were going to war or when they were already in it, it was difficult both for me in the case of the things I heard myself and for those who reported to me from various different places to remember exactly the accurate content of the things that were said. But as it seemed to me, keeping as closely to the general drift of what truly was said, that each speaker would most say what was necessary concerning the always present things, so I have rendered the speeches. [1.22.2] But as regards the deeds of the things that were done in the war, I did not think it a worthy procedure to write by asking for information from the chance passer by [*contra* Herodotus], nor just in accordance with what seemed to me to be so, but both in the case of things at which I myself was present and of things which I learnt about from others, by going through them in each case with accuracy as far as possible. [1.22.3] Things were discovered with much labour, because those who were present at each particular deed did not say the same things about the same things, but in accordance with the individual's sympathy for one side or the other or his memory. [1.22.4] And perhaps the lack of the mythical element in my history will appear rather unpleasing to an audience, but if those who wish to look at [*skopein*] the clearness [*to saphes*: (clear) truth or plausible representation?] both of the things that have happened and of those which, in accordance with human nature, are going to happen again some time like this and in similar form, should judge it useful, that will be sufficient. It is set down as a possession for always rather than as a competitive display for instant hearing.

Thucydides treats speeches first,[18] because speech precedes, and issues in, action or 'deeds'. He regards the ideal to be accurate

---

18. A small selection of the bibliography on this much-debated topic: Gomme, 140–48; G.E.M. de Ste Croix, *The Origins of the Peloponnesian War* (London, 1972), 7–16; P.A. Stadter, ed., *The Speeches in Thucydides* (Chapel Hill, 1973); D. Rokeah, 'Speeches in Thucydides: Factual Reporting or Creative Writing?', *Athenaeum* 60 (1982), 386–401; J. Wilson, 'What Does Thucydides Claim for his Speeches?' *Phoenix* 36 (1982), 95–103; Woodman, *RICH*, 11–15; Hornblower, *Thucydides*, 45–72.

reportage of speeches, as of deeds. But this is impracticable, so his speeches will be an amalgam of a solid factual core and an inevitably subjective reconstruction of 'what was necessary concerning the always present things'. 'What was necessary', even if they did not say it. This may, and often does, produce material that is in one sense historically implausible: diplomats and negotiators may be made to say grossly undiplomatic and offensive things or things of which they could hardly have had knowledge, yet things which are, on another level, historically true, in that they reflect the real logic of their position. 'The always present things'[19] are the real issues, which remained the same: the rights and wrongs of empire, and the struggle between expediency and morality; also, more broadly, the constants of human behaviour. The latter point explains the high degree of abstraction and generalization in the speeches, which is no doubt historically implausible, but which focuses on the eternal questions of human behaviour, that transcend past and present.

Such licence in reporting speeches became accepted historiographical principle.[20] The only later historian to dispute it was Polybius (36.1.7); but even he adopted it in practice, and the only later historian to include verbatim speeches was Cato, whose speeches were his own. In many later historians the licence is extended to allow the actual invention of the fact of a speech, in which practice the Homeric Herodotus had already indulged.[21] But the important point here is that Thucydides' conception of truth is

---

19. Non-classicists are warned that this translation is totally heterodox (the orthodox rendering is 'the particular circumstances'), and is propounded (so far as I know) by only two classicists in the world: Rokeah and (independently) myself. I believe that it is one of those interpretations which are self-evidently true once you see it, and its logic is implicit in my general discussion of Thucydides' prefatory material, but I shall reserve detailed arguments for a more specialized context. N.G.L. Hammond, 'The Particular and the Universal in the Speeches in Thucydides', in P.A. Stadter, ed., *The Speeches in Thucydides*, 49–59, comes close to this interpretation in practice, but without rendering the Greek in quite this way.

20. Occasionally, we can see the licence working in practice, when we have the original text of a speech, as in Tacitus' version of Claudius' speech on the Gallic Senators (*Ann.* 11.24, *Corpus Inscriptionum Latinarum* 13.1668): see M.T. Griffin, 'The Lyons Tablet and Tacitean Hindsight', CQ 32 (1982), 404–18.

21. See, in general, F.W. Walbank, *Speeches in Greek Historians*, J.L. Myres Memorial Lecture (Oxford, 1965) = *Selected Papers* (Cambridge, 1985), 242–61.

becoming something much more complex than mere factual truth. His speech material is a mixture of factual truth and imaginative truth, specific truth and general truth.

Thucydides now turns to his reportage of 'deeds', using the same word (*erga*) as Herodotus had used in his *Preface*. But, whereas in Herodotus, the word has the broad sense 'achievements' (not only 'deeds' but all 'works' of men), in Thucydides it has the narrow sense of 'deeds', the restriction in meaning itself suggesting that his treatment of history will be much tighter and more closely focused than that of the expansive Herodotus.

With the reportage of deeds there is no place for subjective reconstruction. Thucydides' wording here contrasts what is proper for speeches and what is proper for deeds, and also, surely, attacks Hecataeus, who had written things 'as they seem to me to be true'. There can be no reliance, either, on chance passers-by. (This is another jibe at Herodotus, unfair in that Herodotus generally claimed no more than that. Note the brutal economy of Thucydides' targeting, here as in 1.21.1: he blasts Hecataeus with one barrel, Herodotus with the other.) Instead, you need eye-witness testimony, you need to sift even eye-witness testimony, even your own, discounting prejudice and defective memory.

This obsessive stress on truth, on the difficulty of reconstructing it and on the deficiencies of Thucydides' predecessors, sounds pretty grim to an ancient audience expecting pleasure, so Thucydides now states his position on the pleasure principle: 'perhaps the lack of the mythical element in my history will appear rather unpleasing to an audience'; another implicit attack on Herodotus, an enormously successful public performer, unfair in that Herodotus had unified his public lectures into his great history. By contrast, Thucydides' work is less for public performance than for the select and—it is implied—for readers (a small minority even in literate Athens). The emphasis falls on the 'usefulness' of his history—a criterion which many later historians upheld or to which they at least paid lip service.[22] Yet again, Thucydides' stance is ambiguous: he rejects the vulgar pleasure of myth, but hints at pleasure through other channels; he disdains popular acclaim, but modestly says he will be content with . . . his work's immortality.

---

22. Cf., e.g., Polybius 1.4.11, 2.56.10; Livy, *Praef.* 10; Tacitus, *Ann.* 4.32.2; Lucian, *Hist. conscr.* 42.

In what sense will his work be 'useful'? It provides ' "the clearness" both of the things which have happened and of those which, in accordance with human nature, are going some time to happen again like this and in similar form'. The 'clearness' has recently been interpreted by A.J. Woodman as 'a plausible representation'.[23] I believe that this interpretation is untenable. Thucydides' basic argument in the first preface goes like this: in reconstructing past history you cannot discover things clearly (you have to rely on 'indications'), and Thucydides then considers the difficulties of that process. In reconstructing the Peloponnesian War, you can get at the deeds themselves; that is difficult too, of course, but Thucydides' insistence on the supreme greatness of the war depends on its being possible. 'The clearness' of the things that have happened is precisely what you cannot discover in past history, but what Thucydides has 'discovered', though with difficulty, about the Peloponnesian war. 'The clearness' therefore equals the truth—a very common meaning of the Greek word *saphes*. But, while one can obviously talk of the clear truth of things that have happened, how can one talk of the clear truth of things that are going to happen?

Human nature is constant—as Thucydides says here and repeatedly elsewhere (e.g. 1.76.2–3, 2.50.1, 3.39.5, 3.45.7, 3.82.2, 4.19.4), so that things will occur in the future 'like this and in similar form'. Yet there is obviously a difference between the clear truth of things that have happened and the clear truth of things that are going to happen: things that are going to happen will not be precisely the same as the things that have happened. That is, there is a 'slide' in the reference of 'clear truth' in this sentence. Thucydides is grappling with one of the fundamental problems of history—a problem analysed with characteristic acuity by Aristotle in chapter 9 of the *Poetics*.[24]

Aristotle draws a key distinction between the truth of poetry (particularly tragedy) and that of historiography. On the face of it, historiography is much more truthful. But in Aristotle's opinion this kind of truth is trivial: history is about 'what Alcibiades did or what happened to him'—specific truths, what happened to a particular

23. *RICH*, 23–28.
24. I here repeat the discussion in J.L. Moles, *Plutarch: Cicero* (Warminster, 1988), 41.

individual at a particular time. Poetry, on the other hand, is about 'universal truths' ('what sort of person would, as a matter of probability or necessity, say or do what sort of thing'). The tragic poet, while working with material which is broadly historical, yet has freedom to manipulate the material in detail, in order to explore universal truths about human behaviour.

Admittedly, Aristotle's critique of historiography is unfair: he chooses Alcibiades as the archetypal historiographical subject because Alcibiades was a supreme individualist, about whom it was indeed difficult to make useful generalizations. But the basic point is important. If it is to have any meaning beyond the mere recording of specific facts, historiography needs to strike a balance between establishing those facts (so that its raw material is sound) and moving outwards from them to useful generalizations.[25]

This fundamental tension in historiography is exemplified throughout Thucydides' narrative, which records masses of specifics in inordinate detail yet strives constantly to extrapolate general truths. In some ways, the latter requirement pulls against multiplication of material—so that, for example, Pericles to some extent represents the typical Ideal Statesman, Cleon the typical Unprincipled Demagogue, while the politically important Hyperbolus is dismissed parenthetically (8.73.3). Thucydides sometimes resorts also to shorthand formulations such as 'every form of death ensued and whatever is accustomed to happen in such a situation' (3.81.5). In other ways, it pulls towards repetition (hence the endless and shifting debate in the speeches concerning the rights and wrongs of empire, the relationship between expediency and morality etc.) and towards the establishment of recurrent patterns (thus the events of the second half of the history, from 5.25 onwards, in some respects reprise those of the first).[26]

This tension has another aspect: history is concerned both with what is timeless and universal and with what is (in some ways)

---

25. See for instance, on the prefaces to Sallust's monographs, D. Earl, 'Prologue-form in Ancient Historiography', *Aufstieg und Niedergang der römischen Welt* 1.2, ed. H. Temporini (Berlin, 1972), 842–56, at 856: 'Sallust was announcing that what followed was not straight history but a philosophical disquisition on politics and public affairs of which the historical facts were, so to speak, extended *exempla*'.

26. H.R. Rawlings, *The Structure of Thucydides' History* (Princeton, 1981), esp. 38–57.

distinctively different. This explains both the general anxiety of ancient historians to establish the uniqueness of their specific theme and the particular insistence of Thucydides that the Peloponnesian war was the greatest 'upheaval' (*kinēsis*) ever.

Thucydides, then, aims to establish solid factual truth about the war; this allows the deduction of general truths about human behaviour, the contemplation of which will promote understanding of future events, even though they have not yet occurred. At the same time, what is distinctively different about this war facilitates the establishment of what is generally true. The very extraordinariness of the war illustrates human affairs writ large and at their most extreme. Thucydides' views here (and indeed Herodotus') seem to anticipate Aristotelian theory about the supreme cognitive value of tragedy, which is also simultaneously ordinary and extraordinary,[27] though Aristotle, of course, denies this value to historiography.

Thus, Thucydides' ' "clear truth" both of the things that have happened and of those which are going to happen' represents an amalgam of solid fact with less solid generalizing material which is parallel to the amalgam of solid truth and generalizing material in the speeches.

History is composed of tensions: specific factual truths, general truths, what is the same, what is different, what is typical, what is extraordinary, the past, the present and the future. In so far as Thucydides' main theme is both the present and the future, his work is coextensive with them and thus truly a possession for always. As with Herodotus, theme and work are one, but Thucydides' work seems to range through time itself. Indeed, his concern with time as divisible into past-time, present-time, future-time and 'always'-time, and the analogy between his 'always'-theme and his 'always'-work are reminiscent of, and perhaps directly influenced by, the terms in which, some three hundred years before, the poet Hesiod had claimed the Muses' inspiration for his account of the birth of the gods (*Theogony* 31–34): 'They breathed into me a voice divine, that I might celebrate the things that are to be and were before, and they told me to hymn the race of the blessed ones that are for always, but themselves both first and last to sing for always.' If indeed this

---

27. E. Belfiore, 'Pleasure, Tragedy and Aristotelian Psychology', *CQ* 35 (1985), 349–61 at 360.

parallel is directly felt, Thucydides yet again blurs the polarity between the poet and the historian.

This paper began with Lucian's image of the 'mirror' of the historian, an apparently simple image, but one which modern scholars have shown to be capable of fruitful and complex development. Thucydides' remarks at 1.22.4 illustrate some of these complexities.[28] Truth is 'the clearness', what has been *seen* by the historian himself or reliable eye-witnesses (1.22.2–3). Both the historian (1.1.3; 1.22.2–3 by implication) and his readers (1.21.2; 1.22.4) are engaged in a process of 'looking' (*skopein*). Thus the historian's *mimēsis* of events, the product of his 'seeing' and 'looking', is like a mirror, at which he invites his readers to 'look'. But for the readers, as for the historian himself, the process of 'looking' is complex: to 'look' is not only to 'see' in a physical sense, but to 'contemplate', to 'attempt to understand', to 'reflect on'.[29] Hence what the readers see in Thucydides' mirror is not a simple reflection of events but a reflection of specific and general truths, and of the past, the present, and the future. And even this is too simple a picture, as the next section shows.

Having demonstrated the soundness of his historical method for establishing 'the deeds' (1.22.2–3), Thucydides now argues that these 'deeds' prove the supreme greatness of the Peloponnesian war and he ends his first preface by dating the outbreak of war and explaining its causes:

> [1.23.1] Of the deeds before, the greatest that was done was the Median war [the Persian war of 481–479], yet this had a speedy decision through two naval battles and land battles. But in the case of this war, its length advanced to a great size and also it happened that disasters [*pathēmata*] occurred to Greece during it such as did not otherwise occur in the same space of time.

---

28. For stimulating exploration of the image see especially F. Hartog, *Le Miroir d'Hérodote: Essai sur la représentation de l'autre* (Paris, 1980), tr. J. Lloyd as *The Mirror of Herodotus: the Representation of the Other in the Writing of History* (Berkeley, 1988), and 'L'oeil de Thucydide et l'histoire "véritable"', *Poétique* 49 (1982), 22–30. Like Lucian, I am not here concerned with the fact (exploited by Hartog) that if one looks directly into a mirror, one sees, above all, oneself.

29. See e.g. B. Knox, *Oedipus at Thebes* (Oxford, 1957), 120–1.

[1.23.2] For neither were so many cities captured and made desolate, some by barbarians, some by the people themselves as they waged counter-war (some also changed inhabitants when they were captured), nor so many exiles of people and killing, some of it in the war itself, some because of civil strife. [1.23.3] And the things that were before this said by hearsay, but rather rarely substantiated in deed, were established to be not untrustworthy—about earthquakes, which held sway over a very great part of the land and were at the same time most powerful, and eclipses of the sun, which occurred more frequently by comparison with what was remembered from former times, and there were great droughts, and from them both famines and that which did most damage and which did not least destroy: the plaguey sickness. For all these made a simultaneous attack along with this war. [1.23.4] The Athenians and Peloponnesians began it after dissolving the thirty years' truce which they had made after the capture of Euboea. [1.23.5] As to why they dissolved it, I have written first the causes and the discords, so that no one need seek from what so great a war as this came upon the Greeks. The truest cause, though least apparent in men's speech, I believe to have been the fact that the Athenians, becoming great and making the Peloponnesians fearful, pressured them towards going to war. But the causes said in the open on each side were as follows, as a result of which they dissolved the truce and came to the war.

In order to establish the supreme greatness of his war, Thucydides confronts the counter-claims of the Persian war, which (in terms of numbers of men, size of battles, international implications, etc.) was in fact greater than the Peloponnesian. So, inevitably, Thucydides' argument here is untenable—it is like arguing that the Hundred Years War was greater than World War I; again, rivalry with Herodotus produces factual distortion.

The greatness of the war is also manifested in the unprecedented disasters—both man-made and natural—that came with it. The specific claim that 'it happened that disasters occurred to Greece during it such as did not otherwise occur in the same space of time' yet again echoes, and trumps, Herodotus. For Herodotus had maintained (6.98.2) that 'in the time of Darius, son of Hystaspes, and of Xerxes, son of Darius, and of Artaxerxes, son of Xerxes, three successive generations, there occurred more evils to Greece than during the twenty generations before Darius, some done to her by the Persians, others by her own leaders warring for empire.' Not only, then, is Thucydides' war greater than Herodotus', his 'disasters' are relatively more numerous and more concentrated in time. Moreover, Thucydides' description is highly rhetorical, his tone highly emotional, the content itself—disasters, cities captured and made desolate, natural calamities culminating in a great plague—typical of epic or tragedy. Clearly, Thucydides is at least in part here trying to stimulate his readers' emotions with the promise of pleasurable 'tragic history', a useful, if imprecise, term.[30] This is a counterpoise (hinted at in chapter 22) to his austere emphasis on the cognitive value of his work. We may even sense a general contrast in chapters 22 and 23 between *logos* in the sense of 'reason' and *pathēmata* in the sense of 'emotions'.

Exploitation of tragedy is widespread in ancient historiography. In Herodotus we sometimes find tragic language, tragic sentiments, tragic narrative patterning—individuals striving to penetrate the opaque will of the gods, facing great moral dilemmas, moving from ignorance to knowledge, even 'facts' derived from tragedies.[31] In Thucydides' narrative we find harrowing descriptions evocative of pity and fear (for example, in book 7 on the Athenian disaster in Sicily) and tragic narrative patterning (for example, in the account of the Plague and its relationship to the Funeral Speech) and, in the extraordinary Melian Dialogue, something that is virtually formal tragic drama.[32] From Polybius and Plutarch we hear much of the excesses of Hellenistic historians like Duris and Cleitarchus, who

---

30. Woodman, *RICH*, 28–32; in general: B.L. Ullman, 'History and Tragedy', *TAPA* 73 (1942), 25–53; F.W. Walbank, 'Tragic History: a Reconsideration', *Bulletin of the Institute of Classical Studies* 2 (1955), 4–14, and 'History and Tragedy', *Historia* 9 (1960), 216–34 = *Selected Papers*, 224–41; Sacks, *Polybius*, 144–70.

31. See e.g. W.W. How and J. Wells, *A Commentary on Herodotus*, vol. 1 (Oxford, 1912), 21; J.L. Myres, 'Herodotus the Tragedian' in *A Miscellany, Presented to J.M. MacKay, LL.D* (Liverpool, 1914), 88–96; C.C. Chiasson, 'Tragic Diction in Herodotus: Some Possibilities', *Phoenix* 36 (1982), 156–61.

32. Book 7: J.H. Finley, *Thucydides* (Cambridge, Mass., 1942), 321–22, and *Three Essays on Thucydides* (Cambridge, Mass., 1967), 46–49; Woodman, *RICH*, 27 and 60–61, n. 157; plague: Woodman, *RICH*, 32–40; Melian Dialogue: W. Liebeschuetz, 'The Structure and Function of the Melian Dialogue', *JHS* 88 (1968), 73–77 at 76–77; more generally: C. Macleod, 'Thucydides and Tragedy', in *Collected Essays* (Oxford, 1983), 140–58; for the whole approach F.M. Cornford, *Thucydides Mythistoricus* (London, 1907) remains important.

specialized in extreme emotional arousal through protracted and extravagant descriptions of all manner of horrors; such historians were much read. In fact, virtually all ancient historians, even those who claim to be critical of tragic history, exploit tragedy to some degree.[33]

But Thucydides' stress on natural calamities as well as man-made ones conveys a solidly historical point: men are not the only agents of change: they can face forces beyond rational calculation or foresight—a point powerfully demonstrated in the plague narrative. This point is presumably also to some extent directed against Herodotus, whose universe is largely anthropocentric. Moreover, the scale of the disasters meant that 'the things that were before this said by hearsay, but rather rarely substantiated in deed, were established to be not untrustworthy'. Yet Thucydides himself has underlined the difficulty of trusting evidence from the past and distinguished the greater accuracy possible with deeds than with words or speeches: these tremendous events seem to defy historical canons and the historian's attempts to impose order on them. This is very different from the 'clear truth' of ch. 22. Here historiography ruefully contemplates its own inability to comprehend reality.

Then (1.23.4), Thucydides seems to revert to sober history, precisely dating the war's outbreak; he is proud of his chronological accuracy (cf. 1.97.2, 2.1.1, 5.20), which does indeed make a great advance upon any of his predecessors, Herodotus included. He undertakes first to document 'the causes and the discords'. The wording again reflects Herodotus, whose initial preface promised to investigate 'for what cause Greeks and barbarians waged war on each other' and who began his 'sandwiched material' with the words 'among the Persians the learned say that the Phoenicians were the cause of the discord'; it therefore also reflects the beginning of Homer's *Iliad*. Thucydides does this 'so that no one need seek from what so great a war as this came upon the Greeks', the wording of which reflects precisely *Il.* 1.6–7: 'From what [time] Atreides king of men and divine Achilles first stood apart in strife'. Precise historical analysis

---

33. See below, pp. 133–5. For a particular case (Plutarch's *Lives*) see J.M. Mossman, 'Tragedy and Epic in Plutarch's *Alexander*', *JHS* 108 (1988), 83–93; Moles, *Plutarch: Cicero*, 34, 190.

and precise literary imitation here go hand in hand. Again, as in Homer and Herodotus, the search for causation implies investigation of blame. Thucydides would have been astonished by modern claims that he was not a moralist.

The famous distinction between stated causes and the truest cause represents another aspect of the deficiency of speech to express reality, but now *qua* deceptiveness rather than (as in chapter 22) incapacity. Rigorously historical and intellectually penetrating as the distinction may be, it is yet another imitation of Herodotus, who had given the 'causes' that were 'said' before stating what he 'knew' to be true. In the last words of the section, 'they came to the war'; earlier, 'the war came upon them': we see again the tension between human beings as agents and as passive before the agency of inhuman things, but for the moment, and deceptively, the agency lies with humans. Finally, the narrative begins (1.24.1, 'There is a city Epidamnus'), its syntax echoing both Homeric formulations (e.g. *Il.* 6.152, 'there is a city Ephyre') and the beginning of Herodotus' narrative (1.6.1, 'Croesus was Lydian by race'). Later, the formal second preface also imitates Herodotus'.

So is Thucydides' work history or literature, dispassionate analysis or emotional arousal, impersonal or highly personalized, objective or subjective, unbiased or prejudiced, plain or rhetorical, true or untrue? The answer has to be: it is all of these, though Thucydides clearly has a serious concern with truth, and with different kinds of truth at that.

IV

Some questions and conclusions, or inconclusions. Can the literary aspect of ancient historiography be sliced off like icing from Christmas cake? Emphatically, no. You can try to extract factual material from an ancient historiographical text, but (to change the metaphor) it is like cutting a vital organ from the body. You may or may not succeed (that depends on your surgical skill and the constitution of the individual body), but it will always be a messy business: you may take out more than you bargained for, and you cannot always be sure even which organ you should be pulling out. That is not to say that such surgery is unnecessary: modern historians are bound to try to abstract factual data from ancient historiographical texts, their main source of evidence, however recalcitrant;

and for their part modern literary critics cannot properly gauge the originality and creativity of those texts without trying to establish the raw material upon which they are based.

Do ancient historiographers sometimes say things they know to be factually untrue? Emphatically, yes. The accusation of deliberate fabrication is made repeatedly. Herodotus is dubbed the father, not only of history, but of lies; Polybius castigates historians not only for incompetence, but falsehood; Lucian tells of historians who claimed to be eye-witnesses of things they could not possibly have seen; invention and manipulation of factual material is (I believe) demonstrable in Herodotus and Plutarch,[34] as well as Hellenistic tragic historians. The motives vary: some, of course, crudely political—propaganda, flattery, denigration; literary rivalry (to trump one's predecessors, of which we have seen examples even in Thucydides); the desire to spin a good yarn (often important in Herodotus and other historians of the exotic); sometimes (surely) historiographical parody; sheer emotional arousal or entertainment; the need to make moral points or bring out broader patterns or causes behind complicated sequences of events.

Was the whole conception of truth in ancient historiography different from ours? Or, to put it another way, can we produce a theory which will explain untruth in ancient historiography in terms other than lying (excluding, of course, simple error, which poses no theoretical problem)?

One increasingly popular approach is to see Herodotus, in particular, as the product of an essentially oral culture, in whch literacy, though it existed, was only an aid to oral communication. Despite his deployment of a wide range of historical evidence, Herodotus clearly believes in the paramountcy of oral tradition; and oral cultures preserve the past, even the recent past, through stories and anecdotes, all far more fluid and far less concerned with logic and accuracy than the written products of literate societies. Yet such stories themselves embody in some senses 'truths' about the societies that produce them (ways of 'mapping the past', 'structuring reality', and so on). Against such a general perspective, traditional

---

34. Cf. e.g. Moles, *Plutarch: Cicero*, 32–45 and C.B.R. Pelling, 'Truth and Fiction in Plutarch's *Lives*' in D.A. Russell, ed., *Antonine Literature* (Oxford, 1990), 19–51.

accusations against Herodotus of 'lying' may seem inappropriate, because based on cultural misunderstanding.[35]

The 'oral' approach to Herodotus does not seem to me to make traditional questions about his truthfulness nearly as inappropriate as its proponents allege or imply. Oral cultures can be just as concerned as literate societies with basic questions of truth: 'we know how to speak many false things like true things, but we know, when we wish, to utter true things', sang Hesiod's Muses (*Theogony* 27–28); 'you sing of the fate of the Achaeans excellently well, all that they did and suffered and toiled, as if you had been present yourself or heard it from someone who had,' said Odysseus to the bard Demodocus (*Od.* 8.489–91). Such passages and many others like them focus on key historical questions concerning truth, falsehood, plausible falsehood, the reliability of eye-witness testimony, and the importance of learning from eye-witnesses.

Eschewing any great distinction between Herodotus and his successors, Woodman argues that in the Classical world historiography is generally seen as a species of the genus rhetoric.[36] Its detailed categorization varies—it is sometimes categorized as a form of epideictic (formal display) literature, sometimes in terms of forensic, sometimes deliberative oratory, sometimes likened to poetry—but this does not affect the overall picture. Though historiography aims at truth, truth is conceived largely as a matter of the absence of prejudice. It is accepted that truth resides only in a factual core, sometimes very small, which it is the historian's job to build up in a rhetorically persuasive manner; and that the historian may choose (within limits) whether to angle his work towards the encomiastic or the derogatory, these two things representing the main tendencies in ancient literature generally.

How to assess this whole theory? There are obviously things to be said for it. Some people did regard historiography as a rhetorical genre; some rhetoricians did analyse it in this way; poetry can be

---

35. Gould, *Herodotus*, 19–41, 112–34; O. Murray, 'Herodotus and Oral History', in A. Kuhrt and H. Sancisi-Weerdenburg, eds, *Achaemenid History 3: Method and Theory* (Leiden, 1988), 93–115; S. West, art. cit. (n. 5), 304–5; interestingly, West is much less receptive to this approach in her later study (*JHS* 111 [1991], 148–49 and n. 28).

36. I here repeat my discussion in *History of the Human Sciences* 3.2 (1990), 319–21.

part of historiography, as we have seen; rhetorical influence is everywhere in ancient historiography, including Herodotus and Thucydides, as it is in almost all ancient literature. It is broadly true that ancient historiographers fall into two camps: positive and optimistic or negative and pessimistic, and that this is reflected in both content and style. Some historiographers undoubtedly did proceed according to these rhetorical prescriptions. Almost all ancient historiographers would adopt such prescriptions in particular situations which were regarded as fair game for 'big-scene' treatment (e.g. battle narratives or descriptions of sieges or captures of cities).[37]

One big problem is the question of how far this theory can be generalized. (In fact this raises the whole generic problem—how far ancient literature was written according to generic prescription.) Against every single proposition of the theory it is possible to quote programmatic theoretical statements from the ancient writers themselves, some very heavy-weight. Rhetorical though he is, Thucydides makes a firm, though not absolute, distinction between his 'possession for always' and 'competitive displays for instant hearing' (1.22.4). Aristotle's conception of historiography is quite unrhetorical, at least in *Poetics* 9. Lucian insists on the difference between historiography and oratory or poetry (*Hist. conscr.* 8, 39, 45, 50). The rhetorical analysis of historiography seems to have begun in the late fourth century, and while formal rhetoric attempted to engulf historiography, like everything else, its success was never total. Of course, it is possible to argue that in this area, as elsewhere, rhetorical theory merely systematized and developed existing practice; so that, while in one sense it may be anachronistic to apply it to fifth-century historiography, in another sense it may be perfectly justifiable. The question then is how well the theory describes the practice.

In my view, the theory requires at least substantial modification. We have seen that Herodotus' broadly encomiastic stance allows moral criticism of Greeks as well as barbarians. In general terms Thucydides *is* negative and pessimistic, but we are not dealing with a systematic rhetoricizing tendency. As I have tried to suggest, the richness and complexity of both Herodotus and Thucydides makes generalization about them extremely difficult.

---

37. Instructive material in G. Paul, '*Urbs capta*: Sketch of an Ancient Literary Motif', *Phoenix* 36 (1982), 144–55; Woodman, *RICH*, 168–79.

More important, the theory does not actually engage with two key aspects of the truth problem: those cases where ancient historians proclaim the truth of things they know to be untrue (two examples of which I shall consider below), and the many passages where truth is seen not in terms of prejudice but of solid historical criteria such as eye-witness testimony or its absence, paucity or excess of evidence, conflict of sources, carelessness, chronological inaccuracy, dramatic exaggeration and so on.

There are many different types of ancient historians. Some write historiography according to rhetorical prescriptions, some do not, or not to the extent claimed by the theory. Some see truth very largely in terms of prejudice. Some are not interested in truth at all, writing purely and simply to entertain. These latter may fairly be considered as writers of fiction, at least to the extent that historical novelists are engaged in fiction. Whether we say that they are not true historians or allow that ancient historiography is not necessarily concerned with truth, is an almost semantic question, like the question whether untragic happy-ending tragedies are tragedies.

We must also admit that even the most serious and 'historical' ancient historians share characteristics with the most purely 'literary'. The difference between the two is a matter of degree, though there may come a point where quantitative differences become qualitative. Thucydides does differ from Clitarchus, even though there is tragic history in both, because in Thucydides there is also a serious concern with truth, an awareness of the different sorts of truth, an acute appreciation of the difficulties in attaining them, yet a constant effort to do so.

The last problem: why do serious and 'historical' ancient historians sometimes actually proclaim the truth of what they know, or suspect, to be untrue?

Two instructive examples may be cited (with the melancholy but inevitable proviso that some scholars would not accept them as examples). One is from Herodotus: the famous constitutional debate on the merits of democracy, oligarchy and monarchy allegedly conducted between the Persian nobles Otanes, Megabyzus and Darius after the death in 522 BC of the mad king Cambyses. Herodotus introduces it with the words (3.80.1): 'speeches were said which are unbelievable to some of the Greeks, but nevertheless they were said.' This defiant note recurs in his statement that some thirty years later, after the failure of the Ionian revolt against Persian rule, the Persian Mardonius introduced democracy into the Ionian cities (6.43.3): 'when Mardonius sailing along Asia reached Ionia, then I shall describe a great wonder to those of the Greeks who do not accept that Otanes declared his opinion to the seven that the Persians should have a democracy: Mardonius suppressed all the tyrants of the Ionians and established democracies in the cities.' It is intrinsically improbable that the constitutional debate was recorded in any written source, or publicized in any form, before Herodotus himself, a conclusion which seems to be supported by the defiant tone in which Herodotus defends the item, as if his personal honour were at stake. If so, the previous occasion when it excited disbelief was presumably one of Herodotus' own oral performances.

This item poses the most fundamental historical questions of all: did the event take place or not? Is the historian who proclaims the truth actually telling the truth or not? Neither Woodman's conception of truth as the absence of prejudice nor the 'oral-culture' view of Herodotus can cope with the radical challenge posed by these two passages.

There remain scholars who believe either in the historicity of the constitutional debate itself or at any rate that its historicity was believed by Herodotus, despite the obvious impossibility of advocacy by a Persian of democracy at a time when it had not even been invented in Greece. Even such a conservative admirer of Herodotus as A.R. Burn was driven to say that 'if we wish to pillory him as a liar, this is the strongest ground,'[38] while even to argue the weaker case—that Herodotus believed the story—demeans him by making him a much less intelligent man than he was, and much less intelligent than those of his contemporaries who, as he himself admitted, disbelieved in the debate.

Since even the information about Mardonius is either at least greatly exaggerated or totally fictitious,[39] we should be emboldened by the open disbelief of those contemporaries, bite the bullet and say either that Herodotus invented the Persian constitutional debate on the basis of Mardonius' selectively conciliatory attitude to democracy in Ionia, or that he invented both items. Abandonment of

---

38. *Herodotus: The Histories* (Penguin edn, revised 1972), 238 n. 1.
39. How and Wells, *Commentary* vol. 2, 80, remains a sharp discussion.

historicity is counterbalanced by other factors. The fictitious Persian constitutional debate after the death of the tyrannical and deranged Cambyses, in several ways the precursor of Xerxes, invader of Greece, provides an excellent focus for the exploration of several of Herodotus' major themes: the key moment of moral choice, the constituents of good government, the rise and fall of Persian power, the interrelationship between the success or failure of imperial powers and their respective constitutions.[40]

The other example is Plutarch's handling of the certainly unhistorical meeting of Solon the Athenian and Croesus, king of Lydia (a meeting first attested, of course, by Herodotus). Plutarch's discomfort is plain but he cannot formally abandon the story, which he narrates at some length, and he resorts to some obviously desperate expedients to shore up its historicity (*Solon* 27.1): 'As for his meeting with Croesus, some think to refute it by chronology as made up. But for my part, when a story is so famous and has so many witnesses and—what is a greater consideration—is so appropriate to Solon's character and so worthy of his greatness of soul and wisdom, I do not think it right to sacrifice it to any so-called chronological canons, which thousands are to this day trying to correct, without being able to bring their contradictions to any agreed result.' It is the other way round: here historical fact is sacrificed to Plutarch's need to expound universal moral truths.[41]

Why then do Herodotus and Plutarch behave in this way? Serious ancient historians (which both Herodotus and Plutarch intermittently are) face the problem of the eternal see-saw of history: the need to generalize from specifics. No serious ancient historian was so tied to specific factual truth that he would not sometimes help general truths along by manipulating, even inventing, 'facts'. Of course, the requisite manipulation could sometimes be achieved through the medium of 'what-is-said' material, to whose historicity the ancient historian did not commit himself. But there were some occasions when the issues were so serious that it was rhetorically

---

40. Full discussion in Lateiner, *Historical Method*, 147–70 (who does not, however, accept its fictitiousness).

41. Similarly, as Peter Wiseman reminds me, Plutarch refuses to allow chronological considerations to exclude the alleged link between the Roman king Numa and the Greek philosopher Pythagoras (*Numa* 1.2–4, 8.9–10, 22.3–4).

necessary, even at the risk of attack, to maintain the illusion of strict historicity. On those occasions the historian could never admit to manipulation or invention. Such is the tyranny of factual truth.[42]

To return to our initial question: the relationship of ancient historiography to external reality is shifting, ambiguous, multifaceted, messy: in those respects at least, like life itself.

42. Plutarch's wrigglings on these problems are discussed in Moles, *Plutarch: Cicero*, 35–36, 200.

Chapter Four

Lying Historians:
Seven Types of Mendacity

T.P. WISEMAN

I

FOR Seneca, in the first century AD, it was axiomatic that historians are liars. There is a passage in his *Quaestiones Naturales* (7.16.1f.) where, discussing comets, he brushes aside the theory offered by Ephorus with a damning remark: 'It takes no great effort to refute him—he's a historian.' And yet history, of all genres, was supposed to tell the truth. In the only theoretical discussion of historiography that survives from antiquity, Lucian's essay *How to Write History* (*Hist. conscr.*),[1] that principle is stated without irony or embarrassment (39): 'The historian's one task is to tell it as it happened . . . the one particular characteristic of history is this, that if you are going to write it you must sacrifice to Truth alone.'

Seneca justifies his paradox with a sardonic little digression on the practice of history as mere entertainment:

> Some historians win approval by telling incredible tales; an everyday narrative would make the reader go and do something

---

1. Text, translation and short commentary in M.D. MacLeod, ed. and tr., *Lucian: a Selection* (Warminster, 1991), 198–247, 283–302. Detailed commentary in G. Avenarius, *Lukians Schrift zur Geschichtsschreibung* (Meisenheim am Glan, 1956), and H. Homeyer, *Lukian: wie man Geschichte schreiben soll* (Munich, 1965).

else, so they excite him with marvels. Some of them are credulous, and lies take them unawares; others are careless, and lies are what they like; the former don't avoid them, the latter seek them out. What the whole tribe have in common is this: they think their work can only achieve approval and popularity if they sprinkle it with lies.

Writing in a different genre, as the narrator of the 'pumpkinification of Claudius', Seneca gives a brilliant impersonation of the irresponsible historian:[2]

> I want to put on record the business transacted in heaven on 13 October . . . No concession will be made to umbrage taken or favour granted. This is the authentic truth. If anyone inquires about the source of my information, first, I shan't reply if I don't want to. Who's going to compel me? . . . If I *do* choose to reply, I'll say whatever trips off my tongue. Who ever demanded sworn referees from a historian? But if it is obligatory to produce the originator of the account, let the inquirer ask the man who saw Drusilla on her way to heaven.

In the first passage, Seneca has in mind the telling of marvel-stories more appropriate to poetry, and that idea is present in the *Apocolocyntosis* too: the contrast with sworn testimony was usually applied to poets, and Seneca makes one of his characters describe the events as an appendix to Ovid's *Metamorphoses*.[3] However, the reference to Drusilla's apotheosis shows that in the second passage he is thinking mainly of flattery and panegyric.[4]

Those two perversions of history are, in fact, the only items in the 'what not to do' section of Lucian's essay (7–13): if you avoid 'poetic stories' (*muthoi*) and 'praise of rulers and generals', it seems that you have done enough to satisfy truth. But it would be premature to infer that tall tales and flattery of the powerful were the only types of 'lying' that historians were thought to indulge in.

---

2. *Apocolocyntosis* 1.1–2: tr. (slightly adapted) from P.T. Eden's edition and commentary (Cambridge, 1984), 29.

3. Testimony: Cicero, *De legibus* 1.4, Ovid, *Amores* 3.12.19, etc.; D.C. Feeney, *The Gods in Epic: Poets and Critics of the Classical Tradition* (Oxford, 1991), 40. *Metamorphoses*: Seneca, *Apocolocyntosis* 9.5.

4. See p. 94 above on encomium.

Let us move on to the fourth century AD, and listen to a performer every bit as sophisticated as Seneca and Lucian. The author of the *Historia Augusta* presented his thirty imperial biographies under six different pseudonyms, and was unmasked only in 1889.[5] As Sir Ronald Syme put it,[6] 'the *HA* is a genuine hoax . . . the text discloses a rogue scholar, delighting in deceit and making a mock of historians. Perhaps a professor on the loose, a librarian seeking recreation, a civil servant repelled by pedestrian routine.' Such a man's view on history and lies should be worth having.

It comes in the preface to the *Life of Aurelian* (1.1–2), and the setting is perfect:

> On the day of the Hilaria, when, as we know, all deeds and words should be festive, his excellency Junius Tiberianus, Prefect of the City, invited me into his official carriage after the ceremony.

The Hilaria festival was a day of masquerade and disguise; according to Herodian (1.10.5), 'anyone can play the fool by concealing his true identity, making it difficult to tell the real person from the impersonator.' Just as Plato presents his account of Atlantis as a story told at the *Apatouria*,[7] as Virgil's underworld narrative ends with Aeneas emerging through the ivory gate,[8] as (perhaps) Apuleius specifies the first watch of the night for his witch's metamorphosis,[9] so too the author of the *Historia Augusta* leaves a delicate hint, flattering the reader who is alert enough to appreciate it.

The man in the City Prefect's carriage is 'Flavius Vopiscus', one of the *HA* author's aliases.[10] On the way from the Palatine to the

---

5. H. Dessau, 'Über Zeit und Personlichkeit der Scriptores Historiae Augustae', *Hermes* 24 (1889), 337–92.

6. R. Syme, *Historia Augusta Papers* (Oxford, 1983), 221, cf. 62, 128f.; see also Syme's earlier books *Ammianus and the Historia Augusta* (Oxford, 1968), esp. ch. 26, and *Emperors and Biography* (Oxford, 1971), esp. ch. 17. For the psychology, cf. A. Grafton, *Forgers and Critics* (London, 1990).

7. Plato, *Timaeus* 21b; C. Gill, ed., *Plato: the Atlantis Story* (Bristol, 1980), 40.

8. Virgil, *Aeneid* 6.893–8; D. West, *The Bough and the Gate* (Exeter, 1987), 7–14 = S.J. Harrison, ed., *Oxford Readings in Vergil's Aeneid* (Oxford, 1990), 230–8.

9. Apuleius, *Metamophoses* 3.21.3; p. 164 below. Cf. pp. 58f. above, 216f. below on hints of fictionality.

10. The dramatic date is either 291–2 or 303–4: see Syme, *Ammianus and the HA*, 192; *Historia Augusta Papers*, 120 (opp. citt. n. 6 above).

Varian Gardens, he engages the Prefect in conversation about imperial biography. Why, asks the Prefect, doesn't he write a Life of Aurelian? 'I'll even get his Linen Books brought out of Trajan's Library for you.' Linen books (*libri lintei*) were documents appropriate to the fourth century BC, six hundred years before Aurelian's time;[11] but 'Vopiscus' blandly urges his readers to consult them in the Library themselves if they aren't satisfied (1.7–10).

The conversation in the carriage now resumes with a discussion of the work of Trebellius Pollio—who is in fact another of the *HA* author's aliases (2.1–2):

> Tiberianus maintained that much of Pollio's work was brief and careless. I protested that as far as history was concerned there was no author who had not lied about something. I went so far as to cite the places where Livy, Sallust, Cornelius Tacitus and even Trogus were refuted by clear evidence, at which he yielded to my argument and jokingly held up his hand. 'All right then,' he said, 'write what you want. You can safely say whatever you like, and you'll have those admired masters of historical style as your companions in mendacity.'

Here again is the Senecan assumption that all historians lie, but evidently not restricted to Lucian's two categories of panegyric and myth. What sort of examples are we to suppose 'Vopiscus' cited?

The paradox of lying historians needs a wider enquiry. What I hope to do in this chapter is to identify the different definitions of 'lying' that are implied by the various criticisms of historians in the Hellenistic and Roman world.

I shall be emphasizing the influence on ancient historiography of rhetorical and imaginative forms of discourse, and from time to time, as a contrast, I shall use phrases like 'history in our sense'. I realize, of course, that modern historians too necessarily use their imaginations and write to persuade their readers. Rather than invoke literary-critical theory,[12] I cite the experience of a practitioner: 'to

---

11. Livy 4.7.12, 4.20.8, etc.; F. Roncalli, *Rendiconti dell'Accademia Pontificia* 51–2 (1978–80), 3–21.

12. For instance D. LaCapra, *History and Criticism* (Ithaca, 1985), ch. 5, 'History and the Novel', or (in wholly abstract terms) H. White, *The Content of the Form: Narrative Discourse and Historical Representation* (Baltimore, 1987). Cf. p. 85 above.

become intelligible, history has to aspire to the coherence of fiction, while eschewing most of its methods. There is no choice, no escape.' Historians are like novelists to this extent, that 'they too are fabricators and creators of illusion'.[13] That is the mature judgement of a great modern historian of Rome (a connoisseur of Proust and Flaubert), whose own works could not conceivably be read as novels.

Is the inevitable overlap of the genres the same in modern historiography as it was in the ancient world? I think not, and it is the differences that are interesting. I hope that concentrating on allegations of lying will help us to identify some of them.

II

The first and most obvious type of falsehood—tendentiousness—finds its classic statement in the prefaces to the *Histories* and the *Annals* of Tacitus.The twin vices of adulation and malice—flattery of a living emperor, execration of a dead one—militate equally against the truth.[14]   Tacitus regards the phenomenon as peculiar to the Principate, originating in the time of Augustus; the elder Seneca, according to his son,[15] put a little earlier, at the beginning of the civil wars, the point at which 'truth first retreated'. But of course political tendentiousness in historians was familiar long before that. Sallust insisted that his freedom from 'hope, fear and partisanship' enabled him to narrate Catiline's conspiracy 'as truthfully as possible', and a surviving fragment of his *Histories* shows that this work contained a similar declaration.[16] A.J. Woodman has very convincingly argued that Cicero's definition of the fundamental laws of history—never dare to say anything false, never fear to say anything true—refers

---

13. R. Syme, *Roman Papers* 4 (Oxford, 1988), 19; and ibid. 6 (Oxford, 1991), 164—*obiter dicta* from public lectures given in 1982 and 1984.

14. Tacitus, *Histories* 1.1.1–2, *Annals* 1.1.2; F.R.D. Goodyear, ed., *The Annals of Tacitus* 1 (Cambridge, 1972), 96–101.

15. H. Peter, *Historicorum Romanorum Reliquiae* 2 (Leipzig, 1906, repr. Stuttgart, 1967), 98 (Seneca, *De vita patris*); J. Fairweather, *Seneca the Elder* (Cambridge, 1981), 15–17.

16. Sallust, *Catiline* 4.2–3, *Histories* fr. 1.6 Maurenbrecher.

precisely and exclusively to truth in the sense of impartiality and freedom from prejudice.[17]

As it happens, none of these authors uses the word 'lie' in this context, though Tacitus does refer to the 'falsification' of history (*res . . . falsae*). It would be interesting to know if that was deliberate. Polybius, in his polemic against Timaeus, whom he accuses of gross political partiality, distinguishes between pardonable 'lies from ignorance' and culpable 'lies from choice' (12.12.4–5), and undertakes to show that Timaeus' work is an example of the latter. The distinction is reminiscent of Seneca's analysis in the passage with which we began (*Quaest. Nat.* 7.16.2). A late-republican scholar even tried to apply it to the synonyms *mentiri* (to lie) and *mendacium dicere* (to tell a lie): only the former, he said, referred to deliberate lying; the latter he wanted to restrict to the sense of 'telling a falsehood unawares'.[18]

Are we to infer that for some authors, at least, 'lying' was too crude a term for what historians were tempted to do? If so, it was certainly not a general reluctance. Lucian (*Hist. conscr.* 7) had no inhibitions about describing panegyric in history as a lie (*pseudos*). Nor, conversely, had Josephus (*Jewish Antiquities* 20.154–5), in his criticism of historians' malice:

> Many have written the history of Nero. Some have been favourable to him, careless of the truth because he benefited them. Others, out of hatred and hostility towards him, have behaved like shameless drunkards in their lies, and deserve condemnation for it. I am not surprised at those who have lied about Nero, since even in their accounts of events before his time they have not preserved the truth of history.

Naturally, Josephus distances himself from such authors. 'Let them write as they like, since that is what gives them pleasure. As for me, I am aiming at the truth' (20.156)—by which he means impartiality.

---

17. A.J. Woodman, *Rhetoric in Classical Historiography* (London, 1988), 80–3 on Cicero, *De oratore* 2.62; 72–4 on *Ad familiares* 5.12.3. See in general T.J. Luce, 'Ancient Views on the Causes of Bias in Historical Writing', *Classical Philology* 84 (1988), 16–31; and cf. p. 115 above.

18. Nigidius Figulus in Gellius, *Noctes Atticae* 11.11; L. Holford-Strevens, *Aulus Gellius* (London, 1988), 129 n. 17.

Lucian specified only two things that the truthful historian had to avoid—panegyric and *muthoi*. The latter category is our second type; for Roman authors, it provided evident proof that the Greeks were liars.

Valerius Maximus, for instance, in his chapter on friendship (4.7.4), contrasted a true story of Roman loyalty at the battle of Philippi with the tale of Theseus and Pirithous:

> Let Greece talk of Theseus entrusting himself to the kingdom
> of Father Dis in support of the base loves of Pirithous. Only a
> knave would write such stuff, only a fool would believe it . . .
> These are the monstrous lies of a race given to deceit.

'Monstrous', literally—*monstro similia mendacia*. A similar phrase occurred to the elder Pliny (*Natural History* 5.3–4), describing the town of Lixus on the Atlantic coast of Mauretania, where Claudius had founded a Roman colony: according to the 'portentous falsehoods of the Greeks' (*portentosa Graeciae mendacia*), it was the site of Hercules' wrestling match with Antaeus, and of the grove of the Hesperides where dragon-snakes guarded the golden apples.

The objection to such stories was that they involved miracles (*monstra, portenta*). Men do not go alive to the Underworld, trees do not bear golden fruit. The Greeks themselves had two answers to this criticism. First, the historian might include such stories 'not in ignorance of the facts, but inventing impossibilities for the sake of wonder and pleasure'; but he should make it clear that he was doing so, as Theopompus evidently did.[19] Alternatively, he could rationalize the marvellous into the credible, like Dicaearchus in his *Bios Hellados*:[20] 'by eliminating the excessively fabulous one reduces it, by reasoning, to a natural meaning.'

The two approaches could easily be combined, as by Dionysius of Halicarnassus in his account of Hercules in Italy and at the site of Rome. The historian carefully distinguishes the mythical story of Cacus and the cattle of Geryon—which he tells at length—from the

---

19. Strabo 1.35 *ad fin.* (C43): Theopompus *FGrH* (*Die Fragmente der griechischen Historiker*) 115 F 381.

20. Fr. 49: F. Wehrli, *Die Schule des Aristoteles* 1 (Basel, 1944), 24.10. Cf. Feeney, op. cit. (n. 3 above), 31–2 on Palaephatus and Euhemerus, 76 n. 62 on Diodorus.

'more truthful' version, that Hercules was the leader of an invading army, and Cacus a brigand chieftain.[21]

Both strategies were of course familiar to Hellenized Romans. The first, avowed myth for the sake of entertainment, is clearly the *historia fabularis* with which Tiberius used to torment the professors at his dinner table. The second, rationalizing in the manner of Euhemerus, was evidently basic to Varro's *De gente populi Romani*, the fragments of which are full of schematic contrasts between *fabulosa mendacia* and *historica veritas*—respectively the traditional and the rationalized versions of myths.[22]

What lies behind all this is the Hellenistic grammarians' tripartite division of narrative.[23] Our sources, which date from the first century BC, define the three categories in varying terms, as follows:[24]

	1	*2*	*3*
Asclepiades:	true history	false history	quasi-true history
Cicero and *Rhet. Her.*:	history	myth (*fabula*)	plot (*argumentum*)

The criterion for the second category was the familiar one of physical impossibility: Cicero's example is Medea's dragon-drawn chariot; Asclepiades evidently cited the poisonous creatures born from the blood of the Titans, and various stories of metamorphosis.[25] Legends (in our sense) which did not involve such marvels were accommodated in the first category, which included the deeds of gods and heroes as well as men.

Notoriously (it is a recurring theme in this book),[26] the grammarians never mention the novel; perhaps the genre did not yet exist when their schema was first devised. Nevertheless, the third category

---

21. *Roman Antiquities* 1.39–40 (*muthikos logos*), 41–4 (*alēthesteros logos*).

22. Suetonius, *Tiberius* 70.3; Peter, op. cit. (n. 15 above), 10–24, esp. frr. 3, 6, 7b, 8, 13, 14, 17. Cf. E. Rawson, *Intellectual Life in the Late Roman Republic* (London, 1985), 244–5.

23. See R. Meijering, *Literary and Rhetorical Theories in Greek Scholia* (Groningen, 1987), 76–90; Feeney, op. cit. (n. 3 above), 42–4; p. 189 below.

24. Asclepiades of Myrlea, quoted in Sextus Empiricus 1.252–3; Cicero, *De inventione* 1.27; *Rhetorica ad Herennium* 1.13.

25. Sext. Emp. 1.264; Meijering, op. cit., 78–9; pp. 190, 227f. below.

26. See pp. 41, 79f. above, 154, 176f., 232 n. 6 below. Detailed discussion of the problem in H. Kuch, *Der antike Roman* (Berlin, 1989), 11–51.

approximates to our idea of fiction. For the ancient theorists, its function was to account for comedy and mime, where realistic characters and action were invented by the playwright. Tragedy on the other hand, with its traditional plots and characters, and indeed the whole of what we think of as mythology, was divided between categories 1 and 2, according to the absence or presence of the miraculous.

That was the distinction that mattered. It gave rise also to a simpler schema which we know from Servius' commentary on the *Aeneid*:[27]

> The difference between myth (*fabula*) and . . . history (*historia*) is that myth is the report of something against nature, whether or not it happened, as about Pasiphae, and history is whatever is reported according to nature, whether or not it happened, as about Phaedra.

In this version, the truth-value of both categories is explicitly immaterial. Trying to seduce your stepson is according to nature; being impregnated by a bull is not. So Phaedra's story is *historia* and Pasiphae's is *fabula*; whether or not either of them was (in our sense) historical is not at issue.

However, such austere suspension of judgement was not for everyone. Plutarch is a better guide. In his *Life of Theseus*, where he is explicitly rationalizing poetic myths ('purifying the mythical, making it submit to reason and take on the appearance of history'), he has this to say about Phaedra and Hippolytus:

> As for the calamities that befell Phaedra and the son of Theseus, since there is no conflict between the historians and the tragic poets, we must suppose that they happened as all the poets represent them.

For his purposes, and in the absence of any 'more truthful' version, he takes the tragedians' plot as (in our sense) historical.[28]

---

27. Servius on *Aeneid* 1.235—confusingly giving *argumentum* as a synonym for *historia*. Cf. Feeney, op. cit. (n. 3 above), 255.
28. Plutarch, *Theseus* 1.3, 28.2 (cf. 16.3 for Plutarch's rejection of the tragedians' view of Minos). For the important concept of 'true *enough*' in Plutarch, see C.B.R. Pelling, 'Truth and Fiction in Plutarch's *Lives*', in D.A. Russell, ed., *Antonine Literature* (Oxford, 1990), 19–52, esp. 49.

It was an episode in the life of Theseus (p. 128 above) that prompted Valerius Maximus to brand all Greeks as liars. Plutarch's version of it shows how easily 'false history' could be turned into 'true'. Theseus, Plutarch blandly reports (31.4), was imprisoned by Aidoneus, a king of the Molossians who happened to call his wife Persephone, his daughter Kore, and his dog Cerberus.[29]

Type three consists of travellers' tales.[30] From the very beginning, historiography had been concerned with distant and exotic lands. Herodotus, like his predecessor Hecataeus, was a great collector of stories about far-away places (not all of which he believed); a generation later, Ctesias of Cnidos exploited his position as the Persian court doctor to produce a farrago of tall tales about the Persian empire; two generations later again, when that empire fell to Alexander, historians were able to offer eye-witness accounts of the very ends of the known world.

'For the most part,' wrote Strabo in the first century BC (2.1.9, C70), 'those who have written about India have all been liars [*pseudologoi*]'. The Alexander-historians were writing first-hand accounts of contemporary events—about as far from mythography as it is possible to get. But their travellers' tales were as liable as the myths of the distant past to be dismissed as fabulous and incredible. Indeed, the whole story of Alexander, including the wonders he saw in India, was soon converted into pure fiction.[31]

The *locus classicus* for this most elementary category of lies in history is Lucian's preface to his *True History* (1.3):[32]

---

29. On the general theme of this section, see P. Veyne, *Les Grecs ont-ils cru à leurs mythes?* (Paris, 1983) = *Did the Greeks Believe in their Myths?* (Chicago, 1988); also p. 57 n. 45 above.

30. For thrills, wonders and 'the marvellous', see pp. 93 above, 195f. below, and James S. Romm, *The Edges of the Earth in Ancient Thought* (Princeton, 1992), esp. ch. 5, 'Geography and Fiction'.

31. Romm, op. cit., ch. 3, 'Wonders of the East'; R. Stoneman, *The Greek Alexander Romance* (Penguin Classics, London, 1991), and K. Dowden in B.P. Reardon, *Collected Ancient Greek Novels* (Berkeley, 1989), 650–715. For the related genres of paradoxography and utopian writing, see E. Gabba, 'True History and False History in Classical Antiquity', *Journal of Roman Studies* 71 (1981), 50–62.

32. Tr. H.W. and F.G. Fowler (1905), slightly adapted; cf. Romm, op. cit., 211–4. Syme, following Lucian, picked Ctesias as the originator of 'fictional history': *Emperors and Biography* (n. 6 above), 263; *Roman Papers* 6 (Oxford, 1991), 157, 319.

Ctesias of Cnidos in his work on India and its characteristics gives details for which he had neither the evidence of his eyes nor of hearsay . . . Many other writers have adopted the same plan, professing to relate their own travels, and describing monstrous beasts, savages, and strange ways of life. The fount and inspiration of their buffoonery is the Homeric Odysseus, entertaining Alcinous' court with his prisoned winds, his men one-eyed or wild or cannibal, his beasts with many heads and his metamorphosed comrades; the Phaeacians were simple folk, and he fooled them totally.

Like these distinguished predecessors,[33] Lucian is going to tell lies. The difference is that he admits it at the start, in the one true statement of the work: 'My subject is, then, what I have neither seen, experienced, nor been told, what neither exists nor could conceivably do so. I humbly solicit my readers' incredulity.'

The first three categories of lies have been straightforward enough. Now we approach something more complex—the effect of rhetoric and drama. In his dialogue *Brutus*, Cicero represents himself as conversing with his friend Atticus, the author of an outline history of Rome, about Themistocles and Coriolanus. He asserts that the parallels between the two men's careers extend to the nature—suicide, he says—of their respective deaths. He then continues (42–3):[34]

'You have a different account of Coriolanus, Atticus; but you must allow me to acquiesce in this manner of his dying rather than yours.' Atticus laughed and said: 'It's your choice. It's granted that orators may tell lies in historical matters in order to make a point more neatly. Just as you made up a story about Coriolanus, so Clitarchus and Stratocles produced their fictions about Themistocles.'

---

33. For Homer's Odysseus as the lying story-teller *par excellence*, see Juvenal 15.13–26; Romm, op. cit., 183–96.
34. Tr. M. Winterbottom, in D.A. Russell and M. Winterbottom, eds, *Ancient Literary Criticism* (Oxford, 1972), 222. Discussion in T.P. Wiseman, *Clio's Cosmetics* (Leicester, 1979), 31–4.

As Atticus goes on to point out, we know from Thucydides (1.138.4) that Themistocles died a natural death.

> 'But the other two say that he sacrificed a bull, caught the blood in a bowl, drank it, and dropped dead. That, of course, was the sort of death they could give a rhetorical and tragic gloss; the other ordinary kind left no scope for decoration. So since it suits you that everything was parallel in the cases of Themistocles and Coriolanus, you can take the bowl from me too, and I'll give you the victim as well!'

Although Atticus is talking specifically about orators ('concessum est *rhetoribus* ementiri in historiis'), one of the false authorities he quotes on Themistocles was a very well-known historian.[35] So one cannot pretend that this passage is relevant only to the practice of oratory, or to 'histories written by rhetors or sophists' as if they somehow didn't count as historiography.[36] The techniques of history-writing, oratory and poetry (especially tragic drama) over-lapped and affected each other in various ways:[37]

> Though we today see poetry, oratory and historiography as three separate genres, the ancients saw them as three different species of the same genus—rhetoric. All three types of activity aimed to elaborate certain data in such a way as to affect or persuade an audience or readership.

Elaborating the data was what Cicero's Atticus meant by 'giving a rhetorical and tragic gloss' (*rhetorice et tragice ornare*)—like providing Coriolanus and Themistocles with deaths more dramati-cally satisfying than the banal reality. All right for an orator or a tragic poet, but permissible to a historian only with a laugh, to show that he was going beyond his proper function—lying, in fact, for dramatic effect.[38]

---

35. Clitarchus: *FGrH* 137; cf. L.Pearson, *The Lost Histories of Alexander the Great* (Philadelphia, 1960), ch. 9. Stratocles was an orator and politician.

36. P.A. Brunt, in *Philias charin: Miscellanea in onore di Eugenio Manni* (Rome, 1979), 330–3 = *Studies in Greek History and Thought* (Oxford, 1993), 200–2, quotation from 331 = 201.

37. A.J. Woodman, op. cit. (n. 17 above), 95–101, quotation from 100.

38. Others did not make this distinction: see pp. 145–6 below for vivid elaboration as historical truth.

There is a famous passage in Polybius (2.56.10–12), where the historian attacks his predecessor Phylarchus for failing to distinguish between history and tragedy:[39]

> It is not a historian's business to startle his readers with sensational descriptions, nor should he try, as the tragic poets do, to represent speeches which might have been delivered, or to enumerate all the possible consequences of the events under consideration; it is his task first and foremost to record with fidelity what actually happened and was said, however commonplace that may be. For the aim of tragedy is by no means the same as that of history, but rather the opposite. The tragic poet seeks to thrill and charm his audience for the moment by expressing through his characters the most plausible words possible, but the historian's task is to instruct and persuade serious students by means of the truth of the words and actions he presents, and this effect must be permanent, not temporary.

Polybius' standards, however, were unusually austere. He calls Phylarchus a liar (2.56.2); but I think most people in the ancient world would not describe as 'lying' the use in history of such oratorical and dramatic techniques as vivid and imaginative presentation, composition of appropriate speeches, the invention of circumstantial detail *ad libitum*. What Cicero's Atticus calls lying (*ementiri*) is when you know the facts but deliberately substitute a more dramatically effective version.

It is important to remember that episodes of Roman history were regularly represented in the theatre, and that Roman drama was older than Roman historiography. The historians themselves were sometimes conscious of the danger of taking as historical something that had been invented for the stage. Livy, for instance (5.21.8–9), dismisses an episode from the capture of Veii as unworthy of belief; it was 'more suited to a stage show, for the stage delights in marvels'. Ovid (*Fasti* 4.326) neatly confirms Livy's point as he tells a miracle-story about Quinta Claudia in 204 BC: 'it is astonishing, but attested

---

39. Tr. Ian Scott-Kilvert (Penguin Classics). For what Phylarchus was doing, see F.W. Walbank, 'History and Tragedy', *Historia* 9 (1960), 216–34, and pp. 112f. above, 185f. below.

by the stage.' Even Plutarch and Dionysius occasionally suspect the presence of dramatic fiction (*plasma*) in some item of the tradition, though not nearly often enough for modern tastes.[40]

As the Ovid passage shows, this type of dramatic influence was not restricted to the very early period, where it would simply count as 'myth'. Polybius offers a startling example from historians of the Second Punic War, who had Hannibal guided over the Alps by supernatural apparitions:[41] 'they fall into the same difficulties as the tragic dramatists, who all need a *deus ex machina* to resolve their plots, because they are based on false (*pseudeis*) or improbable assumptions.'

Seneca, as we saw at the beginning, was no great admirer of historians. Another passage of his *Quaestiones Naturales* (4.3.1) leads us into a more fundamental definition of lies in history:

> [This is] what historians do: when they've told numerous lies of their own choice, they pick out one thing they don't want to guarantee, and add the phrase 'my authorities must take responsibility for this'.

Ever since Herodotus (7.152.3), it was a commonplace of historical writing to annotate certain items with the plea that 'I'm reporting what I was told, I don't necessarily believe it'.[42] But according to Seneca, historians make this virtuous declaration at random, to give the illusion that the rest of what they say *is* guaranteed.

What lies behind his complaint is best illustrated in the preface of Arrian's history of Alexander the Great (*Anabasis* pref. 1, 3):[43]

> Everything concerning Alexander which Ptolemy and Aristobulus have both described in the same way I have reproduced as being true in every respect; when they have not given the

---

40. E.g. Plutarch, *Romulus* 8.7 (*dramatikon kai plasmatōdes*), Dion Hal. 9.22.3 (*plasmata theatrika, muthoi*).

41. Polybius 3.48.8, taken by Feeney, op. cit. (n. 3 above), 261, as an example of the common ground of history and epic.

42. *Fides penes auctores*: e.g. Sallust, *Jugurthine War* 17.7 (on Africa), Valerius Maximus 1.8.7 (on the migrating Penates), Pliny, *Nat. Hist.* 17.93 (on olive yields). Cf. Curtius Rufus 9.1.3 ('I report more than I believe'), and pp. 95, 120 above.

43. Tr. L. Pearson, op. cit. (n. 35 above), 2.

same account, I have chosen the version which seemed to me more worthy of belief and also more worthy of telling . . . Other incidents recorded by other writers, because they seemed to me in themselves worthy of telling and not altogether unworthy of belief, I have reproduced as being merely 'reported' about Alexander.

Arrian has two criteria for what to include—essentially, credibility and interest, what's worth believing and what's worth telling.

The word Arrian uses for 'more worthy of telling' (*axiaphēgētotera*) is constructed out of *aphēgēsis*, which means narrative, the act of relating. Like its synonym *diēgēsis* (which is now a technical term in modern literary theory),[44] *aphēgēsis* is derived from the verb 'to lead': the narrator, as it were, 'conducts' the listener 'through' the story, or 'from' one event to the next. The origin and truth-status of the events—whether they were discovered or invented—is neither here nor there. *Aphēgēsis* is simply 'story'.

History, as we understand it, originated in the intellectual climate of Ionian rationalism, with Herodotus' 'publication of his research' (*historiēs apodeixis*) into the origins of the conflict between Greeks and Persians.[45] His *historiē* meant not just reporting the stories that were told, but *finding out* by his own enquiries and taking responsibility for the result. Never mind the tales about the rapes of Io and Europa; he will start from Croesus, the man whom he *knows*, from his enquiries, to have originated the enmity (Herodotus 1.1-5).

Historia as enquiry is what sets apart the great historians of classical antiquity (Thucydides, Polybius, Tacitus); but it always had to coexist with *aphēgēsis*,[46] and in many historical authors *aphēgēsis* ruled alone. See, for instance, the preface to Diodorus Siculus' universal history in the first century BC. For him, history is a branch of the art of words: 'there is a harmony between the facts and their literary expression',[47] and it does not occur to him to ask how the

---

44. Four distinct meanings are identified by W.C. Booth, *The Rhetoric of Fiction* (2nd edn., Chicago, 1983), 438 n. 16.

45. See p. 92 above.

46. See J. Gould, *Herodotus* (London, 1989), 47f., who points out that enquiry does not necessarily entail narrative. What made Herodotus 'the father of history' was his brilliant combination of *historia* and *aphēgēsis*.

47. Diod. Sic. 1.2.7: tr. A.J. Toynbee, ed., *Greek Historical Thought* (London, 1924), 32.

facts are achieved. Similarly Lucian,[48] in the second century AD, thought of the historian's mind as like a mirror, reflecting what is already there, and his craft as like that of a sculptor, creating a work of art from material that was already provided for him.

Arrian's two criteria ('worthy of belief, worthy of telling') correspond precisely to these two concepts. The question 'is it true?' addresses *historia*, enquiry or research, what we regard as the historian's proper business; the question 'is it worth telling?' addresses *aphēgēsis*, narration, the business of the story-teller. And to keep them separate, as Arrian very properly does, implies that some credible things are not worth relating, and some incredible ones *are*.

We are now better placed, I think, to see what Seneca was getting at. His sardonic assumption is that all historiography is irresponsible *aphēgēsis*; the historian is merely a story-teller, and story-tellers are liars. Remember Odysseus at the court of Alcinous:[49]

> Alicinous answered: 'Odysseus, as we look at you we cannot think you to be a deceiver and a cheat, though the dark earth breeds a great crop of such, forgers of lies drawn from places beyond our ken.'

Seneca would have agreed with Lucian that the Phaeacians were simple folk.

The most revealing part of his indictment is that historians tell lies 'of their own choice' (*ad arbitrium suum*). Cicero's Atticus used a similar phrase—'it's your choice' (*tuo arbitratu*). 'Write what you want,' said the City Prefect to the imperial biographer; 'you can safely say whatever you like.' Josephus said the same about the historians of Nero. Seneca himself, in his guise as narrator, will say 'whatever trips off his tongue'—a proverbial phrase used also by Lucian to describe what bad historians do.[50]

---

48. *Hist. conscr.* 51: 'what historians have to relate is fact and will speak for itself, for it has already happened' (tr. K. Kilburn, Loeb edn.). Cf. p. 89 above.

49. Homer, *Odyssey* 11.362–6: tr. W. Shewring (World's Classics).

50. Cicero, *Brutus* 42; Historia Augusta, *Aurelian* 2.2; Josephus, *Jewish Antiquities* 20.156; Seneca, *Apocolocyntosis* 1.2; Lucian, *Hist. conscr.* 32.

Historia takes the responsibility for what it tells; *aphēgēsis* has a free and irresponsible choice. The conflict is well expressed by the historian of Zuleika Dobson, describing his heroine's conjuring act:[51]

> Was there ever, I wonder, an historian so pure as not to have wished just once to fob off on his readers just one bright fable for effect? I find myself sorely tempted to tell you that on Zuleika, as her entertainment drew to a close, the spirit of the higher thaumaturgy descended like a flame and found in her a worthy agent. Specious Apollyon whispers to me: 'Where would be the harm? . . . Why not? Your readers would be excited, gratified. And you would never be found out.' But the grave eyes of Clio are bent on me, her servant. Oh pardon, madam: I did but waver for an instant.

III

'You would never be found out.' 'Who ever demanded sworn referees (*iuratores*) from a historian?'[52] But sometimes it does happen.

The disastrous fire at the Bradford City stadium in May 1985 came at a time when the British public was very concerned about the anarchic violence of soccer fans. So when the *Daily Star* reporter linked the tragedy with hooliganism, readers were probably not surprised. Under the headline 'I saw killer smoke bomb', Ian Trueman reported: 'I saw everything, every horrifying second. I saw a smoke bomb thrown by hooligans from a stand adjoining the main building.' The following month, a judicial enquiry into the disaster was set up under Mr Justice Popplewell, and the reporter was called to give evidence and questioned by the counsel for the enquiry:[53]

---

51. Max Beerbohm, *Zuleika Dobson* (London, 1911), 165; cf. 293 for a composite messenger-speech and 'indirect narration'—'Credibility is not enough for Clio's servant. I aim at truth.'
52. Seneca, *Apocolocyntosis* 1.2 (n. 2 above).
53. *The Times* (8 June 1985), 3.

Under questioning by Mr Collins yesterday, Mr Trueman
agreed that he had not seen anything being thrown but after
noticing the trail of smoke in the stand had assumed it to have
been caused by a smoke bomb. He added that he stood by his
story.

He stood by the standards of *aphēgēsis* against the demands of
historia.
Journalism is relevant to our subject simply because it did not
exist in the ancient world. It is essential to remember, as A.J. Woodman has rightly insisted,[54] that much of what happens in Greek and
Roman historiography happens for us in 'the media'. A professional
journalist who systematically monitored a full year of Fleet Street
reporting summed up his results as follows, in terms which could
apply equally to ancient historiography:[55]

Newspapers had lied to entertain, to compete with each other,
to propagate their political convictions, and to persecute those
with whom they disagreed. And when there was no other
obvious reason, journalists continued to lie simply out of habit.

To entertain: *delectatio* (enjoyment) was accepted as one of the
legitimate aims of history.[56] To compete: Josephus (on Greek historians) and Livy and Justin (on Roman ones) make it clear that rivalry
with predecessors and contemporaries was a common motive.[57] To
propagate political convictions: tendentiousness was endemic in
ancient historiography; to the items mentioned above (pp. 126–7),
add the 'democratic' and 'oligarchic' treatments of Athenian history
that were imperfectly reconciled in the Aristotelian *Constitution of*

---

54. Op. cit. (n. 17 above), 207–15; 'From Hannibal to Hitler: the Literature of
War', *University of Leeds Review* 26 (1983), 107–24; and in D.A. West and A.J.
Woodman, eds, *Creative Imitation and Latin Literature* (Cambridge, 1979),
155. Cf. also Veyne, *Did the Greeks . . . ?* (n. 29 above), 5, 9–10, 110.
55. H. Porter, *Lies, Damned Lies and Some Exclusives* (London, 1984), 142.
56. See C.W. Fornara, *The Nature of History in Ancient Greece and Rome* (Berkeley, 1983), 120–34; pp. 184–6 below.
57. Josephus, *Against Apion* 1.24–7; Livy pref. 2–3, Justin pref. 1 (*aemulatio
gloriae*); cf. pp. 99–100 above.

Athens.[58] To persecute: malice too was often complained of in historians, as with Timaeus on Demochares and Agathocles, Theophanes on Rutilius Rufus.[59] Out of habit: that, essentially, was Seneca's charge against all historians.

Then there are the visual media, which achieve what the Greek and Roman historians always strove for, the vividness (*enargeia*, p. 145 below) which could bring a scene to life in the imagination of the audience, or the reader. Consider Polybius' attack on Phylarchus' 'lying' account of the fall of Mantinea:[60]

> Since it was his purpose to emphasize the cruelty of Antigonus and the Macedonians, . . . he introduces graphic scenes of women clinging to one another, tearing their hair and baring their breasts, and in addition he describes the tears and lamentations of men and women accompanied by their children and aged parents as they are led away into captivity. Phylarchus reproduces this kind of effect again and again in his history, striving on each occasion to recreate the horrors before our eyes.

This is what we call nowadays 'good television'.

The other great difference between their literary world and ours is the present-day ubiquity of the novel. The origins of the modern genre were marked by problems and ambiguities about its truth-status which are remarkably similar to ancient views of historiography.[61] And before we smile at the naïvety of those who thought Defoe's fictions were genuine documents, we should remember a scene from only thirty years ago, in the House of Lords debate on *Lady Chatterley's Lover*:[62]

---

58. See P.J. Rhodes, *A Commentary on the Aristotelian Athenaion Politeia* (Oxford, 1981), 15–30, esp. 21–3.

59. Polybius 12.13–15; Plutarch, *Pompey* 37.3.

60. Polybius 2.56.6–8 (n. 39 above).

61. L.J. Davis, *Factual Fictions: the Origins of the English Novel* (New York, 1983); cf. also W. Nelson, *Fact or Fiction: the Dilemma of the Renaissance Storyteller* (Harvard, 1973), and G. Day, *From Fiction to the Novel* (London, 1987).

62. N. Shrapnel, *The Guardian* (15 December 1960), 1; cf. *Hansard* (Lords, 14 December 1960), 530, 561. Cf. p. 179 below: Solon evidently took Lord Teviot's view.

'The story he tells is pure invention!' Lord Teviot said in a tone of outraged wonder at the end of his lashing of Lawrence. 'It never actually happened!' That, Lord Boothby hastened to inform him, is the thing about fiction.

The ancient genre too overlapped with history, as other contributors to this volume demonstrate at length.[63]

It may be helpful to recapitulate the five types of mendacity identified so far, and see where they would be in *our* generic structure. The first is easy: deliberately false historiography is still all too familiar, exemplified in its extreme form by Soviet histories of the Soviet Union.[64] The second and third types, marked as they are by fantasy and 'events against nature', correspond respectively to 'sword and sorcery' novels in the Tolkien tradition, and to science fiction. The fourth is clearly 'docu-drama' or 'faction', that hybrid genre that intermittently exercises media consciences.[65] As for the fifth, most people, then and now, are content with *aphēgēsis* and have no notion of *historia*; we all have in our heads an amalgam of information and misinformation from all kinds of sources which passes for a view of the past.[66]

And yet, beyond all that, there is the sheer intellectual achievement of *historia* as enquiry. Herodotus, Thucydides, Polybius and Tacitus were great historians by any standard. So my two final types of historical mendacity, deliberately antithetical, mark the extremes of the familiar and the alien in ancient attitudes to historiography. They are, respectively, lies defined as too much detail, and lies defined as not enough.

Discussing the size of Hannibal's forces in the invasion of Italy, Polybius contrasts his own accurate information, drawn from contemporary documents, with that of other historians who merely

---

63. See pp. 79–81 above, 186f., 197f., 205f. below.
64. Now of course discredited: see R.W. Davies, *Soviet History in the Gorbachev Revolution* (London, 1989).
65. See for instance P. Fiddick, 'Facts do Furnish a Story . . .', *The Listener* 124 (25 October 1990), 4–6; L. O'Kelly, 'It's Dramatic, but it's not True', *The Independent* (12 May 1991), 15.
66. See D. Lowenthal, *The Past is a Foreign Country* (Cambridge, 1985), ch. 5.

invent details to add verisimilitude (3.33.17); they are, he says, 'plausible liars' (*axiopistōs pseudomenoi*).

That is a very modern type of judgement. It depends on a clear distinction between the historian's type of narration and that which practically all educated men had been trained in at their rhetorical schools. The orator's type of narration depended on *inventio*, which the handbooks defined as 'the devising of matter true or probable [*verum* or *veri simile*] which will make a case appear convincing.'[67] That was what the historians Polybius complained about were doing, and what I imagine most authors and readers would take for granted as acceptable technique; as Christopher Pelling puts it (discussing Plutarch), 'this is not fiction or invention, but creative reconstruction.'[68]

I know of no other passage in ancient literature where that sort of elaboration is explicitly condemned, as Polybius condemns it. The nearest is a quotation that happens to survive from the first book of Ephorus' universal history:[69]

> On contemporary events, we regard as most believable those who give the most detailed account; on events in the distant past, however, we consider such an account wholly implausible, on the grounds that it is unlikely that all actions and most speeches would be remembered over so long a period of time.

The sort of thing Ephorus probably had in mind was his contemporary Clidemus' detailed account of Theseus' battle with the Amazons. Plutarch calls Clidemus' technique 'excessive' (*perittos*)—the word Polybius used to describe a taste for the kind of history he himself did *not* write.[70] No doubt Ephorus, like Plutarch, raised his eyebrows only at such extreme examples as Clidemus. Polybius' uncompromising critical standards, though sympathetic to us, were a rarity in the ancient world.

---

67. Cicero, *De inventione* 1.9, *Rhetorica ad Herennium* 1.3; effects on historiography discussed by Wiseman, op. cit. (n. 34 above), ch. 3, and in *History* 66 (1981), 386–7 = *Roman Studies* (Liverpool, 1987), 257–8. See also pp. 187–8 below.

68. Pelling, op. cit. (n. 28 above), 38.

69. *FGrH* 70 F 9, quoted in Harpocration's lexicon.

70. Plutarch, *Theseus* 27.3–4, 19.4 (Clidemus, *FGrH* 323 F 17–18); Polybius 9.1.4. See Wiseman, op. cit. (n. 34 above), 151–2.

Paradoxically, those whom Polybius castigated as 'plausible liars' could retort that their accumulation of circumstantial detail was not a mere literary device, but actually a way of reaching the truth.

Polybius himself (3.32.6) and Cicero after him (*De oratore* 2.63), both serious and responsible critics, declare that the truth of history,[71] and thus its value for the understanding of public affairs, depends on the detailed analysis of events according to their causes, their accompanying circumstances, and their consequences. It follows

> ... that neither writers nor readers of history should confine their attention to the narrative of events, but must also take account of what preceded, accompanied and followed them. For if we remove from history the analysis of why, how and for what purpose each thing was done and whether the result was what we should reasonably have expected, what is left is a mere display of descriptive virtuosity, but not a lesson, and this, though it may please for the moment, is of no enduring value for the future.

Polybius' concluding remarks here put him explicitly in the tradition of Thucydidean historiography.[72] Like Thucydides, he demands *akribeia*, accurate detail, and that includes the reporting of significant speeches; Polybius insists that 'the historian must devote his whole energy to finding out what was actually said, and repeating the most important and appropriate parts of it' (36.1.7).

Naturally, both Thucydides and Polybius took it for granted that it was only for very recent history that such detailed information could be discovered. They were practitioners of *historia* as enquiry, which meant by personal interview.[73] But their ideal of detailed analysis was taken over by historians concerned with the distant past, who ignored Ephorus' warning about the worthlessness of detail in such contexts.

---

71. Truth: Polybius 3.31.7–8; Cicero, *De oratore* 2.62.
72. Polybius 3.31.11–13, cf. Thucydides 1.22.4 (p. 104 above).
73. Thucydides 1.22.1, Polybius 12.28a.8–10.

The best example is Dionysius of Halicarnassus, an honest man with a serious view of the value of history,[74] but who had little or no conception of *historia* as enquiry. He prides himself on *akribeia*, and insists that what makes history valuable—both for practical politics and for 'philosophical contemplation'—is a detailed account of the causes of events and the manner in which they took place, including, of course, the speeches made at the time.[75] The trouble is, he applies these Polybian precepts to a wholly un-Polybian subject—the early Roman Republic, four to five hundred years before his own time.

Though his sources may have had *some* genuine information about that period (how much, is controversial), all modern historians would agree that the details they supplied were mere elaboration.[76] Dionysius, of course, accepted them in good faith, and used them to provide examples to guide the judgement of statesmen, an aim for which only the truth would suffice.[77]

The conceptual nexus of truth, detail and the value of history is pure Polybius (3.31–2), but detaching it from *historia* as enquiry— the investigation of recent events—brings about the exact opposite of Polybius' view of history and its methods. For Dionysius never asked himself 'how do my sources *know* this?'; he was a professor of rhetoric as well as a historian, and his type of *akribeia*, applied to previous writers' accounts of the distant past, was essentially a rhetorical technique.

Polybius' tripartite analysis of 'what preceded, accompanied, and followed' the events was a standard item in rhetorical handbooks, as a guide to the elaboration of narrative:[78]

> For example, if we are describing a war, we shall first of all mention the preliminaries such as the generals' speeches, the

---

74. See now E. Gabba, *Dionysius and The History of Archaic Rome* (Berkeley, 1991).

75. Dion. Hal., *Roman Antiquities* 1.5.4, 1.8.2–3, 3.18.1, 5.56.1, 5.75.1, 7.66.1–5, 11.1.1–6; Gabba, op. cit., 80–5.

76. See for instance R.M. Ogilvie and A. Drummond, 'The Surviving Evidence', in *The Cambridge Ancient History* 7.2 (2nd edn, Cambridge, 1989), 1–29.

77. *Paradeigmata*: Dion. Hal. 5.75.1, 11.1.5. Truth: 1.1.2 (the source of both practical and philosophical wisdom), 1.5.1–2, etc.

78. Hermogenes 16.22: tr. A.J. Woodman, op. cit. (n. 17 above), 89, cf. 108 n. 79 for other references.

outlay on both sides, and their fears; next, the attacks, the slaughter, and the dead; finally, the victory trophy, the triumphal songs of the victors, the tears and enslavement of the victims.

Dionysius confirms that historians elaborated military narrative in precisely this way, and criticizes them for not doing the same with accounts of political unrest; his own treatment of the conflict of patricians and plebeians, 'characterized by precise detail [*akribeia*] rather than brevity', shows what should be done.[79]

For the rhetoricians, this technique was a means of achieving *enargeia*, the vividness that compels belief. Quintilian explains in his *Institutio Oratoria* (6.2.31–2):[80]

> I am complaining that a man has been murdered. Shall I not bring before my eyes all the circumstances which it is reasonable to imagine must have occurred in such a connection? Shall I not see the assassin burst suddenly from his hiding-place, the victim tremble, cry for help, beg for mercy, or turn to run? Shall I not see the fatal blow delivered and the stricken body fall? Will not the blood, the deathly pallor, the groan of agony, the death-rattle, be indelibly impressed on my mind?
>
> From such impressions arises that *enargeia* which Cicero calls *illustratio* and *evidentia*, which makes us seem not so much to narrate as to exhibit the actual scene, while our emotions will be no less actively stirred than if we were present at the actual occurrence.

Don't tell, show! As we shall see in the next two chapters, the technique Quintilian describes was of great importance for writers of fiction. Certainly it was not confined to oratory: the examples he goes on to give are from Virgil's *Aeneid*, and we know from

---

79. Dion. Hal. 7.66.3 and 5. Cf. Gabba, op. cit. (n. 74 above), 83: 'Such a procedure is fundamentally analogous to that followed by the late Roman annalists, who, in all seriousness and with a wholehearted belief in a substantial continuity of both problems and institutions, reconstructed the ill-known archaic phase of the city by following the political and ideological pattern of contemporary life.'
80. Tr. H.E. Butler (Loeb edn). On *enargeia*, see Meijering, op. cit. (n. 23 above), 29–52.

Polybius' attack on Phylarchus, as well as from many extant examples, that historians used it too.[81]

The Latin for *enargeia* was *evidentia*. For a modern critical historian, what matters above all is the quality of the evidence. A Roman might well agree, but he would not mean the same. In rhetoric, *evidentia* meant 'vivid illustration'; in philosophical discourse, it meant 'self-evidence'.[82] With *evidentia*, there was no need for argument: you could simply *see* the thing was true. And you achieved that end by making explicit 'all the circumstances which it is reasonable to imagine must have occurred'. That is, the invention of circumstantial detail was a way to reach the truth.

And so at last we find our seventh type of mendacity, precisely antithetical to the sixth. On this way of looking at things, lying is the *absence* of elaboration—a view detectable in Cato's account of the unlettered Ligurians' oral traditions, or in the attitude of the cultured world of Lactantius' time to the simple literature and unsophisticated doctrine of the Christians.[83]

I suspect we may be blind to this concept in the ancient texts simply because it is so utterly at variance with our notion of 'the plain unvarnished truth'. One place where it seems to be implied is in that conversation in the City Prefect's carriage (p. 125 above). The Prefect complains about 'Trebellius Pollio' for writing too often in a brief and careless manner (*breviter, incuriose*).[84] But all historians lie about *something*, the pseudo-biographer protests. Lying was brevity and carelessness, because truthful narrative consisted of elaborate detail—what for us the historical novelist supplies.

Our rogue scholar was *perittos*, like Clidemus and the readers of non-Polybian histories (p. 142 above). He and Seneca both affected to believe that all historians were liars;[85] but it turns out that they were complaining about diametrically opposite things.

---

81. Fiction: see below, pp. 185f., 211. History: Woodman, op. cit. (n. 17 above), 84–92.

82. Cicero, *Academica* 2.17; Quintilian 4.2.63, 8.3.61, 9.2.40.

83. Cato, *Origines* fr. 31 Peter (*inliterati mendacesque sunt*); Lactantius, *Divinae Institutiones* 5.1.15–18.

84. Historia Augusta, *Aurelian* 2.1. Thucydides (1.97.2) makes the same complaint about Hellanicus: brevity and lack of *akribeia* (cf. Dion. Hal. 7.66.5).

85. For Seneca, see above, pp. 122–3, 135.

Chapter Five

Fiction, Bewitchment and Story Worlds: The Implications of Claims to Truth in Apuleius

Andrew Laird

THE attempt to reconstruct the ancient understanding of what we call 'fiction' and its relationship to the inducement of false beliefs ('lying') is central to this book. The issue will be approached in the present chapter with specific reference to Apuleius' *The Golden Ass* or *Metamorphoses* (*Met.*), written around AD 160—a text which is now generally classified as fictional. The discussion here will be grounded in a questioning of the modern categories of fact and fiction, and of the distinctions made between them. Some re-evaluation of our own presuppositions may provide us with a clearer and, perhaps, more sympathetic view of those which might have been held in antiquity.

The first section considers some of the rhetorical strategies with which narratives convince their audiences; it also introduces the idea of 'story worlds'. I will argue that the same means of inducing belief are generated by factual and fictional texts alike. These reflections will inform, in the sections that follow, readings of two passages from the *Met.*: the prologue (1.1–2) and the apparent metamorphosis of Pamphile into an owl (3.21–2). It will be maintained that our understanding of 3.22–3, in particular, depends very much on how we read the *Met.* as a whole. The miraculous quality of other events narrated, including even Lucius' own metamorphosis, might consequently be brought into question.

The narrator presents himself as bewitched and confused by the experience he describes in 3.21–2. In turn, he bewitches and confuses his audience, who are denied any precise idea of exactly what is being narrated. It will be shown, in conclusion, that this type of bewitchment—effected through words—was identified by ancient theorists of literature and language. This consideration, in conjunction with the close readings of the passages offered here, may bring us closer to the conception of fiction held by Apuleius' original audience.

I

This is a story about something that happened long ago when your grandfather was a child. It is a very important story because it shows how all the comings and goings between our own world and the land of Narnia first began.

In those days Mr. Sherlock Holmes was still living in Baker Street and the Bastables were looking for treasure in the Lewisham Road. In those days, if you were a boy you had to wear a stiff Eton collar every day, and schools were usually nastier than now. But meals were nicer; and as for sweets, I won't tell you how cheap and good they were, because it would only make your mouth water in vain. And in those days, there lived in London a girl called Polly Plummer.

So begins C.S. Lewis' *The Magician's Nephew*. It has many themes in common with the *Met*. Both stories can be read as religious allegories, of Christianity and of the cult of Isis respectively. Both show a concern with Platonism. Both Lewis' Digory and Apuleius' Lucius are too curious for their own good. Both principal characters have older relatives who are sorcerers, and who prompt them to tamper with magical forces which they cannot control. Both stories end in healing: Aslan gives Digory an apple which revives his dying mother; Isis enables Lucius to eat the roses which turn him back from a donkey into a human being. Finally, both stories have been seen as forms of autobiographical expression by their authors.

The reception of Apuleius in Lewis' work might well be worth investigation,[1] but the passage is quoted here because, as the opening of a narrative which is classified as fictional, it has some interesting features common to a number of stories.

Lewis' use of 'once upon a time' type formulae ('This is a story about something that happened long ago'; 'in those days, there lived in London a girl called Polly Plummer') indicate this is a story. Those formulae are themselves as old as the hills.[2] The old woman opens her story of Psyche in *Met.* 4.28:

> Erant in quadam civitate rex et regina . . .

> [There were in a certain country, a king and queen . . .]

Such formulae by no means suggest that the story to come is a product of mere invention. The writer of Luke's gospel opens his narration in this way at 1.5 (the Vulgate is quoted to highlight the similarity):

> Fuit in diebus Herodis regis Iudaeae sacerdos quidam . . .

> [There was in the days of Herod king of Judaea a certain priest . . .][3]

Set a story in a distant time, or clime, or both, and you are more likely to be believed. (This is the sort of principle at work in the

---

1. See, for instance, Lewis' version of the Cupid and Psyche story in *Till We Have Faces: A Myth Retold* (London, 1956).
2. Aristophanes' *Wasps* (422 BC) 1182 contains the beginning of a fable, 'Once upon a time there was a mouse and a weasel'. The scholiast commenting on the verse remarks that this was a conventional device.
3. Compare Tacitus' opening to his *Histories: Initium mihi operis Servius Galba iterum Titus Vinius consules erint*, 'The consuls Galba and Vinius will be the beginning of my work.' Virgil's narrative in the *Aeneid* gets under way at 1.12–3 with *Urbs antiqua fuit . . . Karthago* 'There was an ancient city . . . Carthage'. (That could be isolated as a factual proposition, though this is not relevant to the plausibility of a fictional text if one conceives of an *a priori* distinction between fact and fiction—see M. Riffaterre, *Fictional Truth* [Baltimore, 1990].) What unites these instances is their function as existential statements of various kinds. G. Genette suggests ('Récit fictionnel, récit factuel' in *Fiction et diction* [Paris, 1991], 89–90) that openings like 'The first time that Aurélien saw Bérénice, he found her frankly ugly'—which we might call temporal statements—presuppose such existential statements. These two types of opening, like the two kinds of story (factual, fictional) they are seen to introduce, are actually of the same order.

third type of 'mendacity' identified by Wiseman in ch. 4.) Lewis, to induce some credibility for his story, chooses Victorian London: a place and time that his intended audience of children may know of, and know to have been real, or at least as real as the world of one's grandfather's childhood can be.

The child reader who does not know about Victorian London is informed of one or two historical 'facts', and simultaneously induced to believe in the reality of the world in which the opening part of the story is set ('our own world' as Lewis calls it, in contrast to the more remote 'land of Narnia'), if not in the story itself.

The mention of Sherlock Holmes and the Bastables prompts a variety of responses:

(i) They might strike a child who knows neither Conan Doyle nor E. Nesbit's *The Treasure Seekers* as further information, which could have the status of historical truth, serving to authenticate the story that is to follow. (Note the effect of referring to '*Mr. Sherlock Holmes*'.) That child might as well have been told that Mr Gladstone was prime minister—for him or her this is only circumstantial detail which will have little bearing on what comes next.[4]

(ii) To the unfortunate reader who is informed and academic, these allusions are indicative of the work's genre. They help him determine that *The Magician's Nephew* is a fictional text, because it suggests the Bastables and Sherlock Holmes are as real as the pennyfarthing and the penny black.[5] He might note the artful *anaphora* in the threefold repetition of 'In those days', which perhaps seeks to achieve an equal kind of truth status for fictional celebrities, the wearing of Eton collars and a girl called Polly Plummer. The reference to E. Nesbit in particular, compounded with the time and place of the story, and the swift

---

4. For circumstantial detail which serves to strengthen the credibility of a story without being directly relevant to the events recounted, see the Gospel according to Luke 3.1f.

5. The fact that letters to Sherlock Holmes still come to 221b Baker St (see J.R. Morgan, p. 197, n. 31 below) may be related to the manner in which the Sherlock Holmes stories are presented. They are narrated in the first person by Dr Watson who has a role in the stories himself. See the discussion of the use of the first person as a claim to truth in the *Met.*, pp. 155–6 below.

focusing on a young girl prompt him to classify the work in the popular genre of nostalgic children's fiction, set, but not written, in Victorian England.

(iii) A third possible response is the most interesting. (I admit that it was my own, to prove it is a possible response.) A second type of child or adult reader knows at least who Sherlock Holmes is, and has read about the Bastable children's treasure-seeking in E. Nesbit. The first reaction of this reader on recognizing the intertextual reference is going to be more inspired: *This is exciting. Digory lived in London at exactly the same time as the Bastables. C.S. Lewis knows about the Bastables. Perhaps Digory or Polly may have bumped into the Bastables without realizing it.* Such a response is presumably the ideal one the text requires.

The point about this third 'ideal response' is not that the reader who has it necessarily believes in *The Magician's Nephew* in the way that he believes he is ten years old (though that is not inconsistent with the real point). The real point is that he has been encouraged by the text to construct for himself, and to construct quite actively, a *world* in which the story takes place.[6]

All of us, whenever we read a book or see a play or film, have to do this passively, if a narrative is going to work on us. But it is not generally a process we notice. The degree of credibility which the opening of *The Magician's Nephew* attains for its ideal reader is not achieved merely by the weaving in of attested information about nineteenth-century London. This degree of credibility is also achieved, and increased, by the very inclusion of details which themselves happen to find their origin in other literary fictions. Holmes and the Bastables make the world of *The Magician's Nephew* more populous and complex, and more plausible. This may well slip the attention of the type (ii) reader, the unfortunate 'academic', for

---

6. My notion of a 'story world' corresponds to Genette's *diégèse* which he defines as 'the spatio–temporal universe designated by the narrative' (with accompanying adjective *diégètique*). This term is often misused or misunderstood, as Genette admits (*Narrative Discourse Revisited* [Columbia, 1988], 17–18). A comparable idea is developed in Pierre Macherey, *A Theory of Literary Production*, tr. G. Wall, (London, 1985), 56–60.

whom information about gas lights and penny farthings is of one order, and information about Holmes and the Bastables is of another.

Not just details from what is perceived as the actual past, but also the cross-referencing to other stories that the ideal reader knows, boost the credibility of this story. Lewis's children are probably justified in feeling that the Bastables are more real to them than Queen Victoria.

In general, for a story to work well it must appear as plausible and true-to-life to its audience as it can. We can see two features by which *The Magician's Nephew* lays claim to credibility, discernible in the passage quoted and applied throughout. These features exist, with varying degrees of intensity or conspicuousness, in *all* stories, whether we call them 'fictional' or 'factual'. They are:

(i) Community with the world of the (expected) reader's experience, beyond the obvious minimum of using his or her language: e.g. reference to known items, places, features of the actual present or past.

(ii) Community with, or reference to, other stories, making the world of the story in question more complex and substantial.

For feature (ii) to work, the other stories referred to do not have to come from other texts (or discourses). The world of a story can be made more complex and substantial just as much by a story embedded within it which is read or heard by a character or characters within that story. C.S. Lewis, like Apuleius, who encloses the story of Psyche within the *Met.*, happens to be fond of using embedded narratives of his own (or *mise-en-abyme* narratives as they are sometimes called).[7] Here at the opening of a book, he saves himself the trouble of devising any new ones or even of cross-referring to his other Narnia stories—something he often does. Instead he conveniently draws from the story worlds of two other authors, without having got very far into his own, and conflates theirs with

---

7. The chapter entitled 'L'Histoire dans l'Histoire' in Jean Ricardou, *Problèmes du nouveau roman* (Paris, 1967) discusses this, but the most exhaustive study is Lucien Dällenbach, *Le récit spéculaire* (Paris, 1977).

his in order to breathe life into the world of *The Magician's Nephew* at a very early stage in the narrative.

These tactics are not unusual and we will see them at work in Apuleius' *Met.* They are the stuff of which most stories are made—stories which we call 'factual' or 'historical' just as much as those which we say are 'imaginary' or 'fictional'. Before turning to Apuleius, however, we should be sure that we know what we mean by 'story world'.

The world of a story is the *mimesis* (or 'poetic imitation') of space, time, values, characters, events, etc. generated by the narrative of a text, and at the same time circumscribed by it. In speaking of 'The world of *The Golden Ass*', I do not mean what Fergus Millar means by it in his article of that title.[8] He is discussing the social conditions of the time in which Apuleius wrote, drawing from other texts and evidence as well as the *Met.* Likewise the 'world of *The Magician's Nephew*' is not Victorian London, however Victorian London may be conceived generally. It is merely what the narrative presents, textually or intertextually.

Such a world is restricted: it depends, at least initially, on the invocations of the narrator. We can generally only talk of what happens or does not happen in it, rather than what could or might happen, or have happened. The narrator himself, however, can use some means himself to encourage readers to speculate on these lines.

Generally speaking, there is no world out there which the narrator presents with relative degrees of fidelity: we have largely what he gives us.[9] The world of a story is what is signified by the language of the narrative, however much that might intersect with other story worlds.

Historical texts and fictional texts have a great deal in common—both kinds of text seek to be believed. To achieve this end, they share many strategies—some mentioned already. We shall consider some of the specific ways in which Apuleius' *Met.* lays claim to credibility. This consideration is profoundly relevant to the problem

---

8. *Journal of Roman Studies* 72 (1981), 63–75.

9. I am allowing for logical closure here—the notion that 'the logical [and maybe a few more] consequences of propositions in a story must also be true in it'. See H. Deutsch, 'Fiction and Fabrication', *Philosophical Studies* 47 (1985), 202. See Don P. Fowler, 'On Closure', *Materiali e Discussioni* 22 (1989), 78 n. 13 for bibliography.

of recovering some understanding of the ancient conceptions of what we now call fiction, as should become clear in the sections that follow.

Our questioning of the conventional modern categories of 'fact' (which I take in this argument to stand for 'factual narrative') and fiction, or at least some realization of the qualities they share as stories, is particularly appropriate for an attempt to reconstruct the way a text like Apuleius' *Met.* might have been understood in antiquity.

The labels of 'novel' or 'prose fiction' have been applied to Latin texts such as Petronius' *Satyricon* (produced some time during Nero's reign in AD 54–68) and Apuleius' *Met.*, and to Greek stories such as Heliodorus' *Aethiopica*, which John Morgan discusses in the next chapter. These labels have been applied rather too readily by contemporary critics and readers. 'Novel' is more often condemned as anachronistic: that term denotes a literary form widely agreed not to have appeared in Europe before the eighteenth century—although firm identification of the first instance of the fully formed 'novel', as opposed to 'romance' or 'history', will always be debated.

The label 'prose fiction' for these ancient texts at least liberates them from direct association with later literary forms. Arguably, it might also be preferable because it does not carry the implication that they are quite so homogeneous—which they certainly are not, as they differ from one another in style, narrative techniques and nature of content. Possibly, the most obvious thing the two Roman texts seem to have in common is their dissimilarity to other surviving literary works in Classical Latin as well as the Greek prose stories.

But 'fiction' is a modern category, not an ancient one. There is a scant framework for criticizing fiction, as we understand it, in ancient terms. Literary critics and theorists in antiquity are notoriously reticent about the genres now referred to as 'prose fiction', 'romances' or 'ancient novels'. Quintilian does not mention them at all in what otherwise appears to be a comprehensive survey of the literary genres in his *Institutio Oratoria* (*The Education of an Orator*) which was written about AD 95.[10]

---

10. The survey begins at 10.1.46. A translation of this part of the *Institutio* may be found in D.A. Russell and M. Winterbottom, *Ancient Literary Criticism* (Oxford, 1972), 387–400.

Macrobius, three centuries after Quintilian, makes at least one interesting remark, referring to the works of Petronius and Apuleius as

fabulae, quarum nomen indicat falsi professionem . . .

['fables'—their name betrays them as the avowal of what is false . . .][11]

I doubt if 'the avowal of what is false' (even if Macrobius made this remark with some irony), would be considered an adequate definition of fiction as we conceive it nowadays. Indeed, the idea that fiction can be a vehicle of truth is widely held. But here we do have a useful hint of what an ancient view might have been of the nature of a story like Apuleius' *Met.*

One important feature of the *Met.* is its use of the first person to induce belief. The significance of this narrative form in the *Met.* itself will not be considered in detail here, but one point relevant to this discussion can be made.[12] First-person fiction in the ancient world was a relative rarity: hardly any fictional narrators tell the whole story themselves. Stories, if they were in the first person, were always told second-hand. Possibly, the convention arose from supposition that what authors invented would otherwise be too easily refutable.[13] No wonder the two hoax accounts of the Trojan war by 'Dictys the Cretan' and 'Dares the Phrygian', rendered into Latin, were so long regarded as authentic.[14] Written in the first person, they were taken to be first-hand sources. So the *Met.*, by using that form too, and by using it throughout without enclosing its principal first-person narrative inside another, might be seen (from the ancient point of view at least) to be aspiring to the status of discourse which we might term 'factual'. The effect of an

---

11. From *In Somnium Scipionis* 1.2.8. See J.R. Morgan, pp. 177–8 below).

12. See A. Laird, 'Person, *Persona* and Representation in Apuleius's *Metamorphoses*', *Materiali e Discussioni* 25 (1990), 129–64.

13. B.E. Perry, *The Ancient Romances: A Literary–Historical Account of their Origins* (Berkeley, 1967), 323.

14. Howard Clarke, *Homer's Readers: A Historical Introduction to the Iliad and Odyssey* (London, 1981) shows just how much and for how long they were believed.

'eye-witness' account is very much constituted by its use of the 'I' form.[15]

Given that there is a virtual absence of any other testimonies to help us recover any ancient categories corresponding to the modern conception of 'fiction',[16] it seems best to go straight to the text of the *Met.* itself. We can try instead to develop an idea of what those categories could have been from closely reading certain passages.

Two sections of the *Met.* will be considered in detail for this purpose—both concerned with the story's claims to truth. In the first (1.1–2), the narrator talks about the nature of the work before commencing his story. In the second (3.21–2) there is a description of an occurrence which would strike modern readers as being indubitably fictional: a human character turns into an owl. I shall look closely at how this event is presented, and seek to establish what it too can tell us about the nature of the text in which it appears.

II

This how the prologue to the *Met.*—a paragraph long—begins:

At ego tibi sermone isto Milesio varias fabulas conseram . . .

[In this Milesian discourse I will put together a variety of *fabulae* for you . . .]

---

15. The deployment of either the first or the third person in narration in all stories, whether they are to be received as factual or fictional, can be regarded as a rhetorical device. The debate about whether to use the first or third person in accounts of fieldwork, which has preoccupied ethnographers and anthropologists, shows that the choice can have serious moral implications. See Tony Free, 'Written or Living Culture?', *Journal of the Anthropological Society of Oxford* 21 (1990), 51–65, at 59.

16. I mean that there is an absence of testimonies about what corresponded to our conception of 'fiction' as a *genre*: there was, obviously, an understanding that some stories were more fanciful than others. Roos Meijering, *Literary and Rhetorical Theories in Greek Scholia* (Groningen, 1987) in her second chapter, 'The Subject Matter of Texts: Fact and Fiction', 54f. discusses *mimēsis* (representation), *phantasia* (visualization), *poiētikē exousia* (poetic licence), *muthos* (plot), etc. This study is confined to what ancient commentators had to say about dramatic texts. See also D.C. Feeney, *The Gods in Epic* (Oxford, 1991), 5–57, which looks at ancient critics' handling of fictional elements in epic.

and ends:

> Fabulam Graecanicam incipimus. Lector intende: laetaberis.
>
> [We are beginning a *fabula* of the Greek type. Pay attention dear reader—you'll enjoy it.]

I.I

These declarations offer a comment—which has to be credible—on the nature of the text that follows. The *Met.* will be a *fabula* or a mixture of *fabulae*: 'fables' or imaginary stories. We are also told something of the work's genre (and therefore how to read it): *Milesia* were scurrilous erotica. Plutarch's *Crassus* 32 mentions that the Roman Roscius read this sort of literature, to his discredit. These declarations in the prologue look as if they are going to be true, and effectively turn out to be so. But, as we read on, we end up being faced with a conundrum of this type: 'If I say from this very moment that I am lying, at which point do you assume I am no longer telling the truth?'[17]

Anyone who contemplates the notion of the historical Apuleius being the speaker of this prologue, even if only to dismiss it later, is caught out, because the speaker has already shown himself to be lying already, by failing to begin after he has just said he is about to: (*Exordior* 'I begin' consitutes the second sentence in the prologue. Eight more sentences follow before the story proper gets underway.) We have been given factual truth about the genre and nature of this text—it is a *fabula Graecanica*, even if that truth means little to us. We do not get it about the name and identity of the author. The lack of that information at least bears out that first truthful claim: we were told we would get fables and fantasies about men changing their shapes. They come perhaps sooner than many readers are ready for them.

---

17. A similar conundrum is to be found in the opening of a Greek narrative, contemporary with the *Met.*, by Lucian, which is aptly entitled *Alethōn Diēgēmatōn* (*True Stories*): 'As I had nothing true to tell, not having had any adventures of significance, I took to lying. But my lying is far more honest . . . for although I tell the truth in nothing else, I shall at least be truthful in saying that I am a liar . . .' (cf. p. 132 above).

This is how the narrative itself begins, in the sentence after the prologue:

> Thessaliam—nam et illic originis maternae nostrae fundamenta a Plutarcho illo inclito ac mox Sexto philosopho nepote eius prodita gloriam nobis faciunt—eam Thessaliam ex negotio petebam.

> [I was bound for Thessaly—for from there my mother's family claims its origin, with descent from the famous Plutarch and then from his nephew the philosopher Sextus, in both of whom we take some pride—so it was to Thessaly I was going, on business.]

1.2

Critics have sensed a disjunction between the voice of the prologue in 1.1 which advertises a blend of various tales (*fabulae*) and the autobiographical voice in what follows. They even seek to ascribe different identities to the two voices.[18] But isn't what goes on here rather comparable to the way C.S. Lewis introduces his account with the curious phrase 'This is a *story about something that happened* . . .'? We are told by our narrator (truthfully) that a story is about to come—that's demonstrable, but then in the same phrase we are told that it 'happened': *did* it happen? When does the narrator begin 'lying'? C.S. Lewis compresses into his first sentence more or less what is accomplished between *Met.* 1.1 and 1.2.

It is not really reasonable to argue that the first paragraph of *The Magician's Nephew* belongs to one voice and the second to another.[19] Likewise, in spite of the more numerous complexities in the opening of the *Met.*, I would prefer to talk of a shift, rather than an actual change in voice, between *Met.* 1.1 and 1.2. There are numerous passages later in the book where the narrator (who certainly need not be completely identified as Lucius the 'autobiographer') engages in conversation with his reader and in other

---

18. For a strong articulation of this view and citation of others, see S.J. Harrison, 'The Speaking Book: The Prologue to Apuleius's *Metamorphoses*' in *Classical Quarterly* 40 (1990), 507–13.

19. However, we should certainly consider V.N. Voloshinov's observation that 'in certain crucial respects paragraphs are *analogous* to exchanges in dialogue' (my emphasis) in *Marxism and the Philosophy of Language*, tr. L. Matejka and I. Titunik (Cambridge, Mass., 1973), 111.

meta-textual activity—the implications of which I have considered elsewhere.[20] On the basis of these passages alone, a claim like Stephen Harrison's (n. 18 above), that there is a separate speaker of the prologue, is not convincing: a tension between sheer story-telling and engagement with the reader or audience, however it is held, is a common feature of literary narrative.

The issue of whether or not we identify a separate voice at the beginning of the *Met.* is thus rooted in confusion about how credible this text is, generated by a claim to truth laid at the very beginning of the prologue.

The same confusion about credibility arising from claims to truth has dogged interpretation of the opening of 1.2, quoted above, in which the narrator claims descent from Plutarch and Sextus. The Sextus referred to is Sextus of Chaeronea, a Platonist and teacher of Marcus Aurelius and Verus, who was in fact the nephew of Plutarch. Plutarch too came from Chaeronea in Boeotia, not Thessaly. Byrrhaena reminds the reader of Lucius' descent from Plutarch, mentioning it to him at 2.3.

This is regarded as a problem, for which two solutions have gener-ally been offered.[21] The first is that, since this genealogy would have little or no interest if it were imaginary, Apuleius must be inserting into the text of his story some autobiographical information about himself. The second explanation is that the supposed original Greek model for Apuleius' *Met.* must have maintained that Plutarch and Sextus were related to the central character.

It is only if one does regard this as a problem passage that such explanations are necessary. Could we not regard Plutarch and Sextus as having a function parallel to that of Eton collars and Sherlock Holmes? It is not so much the historicity of these names as their specificity which is important for a storyteller's strategy of seeking belief by achieving community with the audience's read or felt experience.[22] This view need not be incompatible with the customary

---

20. See further Laird, op. cit. (n. 12).

21. See D.S. Robertson, ed., *Les Métamorphoses*, tr. P. Vallete, Tome 1, (Paris, 1972), 3, n. 2.

22. Cf. n. 3 above on circumstantial detail. A. Scobie, in his commentary on *Met.* 1 (Meisenheim am Glan, 1975) ad loc., says the purpose of these names remains obscure, 'unless it is to give his narrative a contemporary or nearly contempo-rary ring.'

explanations, but it should perhaps be regarded as the primary reaction. Those customary explanations only seem to be called for if the reader of this text expects to be told the truth; and there has been an advance warning that he should not.

A little earlier, I was able to offer, with some confidence, suggestions for three possible responses from readers to the opening of *The Magician's Nephew*. They rest on the knowledge that the book was first published in 1955 and on reasonable assumptions about the type of audience for which it was aimed and how they would have received it. Nothing comparable is known about the *Met.* and the nature of its original readers, though we may make conjectures about the resonance that the names of these second-century thinkers might have had. Perhaps by placing these personages in Thessaly, a place renowned for witchcraft on testimonies other than our narrator's at 2.1,[23] the audience is prompted to expect an account which will blend intellectual sophistication with some hocus-pocus.

In a way, our ignorance of the context and audience for Apuleius' *Met.* helps to make the case that fictional and historical texts are less easily distinguished than they are generally thought to be. One of the most powerful arguments for historiography being regarded as a discourse which is quite different from mere 'literature' is that historical texts are prone to be treated in a quite different way from 'literary' ones. They seem to be automatically subject to either refutation or verification. Nobody, it is maintained, would bother to challenge the truthfulness of a work of fiction.

There is nothing *inherent* in historical texts to evoke such reactions. A text's genre is constituted to some extent by our knowledge (or presumed knowledge) of the climate that produces it and of the audience it is designed for: a history book or a factual journal is subject to refutation because we happen to know in the first place that it is purported to be true.

And we have just seen how only a few sentences into the *Met.* critics have risen to meet the problem of false information—even in a work which has candidly advertised itself as a collection of *fabulae*. When Augustine in his *Civitas Dei*, written in the 420s, discusses accounts of humans turning into animals, he pauses to worry about

---

23. G. Luck, *Arcana Mundi* (Baltimore, 1985), 6. Cf. Lucan, *De Bello Civili* 6.413–830, Seneca, *Heracles Oetaeus* 465–7.

whether or not Apuleius was telling the truth in the *Met.* as a whole.[24] The existence of such responses could well show that the ways in which both 'historical' and 'fictional' texts seek to be believed may not be so dissimilar. The difference between historical and literary investigation does not always reside in the kind of texts which are studied, but in the manner they are approached.[25]

III

For the *Met.* itself, a historian could still argue that, from a common-sense point of view, regardless of Augustine's apparent susceptibility, this particular story is patently far-fetched and fantastic. But even fantastic literature, if it is to work on us successfully, has to be convincing. Todorov has shown that a number of works (he considers mainly nineteenth-century fiction) have sufficient common features to constitute a fully-fledged genre—the genre of the fantastic. It is defined by its capacity to cause the reader to waver in his view of whether what is described is true, and to hesitate between giving a natural or supernatural explanation for the events the narrative presents.

Cazotte's *Le diable amoureux* is one work Todorov considers.[26] The principal character, Alvare, has been involved with a woman for several months whom he believes to be a kind of devil—but he cannot be sure of this. Neither he nor the reader can ever be certain about whether or not his whole experience with her is a kind of dream, and this doubt is sustained right until the end of the story. Either, Todorov concludes, this devil is an illusory imaginary being, or else it exists for real, like all other living things, but is rarely encountered. The fantastic, he argues, occupies this realm of uncertainty: if one actually adopts one or the other interpretation, one

---

24. *Civitas Dei* 18.18. See again J.R. Morgan, pp. 192–3 below.

25. Scobie op. cit. (n. 22 above), 72 shows why the *Met.* is a good case in point. Readers themselves decide on what genre a work is. The factors that make them read a text *P* as genre *x* are often extra-textual. In the ancient world there were fewer explicit signals of genre for prose and even verse texts. See Genette, *Seuils* (Paris, 1987), 89–97. The subscription to the *Aeneid* (*Ille ego qui quondam . . .*) is discussed there in relation to this question.

26. T. Todorov, *Introduction à la littérature fantastique* (Paris, 1970), 28–45.

leaves this genre for one of the neighbouring ones like the 'strange'
(*étrange*) or the 'marvellous' (*merveilleux*).

Apuleius' *Met.* certainly contains elements which would lead us
to regard it as 'fantastic' in this specific sense.[27] Lucius as narrator
applies more care than is generally supposed in describing supernatural or miraculous events. In fact he is pretty sparing of accounts
of anything supernatural actually happening to him, though funny
things certainly happen to other characters like Socrates in Aristomenes' story, which Lucius hears on the road to Hypata (1.5). The
metamorphoses themselves are the only things Lucius says he has
witnessed himself which really stretch our credulity. The manner in
which the first metamorphosis Lucius witnesses, that of Pamphile
into an owl in 3.21–2, is recounted is interesting, and has important
implications for how we should regard Lucius' recounting of his
own conversions into an ass and back again. The excerpt begins at
the point where Photis leads him to see Pamphile's transformation:

Iamque circa primam noctis vigiliam ad illud superius cubiculum
suspenso et insono vestigio me perducit ipsa perque rimam
ostiorum quampiam iubet arbitrari, quae sic gesta sunt. Iam
primum omnibus laciniis se devestit Pamphile et arcula quadam
reclusa pyxides plusculas inde depromit, de quis unius operculo
remoto atque indidem egesta unguedine diuque palmulis suis
adfricta ab imis unguibus sese totam adusque summos capillos
perlinit multumque cum lucerna secreto conlocuta membra
tremulo sucussu quatit. Quis leniter fluctuantibus promicant
molles plumulae, crescunt et fortes pinnulae, duratur nasus
incurvus, coguntur ungues adunci. Fit bubo Pamphile. Sic edito
stridore querulo iam sui periclitabunda paulatim terra resultat,
mox in altum sublimata forinsecus totis alis evolat. 22. Et illa
quidem magicis suis artibus volens reformatur, at ego nullo
decantatus carmine praesentis tantum facti stupore defixus

<hr>

27. Carlos Garcia Gual in his introductory essay to a sixteenth-century Spanish
translation of the *Met.*, 'El libro de oro' in *Apuleyo: El Asno de Oro* (Madrid,
1988), 23–4 conceives of the story as fantastic in Todorov's sense: 'It would not
then be an impossible occurrence, however unlikely or inexplicable, that our
Lucius of Patras or Apuleius of Madaura could have gone about in the shape of
an ass, until Isis, the holy goddess with magical powers, took pity on him and
restored him to his human form; and that all this occurred with the material
help of some ointment and a few roses.'

quidvis aliud magis videbar esse quam Lucius: sic exterminatus animi attonitus in amentiam vigilans somniabar; defrictis adeo diu pupulis an vigilarem scire quaerebam. Tandem denique reversus ad sensum praesentium adrepta manu Photidis . . .

[Now around the first watch of the night, Photis leads me with silent tiptoeing steps to that upper chamber and orders me to contemplate through any chink between the doors what is going on. Now first Pamphile disrobes herself of all her garments and unfastening a particular casket takes out from it quite a number of perfume boxes: after taking off the lid of one of these and extracting the ointment from it which she rubs for a long time with her palms, she smears all of it over herself from the tips of her toes to the top ends of her hair, and conferring much in secret with her lamp, with a trembling upward movement she shakes her limbs. From the gently undulating limbs spring forth soft little feathers, and strong little wings are growing, the nose hardens and curves, nails force themselves into claws. Pamphile becomes an owl! Thus emitting a querulous screech, now making trial of herself, little by little she springs off the ground; and soon lifted on high, she flies out of doors with the full strength of her wings. 22. And she indeed by her own magic arts in accordance with her will is transformed, but I, enchanted by no chanted spell, transfixed into a stupor by the imminence of the event itself, was seeming to be something different from Lucius. Thus driven out of my mind into madness, wide awake I was the subject of a dream; I was trying to know for sure whether I was awake by actually rubbing my eyes for a long time. At last finally brought back to a sense of the imminent events, I snatched Photis' hand . . .]

This may seem to be a tall story, but the telling is so artful that it is hard to establish exactly what it is we are being told. The phrase opening this excerpt *circa primam noctis vigiliam* ('around the first watch of the night') may have more significance than is first apparent. If we go back to read it after Lucius' description at the close of this passage of his musings about whether he was awake or dreaming (*vigilans somniabar . . . an vigilarem scire quaerebam* 'wide awake I was the subject of a dream . . . I was trying to know for sure whether I was awake'), the word *vigiliam* here might have an air of irony about it: the first watch of the night after all denotes, paradoxically, a time when most people are asleep and dreaming. As we shall see, it may not be so unreasonable to ask whether Lucius is too. Note that his timing is not precise: *circa* means 'around' or 'about', not 'at' or 'during'. There were traditions that dreams occurring in the first part of the night were false and misleading.[28] The expression *Circa primam ferme noctis vigiliam* opens Book 11: there, after sleeping, Lucius utters a prayer to Isis who appears to him in a dream.

Lucius observes what goes on through a chink in the door. He is prying into Pamphile's private world, allowing us an intimate view of things that are her concern alone—the first detail presented is her undressing. As the description continues, we almost get the impression that it is Pamphile's experience which is here recounted as much as Lucius' witnessing of it.

Any sense we may have of this excerpt beginning with a really precise description disappears once we look more closely at the language used here: Lucius is watching through '*some* chink in the door' (*rimam ostiorum quampiam*), Pamphile unfastens a '*particular* casket' (*arcula quadam reclusa*), removing from it '*quite a number* of perfume boxes' (*pyxides plusculas*) and takes the lid off '*one of these*' (*de quis unius operculo remoto*). This rhetorical vagueness also helps make the account seem more colloquial and plausible: someone actually recounting such an episode from memory would not record every detail.[29]

Things become more specific once Pamphile softens the ointment and begins to spread it all over herself, but at this point the narrative begins to move towards her own point of view or 'focalization'. This is especially clear with the sentence that begins *Quis leniter . . .*' ('From the gently . . .'). The diminutives *plumulae* and *pinnulae* ('little feathers' and 'little wings') may suggest more about Pamphile's fond and partial attitude to these new attributes of hers than they might about their actual size—the narrator has not been giving us that kind of detail. To call 'small' wings that are strong (*fortes*) and still growing to a sufficient size to bear a body out of a

---

28. See W. Everett's note in *Classical Review* 14 (1900), 153f.

29. Genette op. cit. (n. 3 above), 92, n. 2, notes how a certain kind of precision is an optional index of modern fictional discourse: 'Ten more glorious days without horses! So the second lieutenant Andrew Chase-White, on leave from King Edward's distinguished cavalry regiment, thought to himself as he sat in a Dublin park on a sunny Sunday afternoon in April 1916.'

window seems otherwise a pointless oxymoron. More clinchingly, how could an observer other than Pamphile sense that her feathers are 'soft' (*molles*) or bother to give more emphasis to the phenomenon of her nose hardening (*duratur*) than to its curving? Lucius as narrator may be speaking, but Pamphile as focalizer seems to be the one who is 'seeing' here.

The same could apply to the next sentence *Fit bubo Pamphile* ('Pamphile becomes an owl!'). We could go further, and regard it as Pamphile's actual expression of her own thought, either wholly as an exultant exclamation (direct discourse) or partly, her voice being fused with the narrator's (free indirect discourse). The case for this further supposition is supported by what follows: *Sic edito stridore querulo* ('Thus emitting a querulous screech')—which, if we were really bold, we could render as 'Emitting *that* querulous screech'. *Periclitabunda sui* ('making trial of herself') later in the same sentence might also be read as Pamphile's focalization—would an observer at the scene really know this was the explanation for her springing off the ground in stages (*paulatim*)?

But, it may be argued, if our story-teller seeks to be believed at all, his credibility, which is already flimsy enough by virtue of his saying he saw a woman turn into an owl in the first place, is surely weakened still further by the possible adoption of deviant focaliza-tion through Pamphile, let alone by any presentation of her thoughts. Observers in real life cannot be omniscient narrators: if anything made Lucius' testimony look fictional, it would be this. However, this presentation of affairs from Pamphile's perspective could be the one thing that would make the narration of this incident plausible. It would be plausible in terms of an attempt that has been made to rationalize, rather exotically, such descriptions of metamorphoses accomplished by witches, as I now hope to show.

In Mikhail Bulgakov's novel *The Master and Margarita*,[30] the heroine also covers her naked body with cream from a jar, and trans-forms into a younger woman before flying out of her bedroom window on a broomstick. Like Pamphile, she uses this method to abandon her husband and meet her lover. Either the *Met.* or an inde-pendent folk tradition could have inspired this. Scobie produces

---

30. Tr. M. Glenny, (London, 1988), 263f.

evidence of there being such a tradition—that witches in medieval and Renaissance Europe used hallucinogenic 'flying ointments'.[31]

If the existence of these ointments was acknowledged in the time that the *Met.* was composed, the narrator may be seeking to convey vividly a sense of what was going on without committing himself to testifying that Pamphile was either flying or hallucinating. A tenuous focalization through Pamphile, or even presentation of her discourse, might be the best device to use. A suggestion that the metamorphosis and flight are sensations primarily experienced directly by Pamphile but somehow extended to Lucius could be supported by the first part of the opening sentence of 3.22, which clearly returns to the narrator's perspective as he describes the way he has been affected by what has so far occurred:

> Et illa quidem magicis suis artibus volens reformatur . . .
>
> [And she indeed by her own magic arts, willing it, is transformed . . .]

The word *volens* ('willing it') can be read two ways. It could tell us little more than we think we know already—Pamphile would hardly choose to change her form if she did not want to. Alternatively, if we accept that few words in the *Met.* are ever superfluous, the location of *volens* before the main verb *reformatur* could tell us something about the nature of that transformation—that it really consists in Pamphile's actual willing of it. This could explain the force of *quidem* ('indeed'): it extends what has preceded, to suggest delicately that for Pamphile especially (*et illa*)?—this metamorphosis is real.

More crucially, the narrator's precaution in presenting this whole incident as something which he observed through a hole in a door should alert us to the idea that he is throughout presenting someone else's story. In Petronius and Apuleius (and numerous successors

---

31. Scobie's claims have a bearing on my case for focalization through Pamphile here: 'Many of these preparations contained narcotic stimulants of psychotropic hallucinogens which not only could give the impression of growing feathers and hair but also of flying through the air.' *Apuleius and Folklore* (London, 1983), 101. See also H.A. Hansen, *The Witch's Garden* (Santa Cruz, 1978), 85–102 and H. Biedermann, *Handlexicon der magischen Künste* (Graz, 1976), 156–8.

including John Cleland and the Marquis de Sade) observation through cracks and keyholes is not so much a frequent incident in stories as a narrative technique that allows a story-teller information from which he can provide insight into feelings and motivations of other characters.

However we conceive of this metamorphosis, the most fascinating thing about it is the impact it has on Lucius the narrator himself. It metamorphoses him—well before he is going to tell us that he turned into an ass. He draws a contrast between Pamphile's changed state and his own which turns out not to be much of a contrast at all. She is changed by her magic arts: 'but I,' he says, 'enchanted by no chanted spell, transfixed into a stupor by the imminence of the event itself, was seeming to be something *different* from Lucius' (*quidvis aliud magis videbar esse quam Lucius*). The next word in the following clause is *sic* ('thus'), just as it was after the sentence that conclusively asserted Pamphile's transformation: *Fit bubo Pamphile. Sic edito stridore . . .* And, just as she rubbed the ointment in her palm for a long time (*diuque palmulis suis adfricta*), Lucius rubs his eyes for a long time (*defrictis diu pupulis*).

As well as the sensation of flight, 'inducing stupor' is claimed to be one of the qualities of witches' 'flying ointments'. Could it be just coincidence that Lucius describes himself at this stage as *stupore defixus*? The unfortunate Socrates whom we later find to have been under the lethal spell of a witch is described as *in stuporem attonitus* as he reacts to Aristomenes' reviling of the witch Meroe in 1.8 (cf. *attonitus in amentiam*—also here in 3.22). Anyway, even if Pamphile is not intoxicated and hallucinating, Lucius must be in some sense, unable as he is to work out whether he is awake or in a dream.

Lucius' real, or at least most significant, metamorphosis arguably occurs here at 3.22, rather than at the more celebrated passage in 3.24. Subsequently, the narrator several times expresses anxiety about his reversion to being 'Lucius' again. In 3.23 he asks Photis by what word or action he will turn back into Lucius if he changes himself into an owl (*quo dicto factove rursum exutis pennulis illis ad meum redibo Lucium?*). 'You will turn back into my Lucius' (*in meum Lucium postliminio redibis*), Photis assures him after he becomes an ass. The narrator describes his unfortunate state at 3.26: 'But although I was made into an ass and a beast of burden instead of Lucius . . .' (*quamquam perfectus asinus et pro Lucio iumentum . . .*). But 3.22, when Lucius has witnessed Pamphile's transformation, is the place where that affliction of his lost identity ('being something different from Lucius') is first described.

If Lucius is no longer himself here, our reading of this passage affects our reading of the whole story: his psychological change here could explain all the curious events that follow, including the metamorphosis into an ass, otherwise hard to credit. And of course it may not be that Pamphile has changed into an owl in the sense that most readers and critics have thought she did. Just as Lucius cannot henceforth work out whether he is awake or dreaming, we as readers cannot be sure either. This makes a case for putting the *Met.* into the category of fantastic literature as it was previously defined (pp. 161–2 above).

An obstruction to this argument might be seen to remain. The phrase following that in which our narrator said he was rubbing his eyes to see if he was awake or not, runs thus:

Tandem denique reversus ad sensum praesentium . . .

[At last finally brought back to a sense of the imminent events . . .]

Doesn't this mean that Lucius finally came round and back to his senses? Not at all—though this is a trap into which translators and interpreters of this passage have fallen without exception. The phrase is less determinate. This is revealed by the word *praesentium* which must recall *praesentis* in the previous sentence: the stupor Lucius had in the first place was brought on by the apprehension of what appeared before him. If he was really shaken out of that stupor, we should expect a different choice of word than *praesentium* here: what is *praesens* (i.e. 'immediate', 'instant', 'powerful') is not the same as what is true or certain. Although we may be misled into thinking otherwise, it seems that Lucius in fact abandons his lengthy speculation about whether the events before him are real or not, to concentrate on the events that succeed them, which may also be just as illusory.[32]

---

32. In *Onos*, a supposed epitome of the lost original ass-tale which inspired Apuleius, preserved in the Lucianic corpus, Lucius is not quite sure whether he is awake at the corresponding point in the story (section 12). Apart from this, none of the other touches in Apuleius' narrative of this incident are found in the Greek version. Incidentally there is no equivalent to Apuleius' prologue in the *Onos*. It begins at a point corresponding to *Met.* 1.2: 'Once I was going to Thessaly . . .'; Plutarch and Sextus are not mentioned.

The narrator's transformation back into human form may also have begun before the point where it is generally thought to occur (namely 11.13, when he manages to eat the garland of roses offered him by Isis' priest.) At 11.5, Isis answers our narrator's prayer addressing him as *Luci*. Nobody, including Photis, has before that moment addressed our narrator as 'Lucius' from 3.22 onwards. This is an interesting place for it to happen; while he is officially (or in his own view) still an ass, the narrator is at least able to speak to utter his prayer. Hitherto he has made a great deal of his inability to speak as a dumb ass. What is more, he speaks here at 11.1 with a tearful, and thus presumably more human, face: *lacrimoso vultu sic apprecabar*. In Ovid's *Metamorphoses*, a number of the physical transformations are anticipated by psychological changes in characters who undergo them.[33]

What are we to make of 3.21–2 and its overall implications altogether? As was remarked earlier, it is not so much a case of whether or not we should believe what is related, as one of what it is we are told. Pamphile and/or Lucius are metamorphosed and/or intoxicated. The metamorphosis and/or intoxication work on the reader too, who begins to realize, like Lucius, that the more he attempts to investigate closely what is going on the more confused and stupefied he becomes.

We should bear in mind that the sensations of flight and intoxication or stupefaction were often conjoined as effects of discourse, particularly philosophical discourse, in the ancient world. In Plato we hear Socrates' interlocutors say that they feel stupefied hearing his words;[34] the notion of philosophers or their pupils engaging in

---

33. See e.g. Ovid *Met.* 1. 232–44, 14. 751–8. This is related to the allegorical import which the metamorphoses in Ovid, like Lucius', have. See Forbes Irving, *Metamorphosis in Greek Myth* (Oxford, 1991).

34. See *Meno* 80a–c. Meno says to Socrates, 'I feel you are exercising magic and witchcraft upon me and positively laying me under your spell until I am just a mass of helplessness ... You are exactly like the flat sting-ray that one meets in the sea. Whenever anyone comes into contact with it, it numbs him, and that is the sort of thing that you seem to be doing to me now. My mind and my lips are really numb, and I have nothing to reply to you.' Plato, *Protagoras and Meno*, tr. W.K.C. Guthrie (Harmondsworth, 1961), 127–8.

flight, or at least flight of the mind (*psuchē*) is commonplace—we need only think of Aristophanes' Socrates in *Clouds* 225, 1503 and Plato's *Phaedrus* 246.[35]

Much has been made of the Platonic influences in the *Met.* Purely on the basis of the Pamphile incident, the work could be read as a kind of philosophical text. This incident, and by extension the story that follows, can be seen as raising the question: how do I know I'm not dreaming? Contrariwise, Descartes' *Meditations*, the philosophical text in which that question is most famously posed, could itself be read as a fictional first-person narrative. Again, our sense of that text's genre stops us worrying about whether Descartes' preoccupations were heart-felt, or whether the meditations occurred exactly as he chronicled them.

What we make of the Pamphile incident, and the way we believe in the *Met.* as a whole, depends on our conception of the text's genre—even if that conception is not articulated and the genre not easy to specify. It could be a fantastic text (which like *Le diable amoureux* prompts philosophical speculation): we cannot establish what happened. Alternatively, if we think we are told that Pamphile conclusively turned into an owl and that Lucius conclusively turned into an ass, then we must be reading the *Met.* as a 'marvellous' text, which, unless we are as open-minded as St Augustine, we are unlikely to believe. Or, if we are pedestrian enough to think that Lucius is telling the honest truth about what he thought he experienced 'under the influence', then the *Met.* could be read as a journal recording that kind of psychological experience, a *Confessions of a Carthaginian Opium Eater*.

It is no accident that the Greek word *psuchagōgia* (literally 'the leading of minds', an image not unconnected with flight) is often translated 'bewitchment'. This term is used by ancient literary critics and philosophers for the overwhelming effect that discourse, from poetry to rhetorical or philosophical argument, can have on an

---

35. I am grateful to my friend Mark Edwards for discussing this with me, and for his article 'Treading the Aether: Lucretius, *De Rerum Natura* 1.62–79', *Classical Quarterly* 40 (1990), 465–9, which assembles many more references to flight in philosophical and other texts. A standard treatment is R.M. Jones, 'Posidonius and the Flight of the Mind through the Universe', *Classical Philology* 21 (1926), 97–113. See R.G.M. Nisbet and M. Hubbard, *A Commentary on Horace's Odes* I (Oxford, 1975), 324, on 1.28.5 (the Archytas ode).

audience. It was applied across the board to many or all kinds of efficacious discourse.[36]

A kind of *psuchagōgia* is at work intensely and on many intersecting levels (Pamphile's, Lucius', ours) and perhaps in various forms (magical, pharmacological, rhetorical) in the description of Pamphile's flight. *Psuchagōgia* in the sense of bewitching discourse is operative throughout the *Met.*, as in all stories, causing us to construct imaginary story worlds. In the *Met.* the process is overt, either making us think we know what is going on when we do not, or confusing us by raising questions we cannot answer. *Psuchagōgia* could be regarded as being equally operative in 'historical' and in other 'factual' writing.[37] It makes us think we have a window on to our own world of experience, when we are being presented with a version of it, another story world, conjured up by the journalist or historian.

There might be another route by which this conception of *psuchagōgia* and our reading of 3.21–2 could help us attain an insight into the way our idea of fiction was perceived by the ancients. We have seen how Macrobius, and Lucian and Apuleius in their prologues, have more than implicitly identified the sort of story (*fabula*) we are considering with 'lying', or at least with avowing

---

36. Compare Denis Feeney's discussion at pp. 235–6 below. The mentions of *psuchagōgia* and its cognates discussed most frequently are: Aristotle, *Poetics* 1450a33 (on the effect of reversals of fortune), 1450b17 (on the effect of the visual element, *opsis*, in drama, cf. the discussion of Gorgias and the Plutarch quotation, below p. 172); Plato, *Phaedrus* 261a, 271c (on the effects of speech). P.M. Fraser, *Ptolemaic Alexandria* 1 (Oxford, 1972), 760 shows that Erathoshenes (c. 275–194 BC) saw *psuchagōgia* as 'entertainment', regarding that as the sole end of poetry. He quotes Agatharchides who wrote under Eratosthenes' influence (and incidentally says in the same passage that myths should not be refuted because they should not be believed anyway): 'every poet should aim for *psuchagōgia* rather than truth.' Neoptolemus of Parium also regarded *psuchagōgia* as the end of poetry, but for him it was a *moral* function (see Philodemus, *Peri Poiēmatōn*, ed. C. Jensen [Leipzig, 1923], col. 13, 33). See also R. Pfeiffer, *History of Classical Scholarship*, 1 (Oxford, 1986), 166. Apuleius in the *Met.* as a whole could be seen to achieve *psuchagōgia* in terms of moral instruction as well as entertainment. Like Neoptolemus, Apuleius is a Platonist. His work could well be composed, at least partly, for the purpose of philosophical instruction.

37. On *psuchagōgia* and history see B.L. Ullmann, 'History and Tragedy', *Transactions of the American Philological Association* 73 (1942), 25–53, at 41. See also T.P. Wiseman, p. 140 above.

what is false. In recounting the flight of Pamphile, it was noted that narcotic bewitchment could be affecting Pamphile as the uncanny *sight* of it all bewitches and stupefies Lucius in the story. There may also be a rhetorical bewitchment of the audience or reader accomplished in the narrative.

Drugs, sight (*opsis*), sorcery and discourse are presented explicitly as agents of deception (*apatē*) of the mind (*psuchē*), or 'bewitchment', in a work which combined oratorical display with rhetorical and psychological theory: *The Encomium of Helen*. This was written by Gorgias of Leontini, an influential rhetorician and sophist, in the fifth century BC.[38] While we do not actually find the word '*psuchagōgia*' in this text, all the constituents of it are certainly there. And it is to Gorgias that Plutarch attributes this striking observation on the effect of tragic drama—which could just as well have implications for other kinds of story, including 'prose fiction'.[39]

> Tragedy did flourish, and was famous: a wonderful experience *for the eyes and ears* of that generation. It lent to myth and emotion a *deceit* wherein, as Gorgias says, the deceiver is more just than the non-deceiver, and the deceived is wiser than the undeceived. The deceiver is more just because he has fulfilled his promise; the deceived is wiser, because it takes a measure of sensibility to be accessible to the pleasures of literature (*hēdonēs logōn*) . . .
>
> (*Moralia* 348c)

Gorgias no doubt enjoyed presenting this insight as a paradox by introducing the notion of beneficial deceit. But how else could he express what he meant? Literature can lie, but lies to a pleasing end: it is a lying that can be viewed positively. It may not be coincidence that this comes from a theorist who compares the effects of drugs,

---

38. D.M. MacDowell, *The Encomium of Helen* (Bristol, 1982) provides a recent text, translation and commentary. For an extensive discussion of the theory it contains, see Charles P. Segal, 'Gorgias and the Psychology of the Logos', *Harvard Studies in Classical Philology*, 66 (1962), 99–155.

39. I quote again from a translation in Russell and Winterbottom, op. cit. (n. 10 above). MacDowell, op. cit. (n. 38 above), 16, discusses the relation between speech in general and *apatē* in Gorgias.

sight and speech on the mind. Like Apuleius, he was a professional sophist. Like Apuleius, he may also have been regarded as a kind of wizard.

Perhaps then, the conjunction of elements in *Met.* 3.21-2 bring us closer to an idea of what the ancient conception of fiction might be than we first realized.

Apuleius' story has been used by social historians to attain some insight on life in the period it was written. Some people are still prepared to regard at least part of the *Met.* as autobiographical. The narrator is as scrupulous and persuasive in engineering credibility as any historical narrator could be.[40] Uncanny events are recounted in such a way that they are always 'covered': for example the vision of Isis' epiphany takes place when the narrator says he was actually asleep. The *Met.* is also an accomplished piece of fantastic literature in Todorov's sense, and fantastic literature need not be fictional at all. But the *Met.* advertises itself as a fable. This has caused William Adlington, who translated the *Met.* in 1566, and many in his wake to allegorize it themselves, or to read it as a text which was designed to be allegorical: fictional truths remain whether the story is true or false.[41]

Novel, fantasy, allegory or history—we, almost as much as the ancients, are hard put to classify a story of this kind when so many interpretations have been offered. It is hoped that the examinations of some of the claims to truth in the *Met.* have shed some light, from within, on the genre of that text, and suggested what the conception of fiction may have been for its original audience. It is a *fabula* which should not be subject to refutation on the basis of what actually occurred. Nonetheless, its avowal of what is false is

---

40. There are several places in the text where incidents narrated by characters are supported by what Winkler calls 'evidential accountability': when telling a story, Lucius the narrator always seems to ensure that we are given the source of authority for what is told. See J.J. Winkler, *Auctor and Actor: A Narratological Reading of Apuleius's The Golden Ass* (Berkeley, 1985), 66f.

41. Cf. Apuleius, *The Golden Ass*, tr. W. Adlington, ed. S. Gaselee (London, 1958), xvi: 'This book of Lucius is a figure of a man's life, and toucheth the nature and manners of mortal men, egging them forward from their asinal form to their human and perfect shape, beside the pleasant and delectable jests therein contained . . .'

guarded: the audience is to be given the impression that the things it recounts could have happened.

Finally, the arguments offered here may perhaps reveal something about contemporary literary evaluation. Narratives—historical and fictional—can be regarded as being spread along a scale with fact (or factual narrative) at one end and fiction at the other. These two poles are not contrary opposites, any more than red and violet are, when we place them at different ends of a spectrum. All stories on the scale produce story worlds.

For these story worlds to be convincing, as we saw at the beginning of this enquiry, they must have community with the world of the reader's experience and community with other story worlds. (The two communities amount to the same thing: the world of our shared experience is constituted out of many story worlds which possess elements similar to each other.) 'Historical' stories, because they tend to have a great deal in common with both, are often the most convincing. However, stories which are now held to be purely literary or fictional—and therefore according to most people untrue—seem, strangely enough, still to be evaluated on the basis of how truthful and plausible they appear to the reader.[42] This suggests that our modern category of fiction is in the end as appropriate for a text like the *Met.*—which does aim to convince—as the ancient idea of 'beneficial lying'. The prevalent tendency of calling the *Met.* a 'novel' really indicates that the work is being commended. This shows that it satisfies at least some of our criteria for what makes a good story now.[43]

---

42. On some ancient views of the distinctions between true, false and 'true-to-life' stories, see Meijering op. cit., 76f.

43. I would like to thank Tony Free, Tim Morton and, particularly, Mark Edwards for some useful discussions. I am especially grateful to Don P. Fowler and to the Editors for reading drafts of this piece and suggesting some fundamental improvements.

Chapter Six

Make-believe and Make Believe: The Fictionality of the Greek Novels

J.R. Morgan

EXTENDED non-factual narration in prose—the novel—was the last addition to the family of classical literary genres. We have just five more or less complete examples in Greek, supplemented by a handful of summaries and adaptations, and, within the last hundred years, by an ever-increasing corpus of newly-discovered fragments.[1] What does it mean to call these works fiction? What were the protocols of fictionality controlling their production and consumption? This chapter looks for answers to these questions in two directions: first (I–II), by asking whether there was anything in ancient literary theory that may help to explain the form and practice of the novels; second (III–IV), by examining the attitudes to fiction implicit in the novels themselves. The second stage of the inquiry will turn out to yield rather more positive results than the first.

---

1. The complete novels are those of Chariton (Char.), Xenophon of Ephesus—possibly an epitome—(Xen. Eph.), Achilles Tatius (Ach. Tat.), Longus (Long.) and Heliodorus (Hld.). Translations of these and the most important supplementary material are accessible in B.P. Reardon, ed., *Collected Ancient Greek Novels* (*CAGN*) (Berkeley, 1989). I have used these translations, except where a small modification seemed necessary to bring out my point more clearly.

I

The reason for this is that in antiquity the novel was drastically undertheorized, even to the extent that there was no word for it in either Greek or Latin. There are plenty of words that can be used *of* it, but they all emphasize restricted aspects of the whole and can be applied to other things besides novels. People in the ancient world did, as we shall see, think about fiction, and some of what they thought is applicable to novels. But whereas all novels are fiction, not all fictions are novels. The ancient theories, in other words, were not formed to illuminate or explain novels, nor were they later employed to analyse novels, nor did the theorists ever, so far as we can tell, turn to novels for examples to illustrate their theories. In Bryan Reardon's words, the novel 'was not born in any context of theory or critical interest, but in spite of theory and critics' interests.'[2] Storytelling was no doubt practised throughout antiquity, but narrative fiction remained at an oral, subliterary level until the emergence of the literary romance, perhaps in the first century.[3] Even after that date, there are precious few references to novels, and even those are dismissive and uninformative.[4] We have no direct information as to why novels were written or how sympathetic readers responded to them. We can only assume that the mere existence of these texts indicates a market for them.

From our viewpoint this critical silence is infuriating but intriguing. Fiction is our dominant literary form, the first genre that most

---

2. B.P. Reardon, *The Form of Greek Romance (FGR)* (Princeton, 1991), 50. The discussion that follows is much indebted to Reardon's and should be read more as a supplement than substitute to his. For discussion of the novel from the perspective of ancient genre theory, see also H. Kuch, 'Die Herausbildung des antiken Romans als Literaturgattung', in H. Kuch, ed., *Der antike Roman* (Berlin, 1989), 11–51.

3. Chariton's date is uncertain; opinion ranges between c. 100 BC to c. AD 100; see Reardon *CAGN*, 17. The fragments of the *Ninus Romance* had become waste paper by AD 100, indicating a date of composition possibly in the first century BC.

4. Philostratus, *Lives of the Sophists* 1.524, *Epistles* 66; Julian, *Epistles* 89.301b (see below). The silence may be partly a result of chronology, as argued by E.L. Bowie, 'Who Read the Ancient Greek Novels?', in J. Tatum and G.M. Vernazza, eds, *The Ancient Novel: Classical Paradigms and Modern Perspectives* (Hanover, N.H., 1990), 150–1. But it is hard to believe that, if a critical interest in novels had existed, it should have disappeared without trace.

of us encounter as children, the category of literature that most of us choose to fill our homes with, certainly the source and repository of many of our culture's central icons and myths of the self. We understand almost by instinct how it works, and have no compunction about enjoying it across a wide spectrum of intentions. The ancient novels are not negligible as works of literature. Heliodorus, for one, is a demanding read even for those fully acculturated to following intricate fictional plots, and his novel is clearly presented as an interpretative challenge, intellectually and imaginatively. This sort of work simply would not have been written unless there were sophisticated people prepared to pay good money to read it. But the people who read these novels do not seem to have talked much about them. Macrobius, one of the few ancient critics even to acknowledge the existence of novels, is illuminating here:

> Stories (*fabulae*)—the very name denotes an admission of falsehood—are invented either merely to bestow pleasure on the ear or else to encourage the reader to virtue as well. The ear is delighted by comedies of the type which Menander and his followers produced, or by realistic narratives full of the fictitious adventures of lovers (*argumenta fictis casibus amatorum repleta*), with which Petronius engaged himself and Apuleius, amazingly, sometimes trifled. This whole category of stories, whose only purpose is to delight the ear, a philosophical treatise expels from its holy shrine and relegates them to nurses' cradles.
>
> (*In Somnium Scipionis* 1.2.7–8)

The works of Petronius and Apuleius are not really suitable for the nursery. They are 'adult' literature in the euphemistic sense. Macrobius' point is the limited intellectual capacity of their readers, and the assimilation of their writers to the tellers of old women's tales (*aniles fabulae*), nurses being axiomatically a storehouse of frightening or soothing stories.[5] Only the stupid bother with fiction. Even within his own terms Macrobius' comment is surprising. He goes on to suggest that philosophical allegory is the only form of *fabula* acceptable to a philosopher. That is understandable enough,

---

5. There is useful discussion of this and other contexts for narrative in A. Scobie, 'Storytellers, Storytelling, and the Novel in Greco–Roman Antiquity', *Rheinisches Museum* 122 (1979), 229–59.

but his separation of novels, as vehicles of mindless entertainment, from Aesopic fables, as useful for the philosophically less endowed, suggests that he was blind to the layers of allegory and ethical meaning which we find so obvious in Apuleius.

There is something odd going on. Though people of some sophistication bought and enjoyed novels, they seem to have read them within a frame of cultural values which somehow consigned the pleasures of novel-reading to the categories of the insignificant or in some way ambivalent. This is confirmed by a comment of the emperor Julian in the fourth century, recommending the sort of reading desirable for a pious pagan: history, he says, is useful,

> but we must reject all the fictions [*plasmata*] composed by writers of the past in the form of history [*en historias eidei*], narratives of love [*erōtikai hupotheseis*] and all that sort of stuff.[6]
>
> (*Epistles* 89.301b)

Julian here singles out the two defining characteristics of Greek novels which are most likely to have caused their critical neglect: their content (erotic) and their form, which is what concerns us here. It is not just that they are fictional. The problem is that novels are fictions couched in a form appropriate to and implying something else: factual history. What makes them dangerous is that they blur an essential dividing line between truth and untruth, that they invite a confusion between what is and what is not real. It is not difficult to see what characteristics might promote this confusion: the narrative mode shared with history, and the use of prose for fiction.

'There is some distance between prose and fiction' (Reardon *FGR*, 49). Verse highlights a text's distance from ordinary speech, its artificiality, its status as linguistic construct, the fact that it is not real. Prose, on the other hand, carries implicit claims to factuality. It is conventionally the medium of literature of information and analysis. And because it is closer to the 'natural' language of normal speech, it is able to take itself for granted, to ignore its nature as medium

---

6. That Julian is talking about novels here is confirmed by the recurrence of the phrase *erōtikai hupotheseis* in the Suda's entry on the novelist Xenophon of Cyprus (where it is joined with the word *historia*), and in Photius' summary of Iamblichus, applied to the works of Ach. Tat. and Hld.

and so pretend to a transparency denied to verse. It was thus possible to feel, though admittedly the feeling is not articulated in quite these terms, that fiction in verse foregrounds the telling rather than the substance, opening doors to linguistic and compositional devices (such as allegory, irony, coded self-reference, aesthetic distance) which acknowledge and so partly redeem the text's literal untruth; whereas prose presents the reader with ostensibly unmediated fiction-as-reality. Of course, the very immediacy of the prose medium was one of the romancer's prime assets, allowing direct engagement of reader with the events of the narrative. Instinctively, novelists were drawn to exploit the very possibilities of the genre which most offended unsympathetic observers.

Greek difficulties with fiction go way back. Plutarch tells an illuminating anecdote about Solon, the Athenian legislator and wise man, and Thespis, the originator of tragedy. Solon attended one of Thespis' performances to see what all the fuss was about,

> . . . and after the show he spoke to him and asked if he was not ashamed of telling such great lies [*pseudomenos*] in front of so many people. Thespis replied that there was nothing wrong with doing and saying such things in play [*meta paidias*] . . . 'But,' Solon replied, 'if we praise and honour this play we shall soon find it in our serious business.'[7]
>
> (Plutarch, *Life of Solon* 29.7)

This little exchange, itself a fiction to discredit fiction, is emblematic. From Solon's absolutist viewpoint, an untruth is a lie, regardless of intention, effect or context; Solon's wording does not suggest that Thespis was trying to deceive his audience, nor that the audience was induced to accept falsehood as truth. Any licence granted to fiction is likely to result in similar licence being granted to lying in a context where deception is an issue and unacceptable. Significantly, Solon emerges victorious from the exchange; even in the second century, seven hundred years later, Plutarch's implied reader instinctively endorses the distrust of fiction.

---

7. I translate the text as emended by S.A. Naber. As transmitted, the final phrase reads 'in our contracts'. The basic point is not affected.

But Thespis' side of the dialogue is equally important. He represents the creator of artistic fiction who knows intuitively that fiction and lies are not synonymous but as yet lacks the conceptual vocabulary to give a satisfactory account of the difference. We can help him out: the necessary condition of fiction is that both sender and recipient are aware that it is factually untrue. There is no intent to deceive; but there is also a tacit agreement between the two parties to act as if what they know to be untrue is true. A mutual game of make-believe. This is what Thespis is getting at by using the word 'play', and he has a profound point: fiction for adults continues the imaginative exploration of the self and others begun in children's games of make-believe; it is a necessary tool of self-development. However, the anecdote in which Thespis is cast assigns to the fictional consent a word correlative with the Greek for 'child' (*pais*). The fictional Thespis can do no more than protest the infantile harmlessness of his art, and, as with Macrobius, fiction is relegated, by its own inventor, to the nursery and the weak-minded.

We should not underestimate the persistence of this hostility to fiction. If Thespis offers the germ of one possible defence, there was another, diametrically opposite: for fiction to conceal itself, at least at a formal level.[8] It can be made as factual as possible; authority can be found for it; at the last resort it can be simply held at a distance from the teller. We shall return to this in the novels, but the effect was general. For example, the rhetorician Theon (c. 1–2 AD) giving advice on the use of *muthoi*, which he defines as 'an untrue discourse (*logos pseudēs*) acting as a simile for truth (*eikonizōn alētheian*)' and identifies primarily with Aesopic fables, suggests that a speaker should tell them in the accusative case, that is, in a construction of indirect speech, not in his own person, simultaneously disclaiming personal responsibility for the fiction and implying that it has external authority (*Progymnasmata* 3 = Spengel, *Rhetores Graeci* 2, 72.28–74.27). The striking point is that even a fiction like an animal fable, which had not the slightest intention of being taken as literal truth, should be treated with such squeamishness.

More positive valuations of fiction existed. Gorgias, in the fifth century BC, is reported to have said that the tragic poet who deceives

---

8. Cf. B.E. Perry, *The Ancient Romances* (Berkeley, 1967), 66ff.

is more just than the non-deceiver, and the spectator who succumbs to the deception is wiser than the one who resists (fr. 23). The oxymoron is deliberately intriguing, but makes the exact sense obscure.[9] Gorgias' point may be less sophisticated than we should like; it may be that the spectator's 'wisdom' is the product rather than the precondition of his deception. This would be taking on Solon on his own ground, admitting the identity of fiction and deceit but suggesting that tragedy imparts benefits greater than the harm of the deception: it is a benevolent lie. Gorgias fails to take up Thespis' point that there is a qualitative and moral difference between fiction and lying. On this reading, any Gorgianic defence of the novel as it existed four hundred years later would stress its utility (if any) *despite* its fictionality.

In fact Gorgias' stress on the idea of deception (*apatē*) denies the premiss of fiction. For him, the power of the word is so great as to compel or seduce the audience into taking fiction for fact, so that it ceases to be an audience of fiction at all. Plato, on the other hand, came close to acknowledging that fiction is a game played by two participants. I need do no more here than refer to excellent discussions by Christopher Gill and Bryan Reardon.[10] However, we must note that Plato's thoughts on fiction, ahead of their time as they may be, have to be teased out of their context, and never entered the currency of ancient literary criticism. They are a massive cultural achievement, but not a shaping factor in the horizons of the Greek novel.

More widely influential were the works of Aristotle and his school. The discussion of poetic *mimēsis* (imitation, representation)[11] in the *Poetics* especially presents a compelling defence of fiction. This

---

9. On Gorgias, see T.G. Rosenmeyer, 'Gorgias, Aeschylus and *Apatē*', *American Journal of Philology* 76 (1955), 225–60; C.P. Segal, 'Gorgias and the Psychology of the *Logos*', *Harvard Studies in Classical Philology* 66 (1962), 99–155; W.J. Verdenius, 'Gorgias' Doctrine of Deception', in G.B. Kerferd, ed., *The Sophists and their Legacy* (Wiesbaden, 1981), 116–28; and Denis Feeney, pp. 236–7 below.

10. C. Gill, 'Plato's Atlantis Story and the Birth of Fiction', *Philosophy and Literature* 3 (1979), 64–78; Reardon, *FGR*, 62ff. Gill presents a modified version of his position at pp. 62–6 above.

11. Sometimes explicitly translated as 'fiction', notably by L.J. Potts, *Aristotle on the Art of Fiction* (Cambridge, 1953).

has been so widely discussed that a bare summary will suffice.[12] Aristotle envisaged the poet's task as the construction of a stripped-down version of reality, an action with the contingencies removed so that the operation of universal laws of cause and effect (probability, *to eikos*) become clear:

> It is not the poet's function to describe what has actually happened, but the kinds of thing that might happen, that is, that could happen, because they are in the circumstances either probable or necessary.
>
> (*Poetics* 1451a36–8.)

He is well aware that probability so conceived may result in plots depicting actions of a kind unlikely ever to occur in real life, because actual existence is perpetually choked up with contingencies that may deflect the play of universals. But 'probable impossibilities are to be preferred to improbable possibilities' (1460a26–7). In other words, verisimilitude, in the sense of plausible representation of the way things really are, is rejected in favour of an unrealistic abstraction demonstrating how individual experience is structured by generalities of cause and effect. Fiction mediates between history, whose concern is with the particular, and philosophy, which deals in disembodied universals.

This is potent stuff, but it doesn't get us far with the novels. It is no doubt possible and correct to read the deep structure of the novels as a myth of general reference, at least within the late Hellenistic world.[13] But as individual expressions of that deep structure, the novels are profoundly un-Aristotelian texts. Instead of clarifying the workings of probability by removing particularities, the novelists crammed their texts with contingent detail whose effect is to render the action concrete and specific. The impulse is exactly the opposite of that delineated by Aristotle, and has exactly opposite motives.

---

12. For useful accounts see J.M. Redfield, *Nature and Culture in the Iliad* (Chicago, 1975), 55ff.; K. Eden, *Poetic and Legal Fiction in the Aristotelian Tradition* (Princeton, 1986), 32ff.; R. Newsom, *A Likely Story: Probability and Play in Fiction* (New Brunswick, 1988), 1ff.

13. This is the theme of Perry, op. cit. (n. 8 above), 44ff., restated by Reardon, *FGR*, 28ff.

Whereas tragedy, on the Aristotelian view, strives to reveal the general within the particular for philosophical reasons, the novels strive to clothe the general with particulars to give an illusion of historical reality, and to enable the exploitation of uncertainty about the course of the story for reasons of excitement. Moreover, while Aristotle's focus was narrowed on to a single action (compare his comments about unity of plot at 1459a17ff.), by and large the structure of the novels is multiple and serial. The form denies and avoids rather than seeks and values unity and closure. Thirdly, the Aristotelian concept of probability finds a much reduced application in the novels. With their stress on the unexpected and exciting, what happens to their central characters usually occurs in spite of, rather than because of, their characters and actions. The novelists' search for the drama of surprise promoted the irruption of unmotivated and unforeseen destructive forces, and as a result the hero came to be cast more as destiny's victim than as its agent. Probability made way for coincidence, and profoundly meaningful reversals are reduced to simple misfortunes, which bring no enlightenment in their wake. When hero and heroine are perfect to begin with, there is no scope for tragic error or flaw as motor of the fictional action, nor for learning through suffering.

But if Aristotle's ideas on fiction had little direct effect on the practice of the novels, they did provide the starting point for a series of discussions of fiction in the Aristotelian tradition. Key ideas were chewed over and popularized. Thus the notion of 'cleansing' (Aristotle's *katharsis*, cf. *Poetics* 1449b28) surfaces in a much debased form in the introduction to the last book of the novel by Chariton of Aphrodisias:

> I think that this last chapter will prove very pleasurable [*hēdiston*] to its readers; it cleanses away [*katharsion gar esti*] the grim events of the earlier ones.
>
> (8.1.4)

The conjunction of pleasure and cleansing must be an echo of Peripatetic literary theory, if not of Aristotle himself.[14]

---

14. Cf. C.W. Müller, 'Chariton von Aphrodisias und die Theorie des Romans in der Antike', *Antike und Abendland* 22 (1976), 115–36; A. Rijksbaron, 'Chariton 8, 1, 4 und Aristot. *Poet.* 1449b28', *Philologus* 128 (1984), 306–7.

We do not know exactly how the debate on fiction was conducted in the generations following Aristotle. But among the list of the works of his pupil Theophrastus, Diogenes Laertius preserves an intriguing title: *Peri pseudous hēdonēs*, which seems to mean 'On the pleasure of untruth' (or fiction?). It would also be worth knowing what Theophrastus had to say in his 'On truth and untruth' (*Peri pseudous kai alēthous*). However, Theophrastus' most important influence seems to have been less direct. He is reported to have written a work 'On history' (*Peri historias*), and his pupil Duris of Samos, himself a historian, turns up using the key Aristotelian idea of *mimēsis*, again conjoined with pleasure, to attack the practice of other writers of history:

> Ephorus and Theopompus fell far short of the events. They achieved no imitation/representation [*mimēsis*] or pleasure [*hēdonē*] in their presentation, but were concerned merely with writing.
>
> (Jacoby, *Fragmente der griechischen Historiker* 76 F 1)[15]

Deprived of context, this is very opaque; but at the risk of over-simplification we can hazard something on the following lines. Pleasure is a legitimate function of historiography. It will not be produced if the historian merely writes a text. Instead, he must try to present his reader with a dramatic re-enactment of events, just as for Aristotle tragedy re-enacted or imitated action. Only in this way can the reality of the past be conveyed. Duris' problem, of course, is that historiography cannot be literally re-enactive or representational in the way that drama can, but his ideal seems to be that the text should be so transparent as to belie its status as writing and aspire to the unmediated vividness of dramatic presentation. This cannot be done without the exercise of imagination.

Here we have, apparently, the theoretical foundation for the practice of much Hellenistic historiography. For Duris it was a

---

15. See further H. Strasburger, *Die Wesensbestimmung der Geschichte durch die antike Geschichtsschreibung* (Wiesbaden, 1966), 40ff.; C.W. Fornara, *The Nature of History in Ancient Greece and Rome* (Berkeley, 1983), 124ff.; V. Gray, 'Mimesis in Greek Historical Theory', *American Journal of Philology* 108 (1987), 467–86; L. Torraca, *Duride di Samo: la maschera scenica nella storiografia ellenistica* (Salerno, 1988).

serious question, uncannily reminiscent of modern debate, of how best the true essence of the past might be communicated; but in the hands of less philosophical writers it served rather to legitimize the intrusion of novelistic and sensational material into historiography.[16] Certainly, during the Hellenistic period, the house of history became a home for narrative whose purpose was to give pleasure and which had at least a touch of the imaginative about it. We can get an idea of what was at issue from a passage of the Roman rhetorician Quintilian:

> The mere statement that a town was stormed, while no doubt it embraces all that such a calamity involves, has all the curtness of a dispatch and fails to penetrate to the emotions of the audience. But if we expand all that the one word 'stormed' includes, we shall see the flames pouring from house and temple, and hear the crash of falling roofs and one confused clamour blent of many cries; we shall behold some in doubt whither to fly, others clinging to their nearest and dearest in one final embrace, while the wailing of women and children and the laments of old men . . . will fall upon our ears. Then will come the pillage of treasure sacred and profane, the hurrying to and fro of the plunderers as they carry off their booty . . . the prisoners cowering each before his own inhuman captor, the mother struggling to keep her child . . . All these things are included in the sack of a city, and it is less effective to tell the whole news at once than to recount it detail by detail. We shall secure the vividness we seek if only our descriptions give the impression of truth; indeed, we may even add fictitious incidents of the type which commonly occur.
>
> (*Institutio Oratoria* 8.3.67)

Obviously, from the point of view of strict historical accuracy, such creative historiography can be construed as a deceptive falsehood, in opposition to factual truth. Thus Polybius, in his own field an heir of Solon, introduces his famous attack on the romantic historian Phylarchus by expressing his concern that 'falsehood (*to*

---

16. W. Bartsch, *Der Charitonroman und die Historiographie* (Leipzig, 1934), in showing the proximity of Chariton to historiography, demonstrates even more clearly the proximity of much Hellenistic historiography to fiction.

pseudos) shall not be allowed to enjoy equal authority with truth (*hē alētheia*)' (2.56.2). Would Thespis have granted Phylarchus the licence of play? This depends on the presuppositions brought to a text by its readers. So long as they understood the protocols, the rules by which Phylarchus was playing, so long as they were aware, that is, that any belief they were invited to entertain about the text was itself part of a fiction, then Phylarchus could be called something other than a liar. Clearly in a work that advertised itself as historical, those protocols would become exceedingly delicate, and many must have assumed that they were reading the literal truth, who were deceived by an untruth (compare Julian's touchiness about fiction *in the form of history*).

Nevertheless, even if the fictional conspiracy of writer and reader was not invoked in so many words by historians of this type, it may be held to have been activated by the importance attached to *pleasure* as a function of historical narrative. A reader engaging with a text for pleasure has already effectively conceded that information is at most a secondary function. Hence Polybius' insistence that effects of emotional pleasure are to be grouped with plausibility as characteristic of tragedy, as distinct from history, whose province is truth and utility:

> The tragic poet seeks to thrill and charm his audience for the moment through the most plausible discourse possible [*dia tōn pithanōtatōn logōn*], but the historian's task is to instruct and persuade serious students by means of true actions and words [*dia tōn alēthinōn ergōn kai logōn*] . . . Thus in the first case the supreme aim is plausibility [*to pithanon*], even if what is said is untrue, the purpose being to deceive the spectator, but in the second it is truth [*alēthes*], the purpose being to benefit the reader.
>
> (2.56.11–12)

I think this is crucial for understanding the expectations that were eventually brought to bear on the novel. Without wishing to revert to any evolutionary theory about the origin of the novel,[17] I suggest

---

17. See Perry's polemic against this idea, op. cit. (n. 8 above), 32ff. On the passage just cited, see T.P. Wiseman, p. 134 above.

that it was within historiography itself that the contract of fictional complicity was first extended to narrative prose, thus allowing fiction, recognized and generally, if reluctantly, licensed elsewhere, to enter a new form and generate a new and more equivocal literature of pleasure in prose: fiction in the form of history. We are still a long way from a novel, because the vital ingredient of plot is missing, but it can hardly be coincidental that it is in relation to figures of the historical past that the characteristic romance myth finds its first embodiments: the Ninus Romance, Chariton, *Parthenope and Metiochus*.[18] There is a continuity between historiography and fiction, which was exploited to define and enhance the form of and the response appropriate to realistic fiction.

By this point, Aristotle's notion of *probability* has shifted to something more like *verisimilitude*: a very different proposition both aesthetically and philosophically, whose operation in the novels we shall soon be discussing. However, Peripatetic concerns with history and fiction surface also in the rhetorical treatment of narrative. It will be worthwhile to examine this briefly, if only because rhetoric formed the backbone of the ancient educational system, and it is there if anywhere that ideas familiar to readers and writers of novels are to be found.

The purpose of rhetoric was to teach the art of effective speaking. Rhetoricians consequently devote much attention to the best construction of different types of speech. One recognized element in a court-room speech was the exposition of the facts of the case in the form of a narrative (in Latin *narratio*, in Greek *diēgēsis*). It goes without saying that even here a lawyer's concern would not be for absolute truth but for the success of his case. The *diēgēsis* will be partisan, but it must not be obviously so; it must give the impression of being a dispassionate statement of fact. In short, it must be plausible. In this context, plausibility is more important than truth, and teachers of rhetoric tried to define it and analyse how it could be

---

18. Ninus: P. Berol. 6926 + P.S.I. 1305, Reardon, *CAGN*, 803–8. *Metiochus and Parthenope*: P. Berol. 7927, 9588, 21179, Reardon, *CAGN*, 813–5. There is further discussion of history in these texts below.

achieved. The doctrine remained pretty static over the years; here is a typical example from Cicero in the first century BC:

> The narrative will be plausible [*probabilis*] if in it there seem to be those things which are accustomed to appear in reality [*in veritate*]; if the social standing of the characters is observed, if the reasons for action are clear, if there seems to have been a possibility for acting, if it can be shown that the moment was suitable, that there was enough room and the location was appropriate to the thing narrated; if the event fits with the nature of those who do it, with general custom and with the belief of the audience. By these means it can be made realistic [*veri similis*].
>
> (*De inventione* 1.29)

and a few lines further on:

> That thing is plausible [*probabile*] which generally happens, or which is a matter of general belief, or which has within itself some similarity to these things, whether it is true or untrue [*sive id falsum est sive verum*].
>
> (Ibid. 1.46)

The stress is on producing a narrative which could have happened, that is, one which is a believable reconstruction of particular events at a particular time and place in the past; the action must be accommodated to the particulars of its setting. The contrast with Aristotle's predictive generalities could hardly be greater. Second, there is a clear-headed awareness that non-truths can be made verisimilar, and that truth itself is no guarantee of plausibility. And thirdly, the mechanisms by which the truth-effect can be produced combine correspondence (the ways things happen in reality) with coherence (the story's internal logics of character and situation must be sustained). The importance of circumstantial detail is particularly stressed. The advice would be as useful to a novelist as to an orator, though it is too vague to be of much immediate practical utility to either, and simply systematizes what both would instinctively be doing anyway. But it is enough to note that people were being taught to value and recognize verisimilitude even in a narrative which they knew to be fictional.

Rhetorical interest in narrative is also apparent in the familiar classification of narrative according to its truth-content.[19] This is commonplace among rhetoricians, though with insignificant variations of detail and terminology. It is worth noting that the classification explicitly extends beyond the forensic; although rhetoricians include it because their pupils were encouraged to practise the skills of narration on widely varied material, its concern to categorize the whole of literature, and the frequent use of examples from drama and epic, suggest that it had its origins in a literary theory, most likely Peripatetic.

The essential point of the scheme is that the obvious division of narrative into true and false is refined by sub-dividing the false into the false but like the truth, and the false and unlike the truth.[20] The forensic or the political is sometimes added to these as a fourth category, but, more logically, it is often reserved outside them in a preliminary division into forensic and non-forensic. The three types of narrative are presented as co-ordinate. True narrative is often associated with history (it is termed *alēthēs, historia, historikon*), the false and unlike the truth with myth or tragedy (*fabula, muthos, muthikon*), but is also sometimes designated simply 'untrue' (*pseudos*). A typical definition is that 'it comprises events neither true nor like the truth' (*neque veras neque veri similes continet res*) (*Rhetorica ad Herennium* 1.13).

The third category is the interesting one. It comprises 'made-up events which nevertheless could have happened' (*ficta res quae tamen fieri potuit*) (ibid.). In Latin it is called *argumentum* ('subject, theme, plot'), in Greek we find *plasma* ('invention'), *plasmatikon*, or *hōs alēthēs* ('like truth') or *dramatikon*.[21] When it is illustrated, it is

---

19. On this division, see R. Reitzenstein, *Hellenistische Wundererzählungen* (Leipzig, 1906), 90ff.; K. Kerényi, *Die griechisch-orientalische Romanliteratur in religionsgeschichtlicher Beleuchtung* (Tübingen, 1927), 1ff.; K. Barwick, 'Die Gliederung der Narratio in der rhetorischen Theorie und ihre Bedeutung für die Geschichte des antiken Romans', *Hermes* 63 (1928), 261–87; F. Pfister, 'Isokrates und die spätere Gliederung der Narratio', *Hermes* 68 (1933), 457–60; J. Martin, *Antike Rhetorik* (Munich, 1974), 75ff.

20. It is odd that the logic of the division found no place for the true but like the false.

21. On the history of this word, which in Byzantine writers signifies, more or less, 'novel', see E. Rohde, *Der griechische Roman und seiner Vorlaüfer*, 3rd edn, (Leipzig, 1914), 376ff.

with an example from New Comedy, or else it is simply compared to 'comedy', implicitly of the Menandrian rather than the Aristophanic kind. The terminology is highly artificial; the distinctions made between *pseudos* and *plasma*, or *argumentum* and *fabula*, do not correspond to any inherent nuances in the words. The very arbitrariness of the vocabulary suggests that this is possibly less an attempt to categorize literature in a helpful way than to use literature to illustrate a logical schematization.

What the categorization lacks is any element of intentionality. The true, by definition, is not meant to deceive; the fabulous, again by definition, cannot deceive (though it may try); but is a *plasma* a plausible lie or a plausible fiction? The answer seems to be that it could be either; the classification was simply not framed to deal with that point. Sometimes the third category is glossed with the Greek word *amphidoxon*[22] which can be applied to a person with doubts in his mind or one who causes doubts in other people, like a witness of dubious reliability. This ambiguity makes the whole scheme an inherently flawed tool for thinking about fiction.

Another ambiguity concerns the exact distinction between the fabulous and the lifelike. What are the qualities of an untruth that might make it like or unlike the truth? There is a lot of room for subjectivity at the margin, and the illustrations ignore the difficulty by choosing clear-cut examples. However, we can perhaps say that as the examples from tragedy all concern the supernatural or physically impossible (Medea's snake-drawn chariot, the birth of the Titans, half-man half-snake, Cyclopes and Centaurs) verisimilitude was being conceived in a narrow correspondential sense, not coherentially as a property of plot in itself. So long as each incident stays within the realm of natural or normal possibility, the overall improbability of a story would not disqualify it from being classified as a *plasma* rather than a *pseudos*. Novelists do in fact take pains to observe natural laws, to avoid the supernatural and find rational explanations for every incident. A novel would presumably fit into the category of the lifelike, but it must be emphasized that, although novels naturally tended to operate within parameters of plausibility

---

22. Admittedly only in very late authors. For references see Barwick art. cit. (n. 19 above), 269 n. 2.

made familiar by rhetorical theory, that theory was never explicitly applied to the novel as a literary phenomenon.

In passing, we should mention a peculiar variant of this classification found in virtually identical form in two Latin treatises of the first century BC (Cicero, *de inventione* 1.27 and the anonymous *Rhetorica ad Herennium* 1.12), both presumably using the same lost Greek source. Here the three-fold division in terms of truth is applied only to narrative 'based on actions' (*quod in negotiis . . . positum est*). Against this is set a form of narrative 'based on persons' (*in personis positum*). The way that this is described has made some scholars see a connection with romantic fiction:[23]

> A narrative based on the persons should present a lively style, contrast of character, austerity and gentleness, hope and fear, distrust and desire, hypocrisy and compassion, vicissitudes, change of fortune, unexpected disaster, sudden joy, and a happy ending.
>
> (*Rhet. ad Herenn.* 1.13)

Taken at face value, the classification seems to suggest that this type of narrative works without reference to truth or falsehood. This would clearly be an implication of some significance if we were dealing with an embryonic novel here, but the possibility evaporates on examination. The characteristics of person-based narrative are echoed in Cicero's letter to the historian Lucceius (*Epistulae ad familiares* 5.12), where he is asking for a literarily elaborated and emotionally charged account of his own consulship. This means that the category is not one of pure fiction, and that considerations of truth and falsehood are just as relevant as in event-based narrative. The anomalous division is probably no more than the result of a confused attempt to superimpose two different ways of classifying narrative: the three-fold division according to truth, and a two-fold one, familiar from Plato onwards (*Republic* 392c) of simple narrative against dramatic presentation.

Lastly, we should note a passage of Augustine's *Soliloquies*, where, belatedly, we find a proper recognition of the licence of

---

23. Cf. Kerényi, op. cit. (n. 19 above), 20ff.

fiction. This occurs in a discussion of falsehood, one category of which consists of 'things which feign to be that which they are not'. This category is then subdivided according to intention:

> This type of falsehood [*falsum*] is either deceptive [*fallax*] or untrue [*mendax*]. That is properly called deceptive which has some intention of deceiving [*quod habet quendam fallendi appetitum*] . . . But that which I call untrue [*mendax*] is done by those who tell untruths [*a mentientibus*]. It differs from the deceptive in this respect, that every deceiver intends to deceive but not everyone who tells an untruth wishes to deceive; for mimes and comedies and many poems are full of untruths [*mendaciorum plena sunt*], more with the aim of delighting than of deceiving [*delectandi potius quam fallendi voluntate*], and almost anyone who tells a joke tells an untruth. But that man is properly called deceptive or deceiving [*fallax vel fallens*] whose purpose is that everyone should be deceived. On the other hand those who do it not in order to deceive but nevertheless make something up [*aliquid fingunt*], no one doubts that they are called merely untruthful [*mendaces*] or if not even that, speakers of untruths [*mentientes*].
>
> (*Soliloquies* 2.9.16)[24]

My translation labours to preserve Augustine's etymological connections, but the essential point is clear enough. A clear distinction is made between lying (or deceiving) and fiction, in terms of both the writer's intention and the audience's response (deceived or delighted). This is a significant beginning, though we still need to define the special kind of delight that fiction can impart, and its relation to plausibility and belief. Augustine still does not mention novels, although we know that he had read at least Apuleius' *Metamorphoses*. It seems as if the fictionality of the prose novel was still for him more ambiguous and delicate than that of mimes, comedies and epics. After all, Augustine writes elsewhere as if he

---

24. Cf. Eden, op. cit. (n. 12 above), 120ff.

half believed Apuleius' story, and insofar as he doubted its truth, did not extend any fictional licence to it:

> Apuleius either reported or invented [*aut indicavit aut finxit*] that it happened to him that, having taken a potion, he became an ass, without losing his human mind. These things are either falsehoods [*falsa*] or so abnormal that they are deservedly not believed.
>
> (*Civitas Dei* 18.18).

II

This continuing ambivalence towards novels leads into the theme of the second half of this chapter. The problem is not essentially one of the text's truth-status, since the first condition of fiction is that both sides recognize it for what it is. It is more to do with how a reader is supposed to react to a text which he knows to be fictional, and in particular to what extent and in what sense he 'believes' the fiction. Novels exist for pleasure, and the foremost of their pleasures is vicarious emotional involvement. Readers want to experience from a secure imaginative distance situations and feelings which they are unlikely to experience in their real lives, indeed, which they would often go to great lengths to avoid. It is not easy, however, to see how anyone can experience real emotions about something which he knows to be unreal.[25] 'We are affected only as we believe,' said Dr Johnson; 'disbelieving I dislike,' said Horace.[26] Even in these sophisticated days of post-modernism, the vast majority of readers want their fiction to be believable.

If it makes sense at all to talk about believing fiction, the belief must clearly be different in kind rather than degree from that accorded to straightforwardly factual statements (or lies for that matter). The theme to be explored here is that the reader's belief is

---

25. There is a large philosophical literature about the precise status of belief and emotion in relation to fiction. For recent discussion and references, see G. Currie, *The Nature of Fiction* (Cambridge, 1990), 182ff.; K. Walton, *Mimesis as Make-Believe* (Cambridge, Mass., 1991), 195ff.; Newsom, op. cit. (n. 12 above) is useful from a more literary perspective.

26. *Lives of the English Poets*, Gray, para. 41; *Ars Poetica*, 188.

itself part of the fiction, that, as part of the rules of the game, the reader undertakes imaginatively to believe what he knows to be fiction. This is what most people observably still do when reading novels, and such imaginative belief, make-believe, can (indeed cannot not) exist in tandem with objective and conscious awareness of fictionality. In this respect at least, ancient novels are not so very different from modern ones, and this double structure of belief and disbelief is inscribed, through various devices of proximity and distance, in their very texts.

We are going to be dealing a lot with that mythical creature, 'the reader', so it may be as well to begin with a real reader of ancient Greek novels, whose responses encapsulate the theme. In the ninth century the Byzantine patriarch Photius ran a reading circle. Members read various works of literature which they summarized for the benefit of the others. These summaries and commentaries were recorded by Photius for his absent brother. Among them were a few novels; those by Heliodorus and Achilles Tatius survive, but for others, the *Babyloniaca* of Iamblichus, or the *Wonders beyond Thule* of Antonius Diogenes, Photius provides invaluable evidence. In the cases of Heliodorus and Achilles,[27] he contents himself with designating the works as novels (the word he uses is *dramatikon*) and makes no further comment on their fictionality, confining himself to comments on prose style and morality. These works were unproblematic for him. He knew them to be fictions and the very act of categorizing them as such apparently left him free to discuss them in terms other than truth or falsehood. We have, in effect, a tacit recognition of fiction as a distinct, autonomous literary form.

The prose style of Iamblichus also comes in for praise, but now Photius adds that the author was worthy to demonstrate his powers of style and composition on something more serious than 'frivolous fictions' (*paignia kai plasmata*—still the etymological connection with childishness). On one hand, his phrasing suggests that any

---

27. Hld. is summarized in codex 73 of Photius' *Bibliotheca*; Ach. Tat. in cod. 87. Iamblichus (cod. 94) is in Reardon, *CAGN*, 783–97; Antonius Diogenes (cod. 166) in *CAGN*, 775–82. For a general discussion of Photius' treatment of the literature he summarizes (though without specific reference to the novels) see T. Hägg, *Photios als Vermittler antiker Literatur* (= Studia Graeca Upsaliensia 8) (Uppsala, 1975).

fiction would be a waste of this author's talents; an implied hierarchization of literature with the novel near the bottom. On the other, the way those talents are itemized includes one, construction and disposition of material in narrative form, which seems appropriate only to narrative fiction; in other words, Photius' reservations concerned this novel rather than all novels. Either way, however, Photius was prepared to accord the novel some place, albeit lowly, in its own right and not subject it to an irrelevant judgmental scale of truth and falsehood. His unreflective reaction presumably mirrors that of the countless silent owners of such romantic texts.

However, the codex dealing with Antonius Diogenes demonstrates a rather different and very interesting critical response. Again, the work is categorized as fiction (*dramatikon*), and throughout his discussion Photius repeatedly recognizes its fictionality, even locating it in a literary history relative to other, more canonical novels. As a fiction, it possesses, he says, a particular pleasure in that 'while it is close to the mythical and incredible [*muthōn engus kai apistōn*] it presents the material of its narrative in an absolutely credible fiction and elaboration [*en pithanōtatēi plasei kai diaskeuēi*]' (*Bibliotheca* codex 166.109a11–12). His reading of the novel is poised in a tension between the two kinds of untruth of the rhetorical division, the credible (*plasma* or here *plasis*, glossed with the superlative of the adjective *pithanos*, 'believable, trustworthy') and the incredible (*muthos*, here expanded with a word made from a root meaning 'believe' with a negative prefix).

Fiction and belief are centrally at issue here. Fiction, he seems to be saying, is particularly pleasing if it dances on the edge of the precipice, simultaneously defying and compelling belief. A novel should not try to reproduce the kind of experience available to each and every reader in his daily life; we want thrills and wonders. At the same time, the actualization of the material has to possess believability; thrills and wonders are less exciting if the realistic illusion is not maintained. Plausibility does not produce belief—Photius knew he was reading fiction, and wanted us to know he knew—but fiction's peculiar delight is the illusion of belief, an imagined credence won by the text and willingly given by the reader, but continually subject to inspection. Reader and text are both playing a double game of belief and disbelief, truth and fiction.

Actually, Antonius seems to have been exploiting this doubleness with especial subtlety.[28] The title of his novel, *Apista huper Thoulēn*, plays on two senses of the word *apistos*: (a) untrustworthy, false; (b) amazing, hard to believe . . . but true. There existed a whole sub-genre of *apista* literature, travellers' tales of the 'fact is stranger than fiction' type, the whole appeal of which was that the incredibilia in which it dealt were actually true. This strand begins with Herodotus, and is satirized by Lucian in his *True Histories*.[29] Doubtless many of the marvels were fabricated, but their value as entertainment would be negated if the reader acknowledged it. So to proclaim incredibility was to claim truthfulness. By setting a romantic fiction within this paradoxographical framework, Antonius produced a novel whose plausibility as fiction rested directly on its implausibility as fact. This was reinforced by a convoluted apparatus of authorization, detailing how an autobiographical document had been buried in the protagonist's grave, later discovered, and was now being published for the first time.[30]

At one level, Photius successfully sensed and came very close to articulating the inherent doubleness of plausible fiction. Yet there still came a point when he was deceived into responding to fiction as if it were fact. Eager to date Antonius, he was seduced into accepting the fictional provenance as real, coming up with an answer (Antonius was writing soon after Alexander) which is wildly off-beam. Furthermore, some of his comments on the story itself suggest that he thought he was facing an untruth laying claim to veracity, that is a lie:

> He claims to have seen other similar things, and tells tall tales of having seen men and other things which no one else claims to have seen or heard and no one even imagined. And the most

28. For an interesting view of Antonius, see J. Romm, 'Novel *contra* Encyclopaedia: *The Wonders beyond Thule* of Antonius Diogenes', in Tatum and Vernazza (n. 4 above), 49.

29. The basic survey is K. Ziegler, 'Paradoxographoi', in Pauly-Wissowa *Real-Encyclopädie der classischen Altertumswissenschaft* 18.3 (1949), 1137–66. The word *apista* appeared in the titles of works by, for example, Pytheas of Massilia and Isigonus of Nicaea.

30. On this motif, cf. W. Speyer, *Bücherfunde in der Glaubenswerbung der Antike* (Göttingen, 1970), 43ff. Modern novels like Umberto Eco's *The Name of the Rose* or Milorad Pavić's *Dictionary of the Khazars* exploit the idea in a playful and self-conscious way.

incredible of all, that by travelling to the north they came close to the moon . . . and there they saw the things which it is likely that a man who had already invented such an excess of inventions would see.

(1114a4–11)

It is unclear whether this is aimed at author or narrator, but Photius' indignation is directed not at the implausibility of a fiction but at simple untruthfulness. His difficulties are emblematic. He knew that the whole thing was make-believe, but the text, in trying to make the reader believe, succeeded only too well and ended up forfeiting its status as fiction.[31]

If no one in the ancient world successfully theorized the dynamics of novel-reading, the instinctive competence of actual readers was, as ever, more advanced than any theoretical analysis. The dynamics are clearly written into the novels themselves, which both proclaim and pretend to conceal their fictionality, both make-believe and make believe. In the following discussion, I shall sketch each of these tendencies in turn, and end with an attempt to characterize the tension.

III

The cluster of devices whose function is to win the reader's fictional belief in the fiction can for convenience be called realism.[32] To begin on the most external level, many of the Greek novels have titles which are historiographical in form. *Aethiopica*, *Babyloniaca*, *Ephesiaca* could, and did, serve as titles for both novels and histories. Other novels come to us with titles including the names of hero and heroine, but even these take the form of an ostensibly factual proposition. 'Events concerning Chaereas and Callirhoe', the title of

---

31. Perhaps this is an inevitable hazard of the game of fiction. There are plenty of modern instances of people forgetting the fictionality of fiction. Many people believe Sherlock Holmes to be a real person, partly through the sheer charisma of the character, but largely, I suspect, because of Dr Watson's function as authenticating apparatus. Radio and television serials are notoriously taken as reality. There the medium authenticates itself.

32. There is a good discussion, from a rather different perspective, by K. Treu, 'Der Realitätsgehalt des antiken Romans', in H. Kuch, ed. (n. 2 above), 107–25.

Chariton's novel, for example, implies that events took place. We must not make too much of these titles, because, with the exception of Heliodorus' *Aethiopica*, we cannot be sure whether they are the author's own; but it is still worth making the point that no ancient novel is called anything like *Pride and Prejudice, To the Lighthouse* or *The Code of the Woosters*. An ancient reader looking at the outside of a scroll was holding literally 'fiction in the form of history'.

Within the novels, the represented world is, without exception, explicitly identified with reality. Here are the openings of the narratives of the five extant novels:

> The Syracusan general Hermocrates, the man who defeated the Athenians had a daughter called Callirhoe (Chariton);

> Among the most influential citizens of Ephesus was a man called Lycomedes (Xenophon of Ephesus);

> I was born at Tyre in Phoenicia (Achilles Tatius);

> There's a city in Lesbos called Mytilene (Longus);

> The smile of daybreak was just beginning to brighten the sky, the sunlight to catch the hilltops, when a group of men in brigand gear peered over the mountain that overlooks the place where the Nile flows into the sea at the mouth that men call the Heracleotic (Heliodorus).

Syracuse, Ephesus, Tyre, Mytilene, the Heracleotic mouth of the Nile; in the very first sentence we are in real geography, though, characteristically, Heliodorus takes a little longer to get there than the others. There is no Middlemarch or Casterbridge or Hobbiton here. And, although the plots move out into exotic regions, there is not a single place name in the entire corpus that cannot be checked against genuinely factual literature, even down to Ethiopian rivers in Heliodorus. The entire geography of the novel's world—distances, directions, sailing-times—approximates so closely to reality that there seems nothing odd when the recent Budé Chariton includes a map tracing the fictitious movements of its fictitious characters.[33]

---

33. Edited by G. Molinié (Paris, 1979). The endpapers of T. Hägg, *The Novel in Antiquity* (Oxford, 1983) map the plot of Xen. Eph.

This geography is filled with authentic or—equally good—authentic seeming detail. I have shown elsewhere how the details of Heliodorus' fictional Ethiopia, for example, are drawn systematically from works of history, ethnography and geography familiar to a readership that would readily have accepted their scientific standing.[34] Heliodorus is the extreme case (Iamblichus' *Babyloniaca* looks as if it would have made an interesting comparison but any topographical precision has been lost in Photius' summary), but the principle holds good generally. When Chariton alludes to the administration of the Persian empire, or Longus describes the agriculture of Lesbos, or Achilles the splendours of Alexandria, and even when Xenophon has a caravan of merchants heading for India via Ethiopia, the purpose is to enable the reader plausibly to locate the fiction within the real world or generally held perceptions of it.

Temporal settings are less precise than geographical, and more variably sustained. Chariton's novel takes over characters and historical background from Thucydides' history. The heroine is Hermocrates' daughter, the hero the son of the Ariston mentioned by Thucydides (7.39.2) and Plutarch (*Nicias* 20). Hermocrates' daughter is attested historically, though not named as Callirhoe. She married the tyrant Dionysius (Plut. *Dion* 3), which just happens to be the name of Callirhoe's second husband in the novel. The reader is given the sense that the story is somehow located in the gaps in real history.[35] Not everything ties up; in the novel Hermocrates is alive later than he should be, so that his lifetime overlaps with the reign of the Persian king Artaxerxes. In the later stages of the novel, the hero Chaereas leads an Egyptian revolt from Persia, which looks rather like the actual revolt of 360 BC, with Chaereas playing the part of Chabrias.[36] These anachronisms are not particularly

34. J.R. Morgan, 'History, Romance and Realism in the *Aithiopika* of Heliodoros', *Classical Antiquity* 1 (1982), 221–65.

35. For more details see T. Hägg, 'Callirhoe and Parthenope: the Beginnings of the Historical Novel', *Classical Antiquity* 6 (1987), 184–204; F. Zimmermann, 'Chariton und die Geschichte', in H.J. Diesner, ed., *Sozialökonomische Verhältnisse im alten Orient und im klassischen Altertum* (Berlin, 1961), 329–45; K. Plepelits, *Chariton von Aphrodisias: Kallirhoe* (Stuttgart, 1976), 9ff.

36. P. Salmon, 'Chariton d'Aphrodisias et la révolte égyptienne de 360 avant J.-C.', *Chronique d'Egypte* 36 (1961), 365–76.

important, but they do suggest that the historical material is applied rather than organic to the plot. There is certainly no attempt to accommodate the ethos of the story to its historical setting. Nonetheless, this is a deliberately contrived pretence of historical authenticity.

We know that this was not unique. Papyrus fragments of the romance of Metiochus and Parthenope show that it plundered Herodotus in much the same way.[37] We have a scene at the court of Polycrates of Samos. The heroine is his daughter (historically attested), the hero the son of Miltiades, a refugee from the machinations of his real-life stepmother. Again, the fiction occupies the gaps in the historical record. The very earliest novel we know of, the so called *Ninus Romance*,[38] uses historical figures as its protagonists, though it reduces the formidable legendary rulers Ninus and Semiramis to stereotypical Hellenistic lovers, and the goddess Derceto, in legend the mother of Semiramis, is transmogrified into Ninus' sympathetic auntie.

Heliodorus also gives his novel a setting in the past, during the Persian occupation of Egypt, again not without anachronisms. Achilles' story is set in the contemporary world (the author gets the story from the hero's mouth), but those of Xenophon and Longus are free floating in a timeless Hellenism.

Where the world depicted corresponds to areas within the likely experience of the readership, the novelists stay close to familiar reality. The hardships of rural life, procedures of betrothal and marriage, the legalities of selling slaves, the role of slaves in the economy have all been studied in relation to the novels, with the conclusion that fiction is close enough to social reality to be useful

---

37. H. Maehler, 'Der Metiochos-Parthenope Roman', *Zeitschrift für Papyrologie und Epigraphik* 23 (1976), 1–20; T. Hägg, art. cit. (n. 35 above) and 'Metiochus at Polycrates' Court', *Eranos* 83 (1985), 92–102.

38. See n. 18 above. For the work's relation to historical fact, or rather to Greek perceptions of historical fact, see U. Wilcken, 'Ein neuer griechischer Roman', *Hermes* 28 (1893), 161–93; Perry, op. cit. (n. 8 above), 161ff. Compare also the *Sesonchosis Romance* (P. Oxy. 1826, 2466, 3319), built on the exploits of the semi-mythical Egyptian pharaoh, which is now looking more like a novel, since the latest fragment contains a new element of erotic intrigue. The plot is reconstructed by J.N. O'Sullivan, 'The Sesonchosis Romance', *Zeitschrift für Papyrologie und Epigraphik* 56 (1984), 39–44.

as evidence for it.[39] Likewise, dreams, while forming a staple of conventional plot building, are nonetheless conceived and handled very much in conformity with contemporary theory and belief.[40] In many cases, of course, it may simply not have occurred to a novelist to make his fiction any different from reality; but that is only to say that these novels were conceived of, and intended to be read, within the parameters of reality.

All this is superficial, but not unimportant. Some aspects of a fiction do refer to the real world and occupy a legitimate place along the scale from truth to falsehood. If a reader encounters a proposition which he knows to be factually incorrect, his complaisance in the make-believe truth of the whole fiction may be compromised. Novelists and playwrights go to some lengths to get their facts right; the blockbuster with a heavily researched period setting is a familiar sight on supermarket shelves or in the autumn television listings. But mistakes are made, and there is always some enthusiast waiting to point out that a film set in 1904 uses a type of locomotive not introduced on that particular route until 1906, or to pick up some error of detail in the medals on the hero's military uniform. We laugh, the rest of us, at the naïve pedantry, but to the person concerned a single item, however peripheral, which contradicts his certain factual knowledge can be enough to appear in contravention of the fictional contract. The text has to work hard to make the reader believe in its fiction. And in actual fact we are all prone to this sort of reaction, even in the least naturalistic of contexts. Why else do I find Dick van Dyke's Cockney accent in *Mary Poppins* so offensive?

---

39. Or at least for perceptions of it. Cf. A.M. Scarcella, 'Realtà e letteratura nel paesaggio sociale ed economico del romanzo di Longo Sofista', *Maia* 22 (1970), 103–31; id., 'Les structures socio–économiques du roman de Xénophon d'Ephèse', *Revue des Etudes Grecques* 90 (1977), 249–62; E.L. Bowie, 'The Novels and the Real World', in B.P. Reardon, ed., *Erotica Antiqua* (Bangor, 1977), 91–6; S. Saïd, 'La société rurale dans le roman grec', in E. Frézouls, ed., *Sociétés urbaines, sociétés rurales* (Strasbourg, 1987), 149–71; A. Calderini, 'La *enguēsis* matrimoniale nei romanzieri greci e nei papiri', *Aegyptus* 39 (1959), 29–39; F. Zimmermann, 'Kallirhoes Verkauf durch Theron', *Berliner Byzantinische Arbeiten* (1959), 72–81. For a similar treatment of the Roman novel, see F. Millar, 'The World of the *Golden Ass*', *Journal of Roman Studies* 71 (1981), 63–75.

40. S. MacAlister, *The Dream in Greek Romance* (Ph.D. Diss., Sydney, 1987).

If factual details relating to reality are one sort of truth proposition to be found in novels, another consists in the assertion of what appear to be general truths:

> That was how he spoke to Leonas, but for all that he did not give up hope of winning Callirhoe over. Love is naturally optimistic, and he was confident that by attention to her he could achieve his desires.
> (Char. 2.6.4)

> Dionysius' passion raged fiercely and would not suffer the wedding to be delayed; self-control is painful when desire can be satisfied.
> (Char. 3.2.6)

> She looked up, saw them, and looked down again, quite unperturbed by the strange colour and robber-like appearance of these armed men, quite single-minded in tending the wounded man. So it is that genuine affection and wholehearted love disregard all external pains and pleasures and compel the mind to concentrate thought and vision on a single object: the beloved.
> (Hld. 1.2.8–9)

Sententiae such as these could be multiplied a thousand-fold from the Greek novels. They reach their most extreme form in Achilles, who will quite happily devote a whole page to general reflections about tears (6.7) or kisses (2.8) or sleepless nights (1.6) to substantiate the action. These general truths are statements relating to something outside the fiction, to which the reader is free to assent or dissent independently of the fiction. But they are usually cast in a form with which no normal person would wish to disagree, or else, particularly in Achilles, they are persuasive, framed to win the reader's assent. Their function is to illustrate that the behaviour of the fictional characters and their world conforms to normative statements acceptable as descriptions of the real world. They thus define a plausibility which is relevant to the narrative.

But that kind of plausibility is implicit, even when there is no *sententia* to articulate it. The psychology of Dionysius' love is not made either more or less plausible by Chariton's generalization, but the reader's attention is drawn to the plausibility, which thus becomes an issue in the reading. Actually, the novelists were concerned throughout with plausibility. Realistic fiction has to convince us that the improbabilities, abnormalities, the *apista*, which make up its subject-matter are, step by step, possible. Laws of physical possibility are seldom violated, the supernatural is seldom invoked. The most blatant infringements occur, significantly, in what is regarded, not on this ground alone, as the weakest of the novels.

> They set up the cross and attached him to it, tying his hands and feet tight with ropes; that is the way the Egyptians crucify [researched detail?]. Then they went away and left him hanging there, thinking that their victim was securely in place. But Habrocomes looked straight at the sun, then at the Nile channel, and prayed . . . The god took pity on his prayer. A sudden gust of wind arose and struck the cross, sweeping away the subsoil on the cliff where it had been fixed. Habrocomes fell into the torrent and was swept away—[but our hero is fished out of the river and sentenced to be burned at the stake] but just as the flames were about to engulf him, he again prayed the few words he could to be saved from the perils that threatened. Then the Nile rose in spate, and the surge of water struck the pyre and put out the flames.
>
> (Xen. Eph. 4.2.3ff.)

Even here the action would not violate laws of physics acceptable to an audience with a literal belief in miraculous divine intervention, but it is not typical. In general, the action can be explained at a rational level even when it is overseen by the gods, and is carefully motivated within the text.

For example, Chariton's plot demands that the hero Chaereas should attack his beloved wife and believe he has killed her. To motivate the attack, he is deceived by jealous defeated suitors into thinking that she has a lover in the house. To explain why he fails to notice that she is alone, we are told that the room was in darkness. To explain that, we are told that Callirhoe was so sad at the absence of her husband that she simply had not bothered to light the lamp, and had no time to do so because, at the sound of the familiar footfall and breathing of her husband returning unexpectedly home, she had run to meet him (1.4.11). To explain the effect of the blow, we are told that it landed on her diaphragm and halted her respiration, a plausible medical explanation ostensibly true outside the fiction. The 'corpse'—in fact merely unconscious—is buried with unusual rapidity: necessary for the plot because the hero must continue to believe her dead, but motivated in the story by a general desire that no one should see her beauty impaired by the onset of putrefaction. In the tomb she revives, which is again explained in paramedical terms: lack of food eased the pressure on her diaphragm and so enabled breathing to recommence. At which point tomb-robbers burst in and carry her off; but their arrival at this precise juncture is itself the result of a carefully laid trail of motivation. The whole sequence leading up to the moment of high melodrama is laughably far-fetched when stated barely, but Chariton has made every effort to put together cause and effect so as to render the far-fetched plausible. There is truth both of correspondence to external reality and of coherence of character and setting within the plot itself.

Another, almost self-parodying, version of a similar incident occurs in Achilles. Again the hero has to believe the heroine dead. First she is separated from him when he escapes from Egyptian bandits, leaving her in their clutches. Then, as the authorities move against the bandits, he witnesses a scene where she is staked to the ground, disembowelled, and her entrails cooked and eaten. This appears pretty conclusive to both character and reader, but that only enhances the effect of amazement when (inevitably by the rules of the genre) she turns out not to be dead after all. And there is a rational explanation. The ministrants at her sacrifice, unrecognized because it was dark and they were in armour, turn out to be lost friends, who had fallen into the bandits' hands after the hero escaped. To prove their suitability to join this gang of desperadoes, they had been forced to engage in a little human sacrifice and cannibalism. Recognizing their victim, however, they had contrived an illusion with the help of a false stomach full of sheep's guts and a trick knife with a retractable blade opportunely discovered among the properties of a captured stage-artiste. Of course the effect is one of comic Grand Guignol, and intentionally so. But the imperative to explain action in terms of the physically possible (if statistically improbable) remains.

Of course, in the twentieth century we know that, if Callirhoe's breathing had been stopped for long, she would have been irreparably brain-damaged by the time she revived, but this merely illustrates that perceptions of reality and hence of correspondential realism in fiction alter with cultural determinants. A similar example occurs when Heliodorus' heroine is saved from incineration at the stake because she has on her person a flame-proofing jewel (Hld. 8.9)—within the novel's horizons a scientific explanation. A famous modern example is the spontaneous combustion of Krook in *Bleak House*, whose scientific authenticity Dickens vigorously defended against mounting evidence; it clearly mattered that it should be believable by scientific criteria.[41]

Strategies of realism (make believe) extend to the textual act of representation. Manner of narration, as well as content, is engineered to produce belief.

Chariton poses as a historian (fiction in the form of history). He begins his novel, for instance, with a prologue modelled on those of fifth-century historians, such as Herodotus or Thucydides, in which he introduces himself and his subject, which is a *genomenon*, something that happened:

> This is the production of the enquiry of Herodotus of Halicarnassus, in order that neither should the things which have occurred [*genomena*] fade from mankind through the passage of time, nor should the great and amazing deeds produced some by Greeks, some by barbarians, be without fame.
>
> Thucydides of Athens has compiled an account of the war fought between the Peloponnesians and the Athenians.
>
> I, Chariton of Aphrodisias, clerk to the rhetor Athenagoras, shall narrate a love affair that happened [*genomenon*] in Syracuse.

Not only is Chariton's story set in the fifth and fourth centuries BC, but he pretends to narrate as if he were a contemporary of the events he writes about, as those earlier historians were. Thus, details of the Persian administration, long defunct by Chariton's own time,[42] are referred to in the present tense:

> He decided to march out with the troops already at hand, and to send the order throughout his empire for the army to gather at the river Euphrates. Persia can mobilise its forces very easily.

---

41. G.S. Haight, 'Dickens and Lewes on Spontaneous Combustion', *Nineteenth-century Fiction* 10 (1955–6), 53–63; E. Gaskell, 'More on Spontaneous Combustion', *The Dickensian* 69 (1973), 25–35.

42. This is true of the whole range of possible dates for Chariton; see above, n. 3.

The system has been in force since the time of Cyrus, the first king of Persia. It is established which nations have to supply cavalry for a war . . .

(6.8.6)

He continues in this vein for a whole paragraph.[43]

Critically examined, as we have seen, the pretence is full of holes; one can find reflections of Chariton's own period, places Hellenized before their time, and so on. Nonetheless, Chariton is making a definite effort to adopt a fictitious narratorial persona which contributes to his text's power to make believe. It is at least arguable that the pretence of being a contemporary historian extends even to his prose style, which has features reminiscent of Xenophon's, and to compositional mannerisms, such as the use of strategically placed recapitulations, again recalling the practice of Xenophon.[44] But most importantly, he disposes his material like a historian, even when its substance is most novelistic, self-consciously abjuring emotional tone and the effects of suspense and surprise natural to fiction. He projects himself as an omniscient narrator at pains to *inform* his reader, not artfully withholding information but conscientiously releasing it in due chronological sequence, so that the reader understands, better than the characters, what is happening. We can illustrate this at the very climax of the novel.

Callirhoe has been taken from Babylon in the train of the Persian king as he goes to put down an Egyptian rebellion. Chaereas, in disgust and despair, has joined the rebels, where he has quickly risen to a position of command. The king leaves his queen and Callirhoe on the islands of Arados for safety (7.4). Chaereas is victorious at sea, and takes possession of Arados. There is a small lacuna in the text at this point, but apparently[45] one of Chaereas' soldiers sees Callirhoe among the captive women and reports her exceptional beauty to Chaereas, who sends for her, without knowing who it is. The soldier sent to fetch her speaks of the commander possibly marrying her, much to Callirhoe's dismay (she already has two

---

43. Also 5.2.2, 5.4.5; at 4.6.1 a present tense in the single manuscript is usually emended to an imperfect, but is defended by Plepelits, op. cit. (n. 35 above).
44. Cf. Zimmermann, op. cit. (n. 35 above), Plepelits, op. cit. (n. 35 above).
45. Reconstructed by Reardon, *CAGN*, 109, n. 117, following Plepelits.

husbands and a third would be *de trop*). She refuses to go with the soldier, who duly reports this also to Chaereas (7.6). Now (8.1) Chariton recapitulates the situation and even sketches in the sequel before it happens:

> Chaereas was to have Callirhoe in his possession and fail to recogise her; while taking others' wives on board his ships to carry them off, he was to leave his own behind, not like Ariadne asleep, and not for Dionysus to be her bridegroom, but as spoils of war for his own enemies. But Aphrodite thought this too harsh . . . Having harassed by land and sea the handsome couple she had originally brought together, she decided now to reunite them . . . So I shall tell you how the goddess brought the truth to light and revealed the unrecognised pair to each other.[46]
>
> (8.1.2–3)

Chaereas prepares to leave the island, leaving the reluctant beauty to her fate, but he happens to pass the house where she is confined, and his faithful companion, hoping that he will find something there to console him for the loss of his beloved Callirhoe, urges him to go in and talk to her himself. And at this stage the recognition scene duly takes place (8.1.8–10).

Throughout this sequence the reader is aware of the identity of both general and captive, and of their ignorance of each other. From this vantage point he can savour the irony of the situation. But what is lacking, of course, is the emotional punch of surprise and release of tension. It is easy enough to see how the whole thing could have been contrived differently. The reader need not have been told straightaway that Callirhoe was on Arados, that the beautiful captive was the general's wife. If the narrative had stayed with Chaereas and limited itself to his point of view, it could have re-enacted his despair and joy. Alternatively, in the feminist mode, Chariton could have kept Callirhoe centre-stage, not told us that Chaereas had defected and risen to command the rebels, and piled on the emotion as

---

46. At the same time, of course, the sentiment, the mythological reference to Ariadne and Dionysus (with its punning allusion to the name of Dionysius), and the claim to know the thoughts of Aphrodite mark this out as romantic fiction. It is, in fact, an excellent example of the doubleness of fiction which this paper tries to illustrate.

Callirhoe and reader were both led to believe that destiny was thrusting a third husband on her, with a dramatic reversal when he unexpectedly enters her room.

This is persistently Chariton's manner, however. So, for example, we know that the indications that Callirhoe is being unfaithful are only part of a plot by her thwarted suitors; we know that Callirhoe is not really dead when she is buried, and that robbers are preparing to break into her tomb. But to treat these crises in the plot in a more dramatic, artistic, more superficially effective way would have been to lose the historiographical illusion. Chariton seems to go to such unnecessary lengths to avoid effects of partial cognition (did he really need to tell us that a recognition is shortly to take place?) that it must be deliberate.

I am the more inclined to think that this was a consciously chosen strategy rather than naïve incompetence as a novelist because on one signal occasion Chariton shows that he was well able to control the release of information in such a way as to secure a powerful dramatic effect. Significantly, this is where he breaks with generic expectations and proprieties and his plot takes on a genuine and dangerous unpredictability. After being carried off by the tomb-robbers and taken to Asia Minor, where marriage is proposed to her by the wealthy Dionysius, Callirhoe discovers she is pregnant. This discovery impels her—after a wonderfully well handled internal debate—to accept a second marriage for the sake of her first husband's unborn child, compromising with the conventional moral code of romance in a way unique in the extant canon. But Chariton could have told us long ago that she was pregnant, and could even have used the fact as part of his medical explanation for her apparent death. As it is, we are left, slightly awkwardly, wondering in retrospect whether we are supposed to see a connection or not.

Chariton's stance as all-knowing, all-telling reporter is itself a fiction intended to win authority for the text: the authority of historical record. Other writers aim for similar illusions of authority by manipulating their narrative personae in different ways. One of the most widely employed devices is to provide a provenance for the novel text. Antonius Diogenes uses a particularly intricate mechanism: what the reader has before him purports to be Antonius' publication of letters written by the Macedonian Balagrus to his wife Phila, transcribing wooden tablets discovered in a grave during Alexander's siege of Tyre; these tablets contain the story of the

Arcadian Dinias, as told to the ambassador Cymbas, in the course of which Dinias relates the story of his lover Dercyllis, as told to him by her. This pretence of an ancient text rediscovered is handled with playful ambiguities, not the least of which concerns Antonius' citation of his sources,[47] but it had sufficient fictive force to confuse Photius.

Similar fictions were used to authorize the spoof narratives of the Trojan War transmitted under the names of Dictys and Dares, again with too much success; they came to be regarded as genuine historical documents in the Middle Ages, and better evidence than Homer.[48] The protagonists of the *Ephesiaca* dedicate an account of their experiences in the temple of Artemis at Ephesus, a point curiously unexploited in our possibly abbreviated text, but still sufficient to hint that there is documentary evidence for the novel we have been reading.[49] According to a marginal note in one manuscript of Photius, Iamblichus said that the *Babyloniaca* was one of a number of Babylonian tales told him by his tutor; this seems unlikely to be the literal truth—especially since the novel was 16 (or even possibly 39) books long—but the fictional provenance has found credence with at least one modern scholar.[50] Longus presents *Daphnis and Chloe* as based on a painting which he encountered in real space and time, as elucidated for him by an authoritative exegete. At the end of the novel we learn that the painting was itself a dedication made by the two protagonists, so that (as with Antonius, Xenophon and Achilles) the novel is authorized from within.

---

47. Cf. J.R. Morgan, 'Lucian's *True Histories* and the *Wonders beyond Thule* of Antonius Diogenes', *Classical Quarterly* 35 (1985), 475–90. Photius tells us that 'he cites at the beginning of each book the names of the persons who treated the subject previously so that the incredible events would not seem to lack authority.' This undermines the fiction of the discovery of the text in a tomb, especially as the only source named by Photius, Antiphanes of Berga, was a notorious liar. However, a recently published fragment of the novel (P. Oxy. 3012) appears to come from the beginning of a book, but does not include any citations.

48. W. Nelson, *Fact or Fiction. The Dilemma of the Renaissance Storyteller* (Cambridge, Mass., 1973), 24ff.

49. Similarly, in one of the recensions of the Latin *History of Apollonius King of Tyre*, the hero dedicates one copy of his autobiography in a temple (the same temple, as it happens), and another is lodged in his library.

50. L. di Gregorio, 'Sulla biografia di Giamblico e la fortuna del suo romanzo attraverso i secoli', *Aevum* 38 (1964), 1–13.

Heliodorus' approach is rather different, and less obvious. Among the many poses he affects is one of uncertainty about his own invented facts:[51]

> They were given the warmest of welcomes by their host's daughter, a young lady of marriageable age, and by all the serving-women of the house, who treated their guest just like a father, for such, I imagine, had been their master's instructions.
>
> (2.22.1)

The pretence here and elsewhere is that the narrative can be divided into hard facts and legitimate inference. Acknowledging the 'inference' authorizes the 'fact'. On other occasions Heliodorus obtains the same effect by offering multiple explanations for an occurrence. Again the implication is that the explanations are his but the fact is not. Here is a spectacular example:

> About midnight a section of the dyke, where the previous evening the Ethiopians had begun to dig an outlet, ruptured without warning; it may be that the earth in that section had been piled loosely and not properly tamped down, so that the base gave way as the water soaked into it; or those excavating the tunnel may have created an empty space into which the base of the dyke could collapse; or possibly the workmen had left the place where they had started their digging somewhat lower than the rest of the dyke, so that as the water level rose during the night, causing a fresh influx, the water was able to find a way out and, once that happened, the channel grew deeper without anyone being aware of the fact; alternatively one might ascribe the event to divine intervention.
>
> (9.8.2)

Or perhaps, the reader is left thinking, we have a novelist desperately trying to disguise his control of the narrative; a gloriously double effect where the self-consciousness draws attention to the rules of the game, the first of which is that it is not a game and there are no rules!

---

51. J.R. Morgan, art. cit. (n. 34 above), esp. 227ff.

Apart from the matter of authority, the novels all evince, with, it need hardly be said, differing degrees of success, a striving for the realism of visual immediacy. They pretend, that is, not to be mediated narrative at all but aspire to the status of direct representation of reality. Rhetoricians valued in both narrative and description a quality called in Greek *enargeia*, in Latin *evidentia*. Quintilian defines it as:

> that which seems not so much to tell as to show; and the emotions will follow just as if we were present at the actual events.
>
> (6.3.32)

The text must aim to be transparent, to disappear as medium so that the audience can respond to the subject-matter as directly as to reality. This rhetorical antithesis of telling and showing corresponds to Plato's between *diēgēsis* (narrative) and *mimēsis* (representation), and informs also Aristotle's praise of Homer for speaking as little as possible in his own person, since 'that is not the way to achieve *mimēsis*' (*Poetics* 1460a5–8; see p. 184 above). It lies behind Duris' criticisms of Ephorus and Theopompus, and his development of a new style of history. Exactly the same antithesis was much exploited in the first part of this century, when critic after critic stressed the superiority of showing over telling for the production of realism:

> I speak of 'telling' the story, but of course he has no idea of doing that and no more; the art of fiction does not begin until the novelist thinks of his story as a matter to be *shown*, to be exhibited so that it will tell itself.[52]

In recent years the pendulum has swung away from this sort of mimetic realism. We have learned not to expect our novels to do the impossible, and come to value their reflexive artificiality for its own sake. Novelists have come out of hiding, as it were. But contemporary fashion should not blind us to the fact that many novels were written within a cultural environment where representational realism

---

52. P. Lubbock, *The Craft of Fiction* (London, 1921), 62. On the assumptions and practice of this kind of realism, see W.C. Booth, *The Rhetoric of Fiction* (Chicago, 1961), 23ff.

was expected of the writer and the imaginative leap into belief was expected of his audience. This is demonstrably the case with the ancient novels, although by the strictest nineteenth-century criteria they are desperately flawed. The illusion of reality was a continuing concern in both the visual and the literary arts, if not an exclusive one. I want now to examine three of the novelists as representative of different kinds of mimetic strategies.

Longus, in the prologue, describes the genesis of his novel:[53] it is a response to a painting by which he was deeply moved. The *enargeia* of the visual arts, and the emotive power deriving from it, was widely recognized, and literature often expressly aspired to capture it. Longus' text, however, is something more than a translation of the painter's material into a different medium. He exploits the double sense of the Greek verb *graphein* and its cognates (both 'draw/paint' and 'write') to suggest that his novel, like the painting, is a *graphē*; it claims to share its original's medium, and even to outdo it in that medium. The literary text arrogates to itself all mimetic force and emotive power of a visual artwork—and then some. Although he establishes this visual protocol with an explicitness unparalleled in the novels, Longus exploits it as much for the ambiguities it raises about the relationship of art to nature as for a straightforward motor of realism. In many ways, Longus is the least representational of the novelists.

Chariton's approach is simpler. Narrative itself, whatever its pretensions, cannot actually imitate, because it is a function of language and language is a non-imitative signifier. Narrative must always tell, not show. Except, that is, when it is able to imitate a linguistic object. This was essentially Aristotle's point about Homer: direct speech allows *mimēsis*. Chariton has taken the lesson to heart.[54] Typically, he will narrate events with great rapidity and very little elaboration; then the pace will slow and out of the narrative

---

53. On Longus' prologue, see R.L. Hunter, *A Study of Daphnis and Chloe* (Cambridge, 1983), 38ff.; T.A. Pandiri, 'Daphnis and Chloe: the Art of Pastoral Play', *Ramus* 14 (1985), 116–41; F.I. Zeitlin, 'The Poetics of Eros: Nature, Art and Imitation in Longus' Daphnis and Chloe', in D.M. Halperin et al., eds, *Before Sexuality* (Princeton, 1990), 417–64; D. Teske, *Der Roman des Longos als Werk der Kunst* (Münster, 1991), 25ff.

54. What follows draws on T. Hägg, *Narrative Technique in Ancient Greek Romances* (Stockholm, 1971), 26ff., 89ff.; see also B.P. Reardon, 'Theme, Structure, and Narrative in Chariton', *Yale Classical Studies* 27 (1982), 1–27.

will grow a scene, playing more or less in real time. The viewpoint shifts from that of omniscient narrator to that of the characters, and we are given their emotions, thoughts, and, most important, their words, in dialogue or soliloquy. The narrative complex of 3.5ff. will serve as example.

The truth of Callirhoe's disappearance has been discovered; Chaereas' eagerness to sail in search of her and the equipping of his ships are dealt with summarily, then Chariton slows into a scene on the day of departure, with tearful farewells in direct speech from the hero's parents, and noble sentiments from hero and his companion. The passage to Ionia is dismissed in two and a half lines (3.6.1), leading to an emotional scene when Chaereas discovers Callirhoe's image in the temple of Aphrodite. Detailed description of his reaction and lamentations in direct speech cover the next page. By contrast, the recognition of Chaereas' ship by the steward Phocas, its destruction by the Persian army, and the capture and enslavement of Chaereas and his companion are covered in a few terse sentences. Then comes a scene where Callirhoe dreams of Chaereas, laments, and so arouses jealousy in her new husband Dionysius. Time then passes rapidly. Callirhoe's child by Chaereas is born with the minimum of narrative fuss, but in 3.8 comes a protracted scene, extending over several pages, beginning with Dionysius' prayers to Aphrodite when the child is first presented in public, Callirhoe's more tearful private prayers, a conversation with the priestess in which she learns of the destruction of a Greek ship and suspects that the handsome stranger who wept at the sight of her image was her own husband, and a dialogue in which Dionysius interrogates Phocas.

It should be clear from this that the scenes occupy the emotional cruces of the plot. It has been calculated that they comprise something like 90 per cent of the total text, about half that in direct speech. The effect is like a series of filmed highlights held together by a continuity announcer. When it really counts, the narrator disappears, stops telling and starts showing.

Heliodorus is technically far more sophisticated than this.[55] His novel begins with a mysterious tableau: an empty ship, dead bodies,

---

55. For fuller treatment see J.R. Morgan, 'Reader and Audiences in the *Aithiopika* of Heliodoros', *Groningen Colloquia on the Novel* 4 (1991).

the remains of a feast on the beach, an indescribably beautiful girl tending a wounded man. These things are not described directly but are channeled through the perceptions and inferences of a party of Egyptian bandits, whose ignorance and puzzlement at what they see forge an identity between them and the reader. These twin audiences, reader and bandits, confront the world of the fiction in parallel; the Egyptians function as a locus for the reader's visual acquisition of knowledge, giving him imaginatively a physical and cognitive presence within the represented world, and so setting him in a much more direct relation to the substance of the fiction. Of an omniscient narrator there is no trace, facilitating the pretence that there is no author and that the text is a transparent mimesis of reality. As far as he exists at all, the narrator is just a more articulate version of the reader. Here, *enargeia* is produced by the duplicitous evasion of omniscience and the use of in-text reflectors to process raw visual data, devices familiar to us from modern novels but unique in the ancient form. Heliodorus' *praxis* outstrips the conceptual power of ancient literary analysis, but the effects do not need to be analysed to be felt. The novels, especially Heliodorus', imply a competence in reading fiction far more sophisticated than any contemporary critical formulation.

If the brigands of the opening scene are the most obvious example of this technique, they are not the only one. Other figures in the narrative are employed to enact the response elicited from the reader inside the world of the fiction, thus providing him with a focus of identification. But by becoming, as it were, part of an audience inside the fiction, the reader finds that, by analogy with his fictional counterparts, he is implicitly responding to a visually perceived reality rather than to a verbally mediated fiction. Heliodorus is fond of retrospective explication, so that the reader knows what happened before he knows why it was going to happen. This re-enacts textually the way in which we subjectively experience the real world; the effect is of an unauthored reality playing itself out before our eyes.

This strategy is the opposite of Chariton's, but the purpose is closely related. Both pretend to have abjured artifice—a pretence which is of course itself the nth degree of artifice. Chariton masquerades as an artless historian, having renounced tawdry effects of surprise and suspense in favour of a sober and fully explicative narrative mode. His presence in the text is constant, but as reporter of objective fact, not as organiser of a controlled fiction, Heliodorus, on the other hand, subtracts himself from the surface of the text in the cause of immediacy directly experienced, interpreted from within, which, like the present-tense real world, can often be understood only partially, provisionally or retrospectively. In both cases the fictionality of the fiction is camouflaged.

Fiction's willed blindness to itself is at the heart of realism, a strategy to make the reader in some sense 'believe' what he is reading. This is one defence against Solon's puritanical absolutism: the fiction presents itself as a communication between a truthful (implied) author and a believing (implied) reader. The charge of telling untruth is avoided by pretending to tell the truth. 'Truth' in fiction depends on belief in fiction and 'belief' is an important dynamic of the reader's pleasure, as Photius saw. Given that the primary function of these texts is to please, not to theorize on their own nature, we should nonetheless have expected them to play with, and exploit, systems of 'belief'. The exact nature of that 'belief' we shall examine shortly. But so far we have only told half the story.

IV

We are accustomed now to novels which make no attempt to be plausible or realistic, which revel gleefully in their artificiality and defy anyone to believe them. But belief in even the most realistic novel is never real belief and, in Riffaterre's words, 'a novel always contains signs whose function is to remind readers that what they are being told is imaginary'.[56] For the two very good reasons that a novel is a text and exists to give pleasure, novels always offer pleasures which are specifically textual. Even the most thoroughgoing realism is ultimately self-regarding; we are supposed to admire the author's skill or research in creating the illusion. Even as we believe, we can stand back and enjoy from the outside. In the Greek novels, side by side with the realistic elements so far discussed marches a second army of phenomena, which are there to draw attention to the textual surface and the artfulness of the artefact, and which thus locate the reader precisely as *reader*, a person with a book in his hand, reminded continually of the conventional, imaginary and

---

56. M. Riffaterre, *Fictional Truth* (Baltimore, 1991), 1; cf. ibid. 21: 'narrative verisimilitude tends to flaunt rather than mask its fictitious nature.'

playful nature of the activity in which he is engaged: it is, they say, only make-believe. This is Thespis' defence against Solon, and one taken up famously by Sir Philip Sidney:

> Now for the poet he nothing affirmeth and therefore never lieth . . . though he recount things not true, yet because he telleth them not for true, he lieth not.[57]

From the very beginning of a Greek novel, the reader is alerted to the fact that it is a novel he is reading, not through explicit statement of course, but through conventional cues. Thus, even in the historiographical prologue already quoted, Chariton designates his subject as a love affair, *pathos erōtikon*, so aligning himself with love poets, like Parthenius who wrote a little book of stories suitable for poetic treatment called *erōtika pathēmata*. Despite the manner, our attention is drawn to the distance in subject-matter and ethos from military and political history. Xenophon begins in a way irresistibly reminiscent of the 'once upon a time' formula with which fairy tales signal their nature and define their audience's expectations. Longus, as we shall see, uses his prologue to stake out his ground as a second-order imitator, while Heliodorus' plunge *in medias res* is a strategy of epic poetry rather than of any literature of reality. For all its mimetic qualities, no one could mistake the opening of the *Aethiopica* for a factual document. By the Renaissance, in fact, critics had come to recognize such temporal inversions as a conventional sign of fictivity.[58] Achilles' first-person narrative, while self-authenticating, is again a poetic rather than a documentary sign.

Overt self-reference in the novels is rare, but within the fiction the reader's attention is often drawn to the miraculous or incredible nature of the plot. Here is Chariton at one of his climaxes, speaking directly to his reader:

> Who could fitly describe that scene in court? What dramatist ever staged such an astonishing story [*paradoxos muthos*]? It was like being at a play packed with passionate scenes, with emotions tumbling over each other—weeping and rejoicing, astonishment and pity, disbelief and prayers.

(5.8.2)

---

57. *An Apology for Poetry*, ed. G. Shepherd (London, 1965), 123–4.
58. Nelson, op. cit. (n. 48 above), 38ff.

This only just maintains the pretence that Chariton is a mere reporter. The comparison to drama draws attention to the theatricality of the invention. And the story, while not itself a *muthos* (a self-acknowledging falsehood on the rhetorical schema) is similar to one. The reactions of people within the fiction are listed to guide the response of the reader: they include astonishment and disbelief.

Likewise the ego-narrator of Achilles Tatius comments on the nature of his experiences, which he says are like *muthoi* (1.2.2); his narratee, the author, responds eagerly, and takes him to a park, a suitable setting for *muthoi erōtikoi* (1.2.3). It would be possible to multiply references where a character in the plot comments on the paradoxical or unbelievable nature of events, or where secondary narratives are greeted with disbelief.[59] These are clearly cues of some kind for the reader, though often of an ambivalent or ironic kind. He is made to savour the fact that fiction enables him to believe things that in another context—reality—would be incredible; but because he knows that in the world of the fiction the incredible is true he is also placed in a position of detached superiority to those who cannot see the truth. The novels dance around the doubleness of truth and fiction.

The metaphor of the theatre is taken to its highest point by Heliodorus,[60] who exploits it simultaneously to validate and destabilize his narrative. An instructive and prolonged example occurs at 7.6ff. Two brothers are re-enacting the scene from the *Iliad* where Achilles pursues Hector around the walls of Troy (here Memphis); at the crucial moment their father returns from exile:

Round the walls they sped, once, twice, but towards the end of their third circuit, with Thyamis levelling his spear at his brother's back and threatening to strike him dead if he did not stand and fight, with the entire population of the city lining the walls watching like the presiding judges in a theatre—at that very moment either some divine power or some fortune that arbitrates over human affairs made the drama take a new and

---

59. Char. 3.2.7, 3.3.2–4, 2.5.9, 2.8.3, 8.6.6; Ach. Tat. 6.2.3; Xen. Eph. 5.12.2, etc., etc.

60. The standard discussion is still J.W.H. Walden, 'Stage-terms in Heliodorus's *Aethiopica*', *Harvard Studies in Classical Philology* 5 (1894), 1–43.

tragic twist, almost as if bringing a second drama on stage to compete with the one already in progress; by a miracle of stagecraft it brought Calasiris on to the scene . . . [A recognition scene ensues, including the reunion of Theagenes and Charicleia, the hero and heroine.] The struggle, which had seemed set to be settled by the spilling of blood, changed at its denouement from tragedy to comedy . . . but all were agreed that the high point of the drama was its romantic side.

There are several levels in play here. Firstly, the sustained theatrical metaphor sets us in a context where the exceptional is to be expected, and highly emotional responses are in order. By being very clearly metaphor it distances the truth to which it is applied from 'mere' drama. At the same time, however, particularly when we are already in an allusive climate, it draws attention to the fact that Heliodorus' plot is using the staples of romantic melodrama: hair's-breadth escapes, miraculous interventions *ex machina* and recognitions. And thirdly it presents an audience within the frame whose responses are already modified by aesthetic distance, who are not simply moved, but are there to judge the artistic merits of Destiny's drama and to rank its excellences. In so doing, they signpost the reader to an artistic appraisal of Heliodorus' creation.

The prologue to Longus' novel is complexly self-referential. Not only does it predispose towards a visualization of narrative as picture, it simultaneously distinguishes the object of the narrative's mimesis, as an artwork, from nature, or reality. It is the author's response to art, not reality, which is offered as an appropriate analogue for the reader's to the text. Throughout the novel, the focuses of nature and art are mediated by *mimēsis*—in symbolic gardens, in love, in the whole business of growing up—and it is hard not to see this equation as a self-reference to the novel's own relationship both to reality, held at an aesthetic distance by the very process that ostensibly embodies it, and to the literary traditions that Longus imitates. The same prologue also contrives to communicate the groundrules of the novel's hermeneutic dynamics. The need for an exegete to interpret the painting suggests that the novel also has layers of meaning and connection beneath its obvious surface; and Longus' remarks on utility, which slyly invert those of Thucydides on history, hint that the particularities of the story have a universal application. Readings as allegory and parable are thus invited.

During the body of the work the author recedes, but still suggests that this is not a window on the real world. Apart from literary allusion (discussed below), there are moments such as when Daphnis' foster-father at last reveals the truth of his discovery, only for the real father to 'question him again, telling him to tell the truth and not to make up tales like myths [*homoia plattein muthois*]' (4.20.1). And, most strikingly, when Chloe has been abducted, Pan appears to the leader of the raiders and accuses him of carrying off 'a maiden from whom Love wants to make a story [*muthos*]' (2.27.2), this *muthos* being nothing other than *Daphnis and Chloe* itself.

There is every reason to think that these writers were not only themselves aware of and interested by the process of fictional representation, but that they expected their reader to be so also.[61] Heliodorus repeatedly contrives situations of imperfect cognition where fictional characters engage in partial and distorted interpretation, paralleling that of the reader, who is trying to second-guess the development of the plot. The plot itself is assembled around an armature of predictive dreams and oracles, which not only clarify its movement and structure but delineate, often misleadingly, areas where uncertainty and suspense can be forestalled by intelligent interpretation on the reader's part.

The temporal inversion of the narration necessitates the use of a secondary narrator to fill in the earlier part of the story. This role is assigned to Calasiris, an Egyptian priest who is anything but a straightforward purveyor of facts. He is a showman, prepared to exploit dramatic illusion to achieve a higher end, aware that his way of telling the story might appear sophistic and tricksy (2.24.5). He withholds information to generate suspense and surprise. Dramatically, but duplicitously, he uses the narrative to re-enact the acquisition of the knowledge which gives him narratorial authority. Calasiris is there as Heliodorus' commentary on the art of narration, to draw attention, dramatically, to what the author is doing himself.

---

61. For such a narratological reading, cf. J.J. Winkler, 'The Mendacity of Kalasiris and the Narrative Strategy of the *Aithiopika*', *Yale Classical Studies* 27 (1982), 93–158.

His narratee, Cnemon, is likewise an inscribed, but ironized, version of the reader of Heliodorus' novel, with his curiosity, emotional reactions, romantic sensibilities and desire for expansive detail.[62] The heroine herself understands the principles of the plot in which she finds herself enmeshed, and lectures her consort at some length (9.24) on the need for postponement and complexity rather than precipitate resolution. But the complexity is nothing other than the structural complexity of the novel itself, and her strategy for life is Heliodorus' for his fiction.

This degree of reflexivity about fiction is exceptional. The more general point is that all the novelists allow themselves to be writerly. They appeal as such to an aesthetically distanced reader, invite response to textual surface and so subvert the illusion of a self-narrating mimesis. At the most superficial level (I do not mean that pejoratively), they are all interested in style and diction. They avoid hiatus.[63] Chariton is careful about his rhythmic clausulae. Xenophon is just drab, but Longus alternates between a mannered simplicity and passages of almost incantatory poetry. Achilles and Heliodorus use all the rhetorical tropes they can get their hands on. Indeed, the latter's linguistic artificiality was a paramount influence on the English euphuists, such as Lyly.

More interestingly, perhaps, the plots are replete with intriguing patterns and symmetries which suggest artistic control of significa-tion. In Chariton, for example,[64] the heroine's story is built around a series of men who love her. In themselves they form a meaningful hierarchy: private citizen, provincial bigwig, satrap, King of Persia, and finally her first husband again, the only man she has ever really loved. His place at the head of the hierarchy not only produces an aesthetically satisfying cyclical form, but makes the basic structure of the text into a statement of a value-system which ranks true love above position and wealth. Likewise, in Heliodorus, Charicleia's life is guided by a succession of priestly father-figures, forming an ascent towards wisdom and spirituality.

---

62. See Morgan, art. cit. (n. 55 above).
63. See M.D. Reeve, 'Hiatus in the Greek Novelists', *Classical Quarterly* 21 (1971), 514–39.
64. The symmetries of Chariton are revealed with especial clarity by the diagram-matic analysis in G. Molinié's Budé edition, 14–21.

Let us take another example from Chariton. After being entombed alive, Callirhoe is stolen by tomb-robbers, leaving her husband to lament beside the empty tomb (3.3). He sails in search of her, but is ambushed and sold into slavery. Believing him dead, Callirhoe has a cenotaph built in which she entombs his image. Then she laments beside the empty tomb, and in so doing draws our attention to the parallelisms:

First you buried me in Syracuse, and now I am burying you at Miletus. Our misfortunes are not merely great, they are also hard to believe [*paradoxa*]—we have buried each other! Yet neither of us has the other's dead body! Malicious Fortune! You do not even let us share a tomb in death! You have exiled even our dead bodies!

(4.1.11)

In enjoying the parallelism and recognizing its improbability, the reader becomes conscious that this is a *plot*, controlled and contrived by an author: fiction. Such parallelisms abound in the novels, constituting one of their principles of construction, and they generally carry an implication of significance.

So, in Heliodorus, the hero competes with an Arcadian athlete (4.1ff.) and an Ethiopian wrestler (10.30ff.). The two contests are linked by verbal allusion and by the contemptuous arrogance of the hero's antagonists, and they occupy symmetrical places at the beginning and conclusion of the love story. Charicleia, for her part, is given two scenes of iconic purity and radiance, one when she fails to be incinerated at the stake (8.9), the other when her virginity is proven by the Ethiopian fire-ordeal (10.9). The first marks her victory over the immorality of the Persian court and its attempts to destroy her physically and morally, the second her triumph over malicious fate and its threats to her chastity. But in both cases her vindication is the prelude to mortal danger. Even Xenophon of Ephesus is capable of such effects. His heroine Anthia is successively immured in a pit with starving dogs (4.6) and in a brothel (5.7), the carnal bestiality of whose clients is figured in the symmetry. In all these cases the reader's satisfaction results from an appreciation of the text's artistry, a pleasure opposite to that of realistic engagement.

Similarly, self-conscious elaboration of plot leads to appreciation of the cleverness with which the cogs of the narrative machine are made to mesh, but that in itself distances the reader.

The novels are thoroughly allusive. The novel has always been the most polyphonic, heteroglossic of genres. Some modern theorists suggest that its success is due to its omnivorous ability to absorb and adapt stimuli from a wide range of literary forms. The Greek novels exploit the broadest possible spectrum of intertexts, and in doing so proclaim themselves as literature within a literary tradition.

Longus recast Theocritean pastoral into narrative.[65] His story is set in an ambience which is avowedly artificial, and he enjoys playing with its nature as fantasy by lifting the curtain occasionally to show hard and dirty realities of rural life behind the sanitized niceness of pastoral. Chariton is constantly quoting Homer,[66] not in a purely decorative way but using Homeric lines as organic parts of his own storytelling. Again, attention is drawn to the work's status as literature.

Heliodorus also looks to the Homeric poems. The Odyssey is evoked by the plunge in medias res and the use of a secondary narrator. Calasiris, equivalent to Odysseus in this structure, is an Odysseus-like, ambivalent figure. The analogy is made palpable when he introduces his retrospective narrative by alluding to the first words of Odysseus in his retrospective narrative (2.21.5 cf. Od. 9.39). In the course of his story, he is visited by a dream of Odysseus, who compares their experiences (5.22.3), and then casts the heroine in the role of Penelope. Earlier, Calasiris in his elusiveness has been compared to another Odyssean figure, the shapeshifter Proteus (2.24.4). Theagenes, the hero, is assimilated to both the Homeric heroes. His ancestry is traced to Achilles, of whom he is suggestive physically (2.34–5); he leads a sacred mission to Delphi to honour Achilles' son, and in the procession carries an Achillean

---

65. For details see G. Rohde, 'Longus und die Bukolik', *Rheinisches Museum* 86 (1938), 23–49; M.C. Mittelstadt, 'Longus' *Daphnis and Chloe* and the Pastoral Tradition', *Classica et Medievalia* 27 (1966), 162–77; id., 'Bucolic-lyric Motifs and Dramatic Narrative in Longus' *Daphnis and Chloe*', *Rheinisches Museum* 113 (1970), 211–27; L.R. Cresci, 'Il romanzo di Longo Sofista e la tradizione bucolica', *Atene e Roma* 26 (1981), 1–25.
66. Cf. Müller, art. cit. (n. 14 above).

ash-wood spear (3.3.5). As a second Achilles, he is swift of foot and wins the palm in the race in armour at the Pythian Games (4.2ff.); as he stands at the starting line, he is compared to Homer's description of Achilles fighting the river (4.3.1). But Theagenes is also Odysseus to Charicleia's Penelope. He can be recognized by a scar on his leg which he got hunting boar (5.5.2), evoking the very passage of the *Odyssey* where the hero's essence is encapsulated in his naming. And so the happy ending of the novel re-enacts the union of Odysseus and Penelope at the end of the *Odyssey*.

Other incidents are built on tragedy. Charicleia is the physical image of Andromeda, whose whiteness in Ethiopia seems to have played a part in Euripides' play. The final episode, where hero and heroine face human sacrifice at the ends of the earth evokes *Iphigenia in Tauris*. Phaedra from the *Hippolytus* appears twice over, as Cnemon's lascivious stepmother (the parallel is drawn for us at 1.10.2) and as the nymphomaniac princess Arsace (with quotation from Euripides at 8.15.2). Chariton points a similarity to Medea at the point where Callirhoe is contemplating aborting her unborn child (2.9.3).

There are other analogues too numerous to mention here, but my point is that these novels are desperately concerned to be part of Greek literature. Their whole fabric is shot through with motifs and patterns which their readers would recognize as deriving from the masterworks of the classical period. Scholars used to try to explain the origin of the novel in terms of evolution from another genre. Erotic narrative poetry, New Comedy, rhetorical exercise, epic, historiography were all canvassed as its parents. But perhaps it is better to argue that the polyphony characteristic of all novels expresses itself by an incorporation of virtually all previous literature.

At the same time, the novel constituted a generic unity of its own, and the leading voice in the intertextual orchestra is always that of the genre itself. The restricted repertoire of motifs and plot-units means that the novels seem to be playing variations on the same inherited theme. Anyone reading them presumably knew pretty well what to expect, and reaction to, and appreciation of, them will have been determined to a very large extent by expectations derived from a pre-existent corpus.

Many effects derive from exploiting or thwarting these expectations. Even in the earliest surviving novel, Chariton's, Callirhoe's pregnancy and second, bigamous marriage are best read as deliberate infringements of generic rules, for it is precisely when she transgresses generic conventions that the heroine becomes individual and morally interesting. Chariton equivocates still further by making her second husband, who in generic terms is a structural obstacle to the required happy ending, into a sympathetic and human character. He seems, in other words, already to be examining the novel's conventions by exploiting his reader's familiarity with them. Achilles and Heliodorus are immensely sophisticated at doing this.[67] They use the reader's own reading competence to lure him into assumptions about the course of the plot, only to prove him wrong when the conventional signposts turn out to mean something quite different. The reader of these novels knows how they are going to end almost from the first page, and knowledge of the intertextual archetype is a crucial element in a play of expectations designed to keep him guessing as long as possible.

All of these things denote an awareness of the text as text. As far as they draw attention to the literariness of the novel, they open the way to interpretation. Umberto Eco has called the novel 'a machine for generating interpretations'; but it must first be recognized as a novel. All interpretation rests on the assumption that the work is purposefully organized, without the random contingency of reality. In this sense, any impulse to interpret denies reality. Through their control of structure, the novelists were able to suggest 'truths' in the Aristotelian sense, but at the cost of a literal verisimilitude.

V

Where does all this leave us on the question of the concept of fiction inherent in these novels? The obvious point is that there is a lot which is in excess of ancient theory, but that just means that theory had not caught up with practice. My argument has been that the novels comprise two antithetical but interdependent systems of belief and disbelief which answer to the opposing positions in the

---

67. This is explored at length by S. Bartsch, *Decoding the Ancient Novel* (Princeton, 1989); and by J.R. Morgan, 'A Sense of the Ending: the Conclusion of Heliodoros' *Aithiopika*', *Transactions of the American Philological Association* 119 (1989), 299–320.

anecdote of Solon and Thespis, and which underlie Photius' problems with Antonius Diogenes. There are two defences for fiction against the charge of lying: the first is to pretend that the fiction is not untrue at all, the second to deny any intention to deceive. For a logician these are incompatible, but a novelist and his readers seem to be able to have it both ways. To see how that can be, we must return to what it means to 'believe' a fiction. It is obviously something quite different from believing a lie.

We all know the mythical child who watches *Dr Who* from behind the sofa. He is driven there by a real fear: he is not just pretending to be afraid. But if he really believed in what he feels threatened by, he would be out of the room and running for his life. He is held by a desire to know what happens next, and, at one level of his consciousness, by the secure knowledge that he is watching fiction. Novel-reading, I suggest, is like that. We turn to a novel for the imaginative pleasure of being able to enter a world of vicarious experience and live it from the inside, to experience it with real emotional involvement, to believe it. Yet many of the experiences we enjoy vicariously are ones we would seek to avoid in real life. We can only abandon ourselves wholeheartedly to the novel's imaginative power because we know there is no real cost or risk to ourselves. So the novel has to reassure us constantly that it is only fiction, and it does this by keeping at least one part of the reader consciously in the real world, where he can watch from an aesthetic distance.

We must believe to be moved, and yet we find it comic or pathetic when the fictivity of the belief is forgotten. As early as *Don Quixote*, novelists were concerned by the protocols of belief in fiction, and the problem is still with us. Seven hundred people a year write to Sherlock Holmes in Baker Street, in the belief not only that he was a real person but that he is still alive; fiction's power can convert past tense to present. When a novel is read properly, the reader does believe, but only with the imaginative part of himself that has entered the world of the novel. Within this world the statements that make up the novel are fictionally true; outside it they are factually untrue, and both writer and reader acknowledge them to be so in their rational minds.

It is helpful to use the commonplace metaphor of games with rules. Indeed, fiction begins in childhood as a game of make-believe, vital for cognitive and affective development. The rules of soccer impose unnatural forms of behaviour on its players; the central fiction is that the ball cannot be handled. If the rules are not observed, the game cannot be played. But even while he is playing, the soccer-player knows that the rules do not apply outside the game, and may even infringe them for advantage within the game. So in a novel the reader has to believe. Coleridge called this 'the willing suspension of disbelief'; I have used the more positive idea of make-believe. Without it the game is no fun; but, even when playing, the reader cannot forget that the central rule of the fictional game is itself a fiction. Believing and knowing that it is only make-believe are inseparably twinned. Obviously, the balance of awareness and surrender varies from reader to reader, from text to text, and from period to period, but to neglect one or the other side of the equation is, it seems to me, to falsify the experience of reading a novel.

However, the reader's belief cannot simply be willed into being. It is a response to a certain quality in the writer's invention: believability. It is the writer's task, within the rules, to make the reader 'believe', and if the reader ever feels that the imaginative leap he is being asked to make is too great he is likely to withdraw from the game. The game is refereed by subjective criteria of plausibility, although the referee may well be swayed by the persuasive power of a certain piece of writing into accepting as believable statements which in any other context he would have adjudged foul play.

What do we mean when we talk of a fiction being believable?[68] I have argued that readers believe; but it is hardly sensible to ask whether something you believe is believable. Equally, I have argued that fiction also entails an awareness of its untruth; and again it seems inappropriate to ask if something you know for certain to be untrue is believable. The idea of 'believable fiction', then, does not make sense from either of the reader's two perspectives in isolation. Rather, it is what mediates between and unites his two worlds. In monitoring a novel's believability, the reader is in a continual process of moving backwards and forwards between the world of the fiction and the world of reality, checking that the correlation is sufficient to allow the game to go on. There is a chain of relativities: fictional

---

68. Newsom, op. cit. (n. 12 above) is fundamental here.

pleasure requires belief, belief implies believability, but believability requires the evaluative distance of objective disbelief. The paradoxes cohere and make sense around the reader's double aspect which I have tried to illustrate in the Greek novels.

However, it is a common criticism of the Greek novels that they are incredible. Modern readers feel that the invention contravenes their view of reality, and that the texts are not persuasive enough to adjust that view. But this is merely to say that the implied view of the verisimilar differs from generally held modern ones. This is worth stressing, because it is here, rather than on the fundamental questions of what fiction is and what it is for, that the Greek novels are foreign to us.

We are used to evaluating plausibility in fiction broadly in two ways.[69] First by correspondence: by the extent to which there is a straightforward coincidence between the fiction and reality. And second, by coherence: that is, the extent to which the fiction is maintained within the logic of its own premises. This latter sometimes enables us to assent to a fictional situation quite unlike anything in our own experience: science fiction or Tolkien's fantasy world would be good examples. In more traditional novels, it is this second type of plausibility which governs plot-building, where we tend to expect tight construction with a minimum of contingency. The modern mode of plausibility is tied up with mathematical or statistical probabilities. Though there is no difficulty about accepting a statistically improbable incident, such as a mysterious death, we look for the likelihoods within that category to be observed, and feel that believability decreases geometrically as improbabilities are conjoined. We look also for verisimilitude on levels such as that of character, which plays an important causal role in the modern novel and often persuades that some unlikely action is in fact probable in certain circumstances.

Ancient concepts of verisimilitude, as voiced by the rhetoricians and reflected in the novels, seem less complex. Both correspondential and coherential forms are recognized, but the division between *muthos* and *plasma*, for example, seems to reside in little more than physical possibility. So long as an incident did not contradict

---

69. Cf. K.K. Ruthven, *Critical Assumptions* (Cambridge, 1979), 164–80.

observable physical laws, it was inherently acceptable, and could be persuasively enhanced by the application of *enargeia* and other techniques of presentation. This approach to verisimilitude, by remaining at the level of the individual incident, encouraged the multiplication of unlikelihoods within the bounds of possibility. The effect of this is readily observable in the plot structure of the romances, which, in its simplest form, is an infinitely extensible chain of thrilling episodes between the loss of felicity and its recovery.[70] In fact, the emotive power of each incident and of the plot as a whole is enhanced by their extremity and statistical improbability. 'The highest degree of perfection is when the marvellous and verisimilar are joined together'.[71]

Perhaps most alien of all, the ancient novels do not exploit the interiorities of character as a means of enhancing the believability. As early as Aristotle, probability was connected with character, but the connection tended to be conceived in terms of generic appropriateness rather than psychological individuality. Kings must act like kings, slaves like slaves. Chaereas' characterization is more a matter of what he is than who he is. The ancient novelists seem hardly to have recognized the possibility that Chaereas might act as he does because he is Chaereas. They did not need individuation of character to engage their readers' belief, and so their interest was concentrated more on manipulation of plot than on observation of humanity. The action of a Greek novel is not powered by the indivduality of its actors. To us, they do not ring true, maybe, but there is no reason to project that feeling back on to their original audience.

This paramountcy of plot over character leads to one final point. Self-conscious manipulation of plot exposes, I have argued, the controlling mind behind the fiction, and hence its fictionality. This guarantees that there is a plot, a narrative structure, at all, and that this structure will, in the end, make sense, both artistically and morally. Within the text, the controlling intelligence can be figured

---

70. This potentially infinite chain of adventures occupies what Bakhtin termed the 'chronotope of atemporal adventure-time'; see the important discussion in *The Dialogic Imagination* (Austin, 1981), 84ff.

71. Quoted from Torquato Tasso's *Discorsi dell'arte poetica e del poema eroico* by Newsom. The whole of Tasso's remarkably shrewd discussion of the verisimilar in poetry, contained in Bk 2, is worth pondering. The underlying aesthetic is drawn from classical literature, and seems to me to make a great deal of sense as a reconstruction of ancient assumptions.

by the metaphor of the divine. As arbiters of human destiny, the power of the gods within the fiction is identical to that of the author over his creation. This identity can be used for camouflage, as in the case of Chariton, who invokes the divine at precisely those moments when he is himself most active, as at crucial changes of plot direction. This avoids the direct admission that things happen simply because he chooses to make them happen. Alternatively, the divine apparatus can be exploited as a means of self-reference, as Heliodorus does.[72] Either way, the prominence of the gods guarantees the sensefulness of the fiction.

The problem with the Greek novels is that they depict not the world as it is, but the world as it ought to be. The good reap the fruits of their goodness, their ordeals only prepare for final, immaculate happiness. Life is not like that. The more arbitrary and unfair reality seems, the more people need to believe in some ultimate viewpoint from which the patterns will become clear. The Greek novels offer that, as does much popular fiction still. Religion and the novel are in the same market, and the parallel was not lost on the Greek novelists. There is comfort in the knowledge that everything is safe in the hands of a rational power, and in a novel that means awareness of fictionality. The comfort is a naïve one, and, though pleasant to entertain imaginatively, it would be foolish to import it wholesale into one's real life. The awareness of make-believe confines to a textual experience the desire to relinquish control, to trust to the benevolence of things. It is an observable fact that people do not lead their lives by the values enshrined in even their most treasured art.

And yet . . . there is an ache for life to make sense as fiction does. If not today, then perhaps tomorrow. If virtue is not rewarded, then perhaps it might be under an only slightly different dispensation. The realism, the *make* believe, of the novels functions to tell us that the world in which things come right in the end is not after all so very different from our own. It takes only a little help and a little imagination to believe, to experience that world from the inside. The realism is an apparatus of optimism; the reader's belief is made to coalesce with his hopes. To read and believe is a gesture of faith: faith in the possibility that reality could be like a Greek novel.

---

72. Well argued by Bartsch, op. cit. (n. 67 above), 135ff.

Epilogue

Towards an Account of the Ancient World's Concepts of Fictive Belief

D.C. FEENEY

> What to believe, in the course of his reading, was Mr Boffin's chief literary difficulty indeed; for some time he was divided in his mind between half, all, or none; at length, when he decided, as a moderate man, to compound with half, the question still remained, which half? And that stumbling-block he never got over.
>
> Charles Dickens, *Our Mutual Friend*

THE problem of the kind of belief which is generated or invited by fiction is a very large and strange one, which has been with us for a very long time. What we do when we 'believe fictions' is, after all, a most mysterious business.[1] What do we mean when we say 'Evander, or Chloe, or Little Dorrit, did this

---

This chapter may be regarded as a supplement to the discussion of belief in Ovid's fictions in *The Gods in Epic: Poets and Critics of the Classical Tradition* (*GIE*) (Oxford, 1991), 225–32. A draft of the paper was read by Charles Martindale, John Morgan, Christopher Rowe, and Michael Wood, who made very helpful comments. They remain, of course, innocent of any responsibility for the use I have made of the aid they have given me.

1. These issues have, naturally, been intensively discussed, and a useful biblio-graphical discussion may be found in W. Rösler, 'Die Entdeckung der Fiktionalität in der Antike', *Poetica* 12 (1980), 283–319, at 283–5 (hereafter Rösler, 'Entdeckung'). Two highly important recent studies (themselves

or that', and how are these utterances different from saying 'Hitler, or Caesar, or John Major, did this or that'? What are we doing when we even act upon these beliefs, visiting, for example, the Palatine Hill, or the Cobb at Lyme Regis, or the sights of London or Bath, imagining in all these places the scenes taking place which we first imagined when we read Dickens, Jane Austen, or Vergil? The very existence of a *Blue Guide to Literary Britain and Ireland* is a thought-provoking phenomenon. What kind of statements are they, these fictional statements which make people want to write and read such a *Blue Guide*? What kind of reality do the fictive events of these statements have, and what kind of belief do readers or listeners entertain in that reality, as they are moved to laughter, rage, or tears by things that never happened?[2]

Even in proposing to concentrate only on the problem of belief, I am conscious of biting off more than anyone could reasonably hope to chew, and the impression of the enquiry's rashness may perhaps be increased, from a classicist's point of view, by the notorious problem of whether or not the ancient world even had such a thing as a concept of fiction. For my part, at least, I think it has been established, from various perspectives, that the ancient poets and critics developed a range of concepts which may usefully be compared to what we call 'fiction', even if there is no precise fit between our word or concept 'fiction' and their *fabula, plasma, mimēsis, muthos, figmentum* ('fable, moulding, imitation, myth, forming'). We should not indeed, be too exercised by this lack of a precise fit. Quite apart from the question of whether any such fit is possible between any two concepts or words in different cultures, one of the aims of the present paper is to suggest that an exact overlap in the concept of 'fiction' between any two cultures would be theoretically impossible, since even within any one culture

containing up-to-date bibliographical discussions) deal in particular with the issues of belief which engage me here: R. Newsom, *A Likely Story: Probability and Play in Fiction* (*LS*) (New Brunswick, 1988); K.L. Walton, *Mimesis as Make-Believe: On the Foundations of the Representational Arts* (*MMB*) (Cambridge, Mass., 1990), esp. 190–289; cf. G. Currie, *The Nature of Fiction* (*NF*) (Cambridge, 1990), ch. 5, 'Emotion and the response to fiction', 182–216. See, too, the diverting collection of opinions in K.K. Ruthven, *Critical Assumptions* (Cambridge, 1979), 164–80 ('Truth and credibility').

2. On emotional response to fictions, see Currie, *NF*, 182–216; Walton, *MMB*, 385, 430.

different concepts of fiction will emerge and fade over time, and be in play at any one time.

To show that it is provisionally worthwhile, before putting the concept under any kind of pressure, to talk about something corresponding to fiction in the ancient world, let us begin by taking as a rule of thumb the definition of fiction given by Halliwell: 'a relation between poetry and its objects . . . which can be described neither as a simple transcription of the truth, nor as the invention of untruth masquerading as reality'.[3] Against this yardstick, it is tolerably clear that Aristotle's account of poetic mimesis ends up describing what we would recognize as a theory of fiction.[4] Similarly, the tripartite divisions of narrative, with their criteria of variation in correspondence to reality, assume a sliding scale of fictiveness, as may be seen from the formulation of Quintilian: 'we have three types of narrative: myth, which you get in tragedies and poems,[5] and which is removed not only from truth but even from the appearance of truth; fictitious story [*argumentum* = Greek *plasma*], which comedies invent, false but verisimilitudinous; and history, in which there is an exposition of something which actually happened' (2.4.2). Ancient novels, to take a concrete example, are usefully described by Reardon as 'narrative fiction in prose—imaginative, creative literature'.[6]

Even epics or tragedies, which Reardon on the same page describes as 'in principle . . . not fictitious', since 'they are always in some sense based on real things, historical events or figures', were regarded by the critical tradition as being, in important senses, 'fictitious'. This is true not only in the rather casual sense by which, as Reardon himself says, 'the *Odyssey* itself is a prime example' of

---

3. S. Halliwell, *Aristotle's Poetics* (*AP*) (London, 1986), 12.
4. Halliwell, *AP*, 12–13, 21–3; id., *The Poetics of Aristotle; Translation and Commentary* (London, 1987), 72–4, 172, 177–9.
5. By 'poems' (*carmina*) he means, above all, epics.
6. B.P. Reardon, ed., *Collected Ancient Greek Novels* (*CAGN*) (Berkeley, 1989), 1. John Morgan raises with me the question of why ancient critics, if they had a relatively well developed theory of fiction, disregarded the novel so completely (see his ch. 6 above); at the moment, I have no answer beyond a reference to the canonical frame of mind of ancient critics, who might have found it difficult to accommodate new forms to their inherited apparatus.

'embryonic narrative fiction',[7] but in more fundamental ways as well. Even though Ajax or Achilles may have been thought of as actual people who had once lived, even receiving hero-cult in historical times, the acts and speech posited of such characters in epic or tragedy were openly regarded as fictitious: their deeds could be rationalized at any stage by critics or historians, and it was taken for granted that there were competing representations of what their deeds might have been. Right at the beginning of Greek criticism, Herodotus, for example, could explain away such a basic part of the tradition as Helen's presence at Troy on the grounds that it was entirely a question of Homer's poetic preference, since Homer knew that Helen had really been in Egypt the whole time (2.116).

According to the mainstream critical opinion as represented by the grammarians and rhetoricians, the difference between history and epic had nothing to do with what we might label 'historicity' (whether something had happened or not), but was rather a question of the mode of treatment, the degree of 'fictiveness' which was applied in the narrating.[8] This critical dogma may be regarded as a watered down version of the more comprehensive insights of Aristotle, in whose description of poetic fiction's universalizing power the proper names of the characters of panhellenic myth are mere epiphenomena (*Poetics* 1451b10, 15–16). We encounter the Aristotelian insight again (though with typically Renaissance didactic colour) in Sidney's *Defence of Poesie*, in the famous section where he rebuts the charge that poets are liars ('the poet . . . never affirmeth'). To the specific charge that poets lie when they 'give names to men they write of', he replies with a question:

And doth the lawyer lie then, when under the names of *John-a-stiles* and *John-a-nokes* he puts his case? . . . We see that we cannot play at chess but that we must give names to our chessmen; and yet, methinks, he were a very partial champion of truth that would say we lied for giving a piece of wood the

---

7. Op. cit., 6.
8. Feeney, *GIE*, 44–5, 253–6, 261–4.

reverend title of a bishop. The *Poet* nameth *Cyrus* and *Aeneas* no other way than to show what men of their fames, fortunes, and estates, should do.[9]

It is certainly true that the ancient critics had very different priorities from modern ones. They were, in particular, much more concerned about the moral worth and philosophical value of making fictional statements than about the logical status of those statements, the nature of their reality, whereas the mainstream of modern criticism has the reverse priority.[10] Still, having provisionally established that there was some kind of interest in a category of fiction in the ancient tradition, we may now move on to note that this interest extended to the issues of belief which concern us here. Ancient poets and critics mentioned many factors as being operative in fostering the fictive illusion, in keeping an audience involved, maintaining its assent in the representation. In the higher genres especially, the qualities of elevation and sublimity were singled out as ways of keeping the audience enraptured;[11] authenticating detail, and the apparatus of probability, were regarded as especially powerful factors in inducing belief.[12]

---

9. K. Duncan-Jones and J. van Dorsten, eds, *Miscellaneous Prose of Sir Philip Sidney* (Oxford, 1973), 103. Earlier, Sidney paraphrases Aristotle's point about names in such a way as to show that he sees the poet's naming as a function of the universal nature of poetry (88.6–7). Coming at the problem from the other direction, Currie (*NF*, 146), makes the point that 'there is no necessary connection between writing fiction and using fictional names.'

10. Indeed, according to Newsom (*LS*, 108), the 'premodern' ranking of priority persisted up to the nineteenth century. Walton *MMB* is a very successful attempt to provide an 'integrated theory' to bridge the 'remarkable and unfortunate separation between . . . *aesthetically* and *metaphysically* oriented theorizing about fiction' (6; his italics). Charles Martindale, meanwhile, makes me realize that much modern criticism is more 'moralistic' than its overt programmes would imply: for a fine attack on the 'secularized puritans', see B. Harrison, *Inconvenient Fictions: Literature and the Limits of Theory* (New Haven, 1991), 61–70.

11. N.J. Richardson, 'Pindar and Later Literary Criticism in Antiquity', *Papers of the Liverpool Latin Seminar* 5 (1985), 383–401, at 386; 'Longinus', *On Sublimity*, esp. ch. 15, on *phantasia* ('fantasy, visualisation').

12. A.J. Woodman, *Rhetoric in Classical Historiography: Four Studies* (London, 1988), 85–6; Feeney, *GIE*, 28–9, 49–50. The coexistence of two such different factors as elevation and detail shows up interesting fissures in the entire problem of belief, to which we shall return shortly.

The main emphasis, however, was on desire, on the enthralling, seductive power of speech, and the desire for pursuit, consummation and satisfaction which speech quickens in its audience.[13] Peitho, the very goddess 'Persuasion', was, after all, 'a divinity whose province was the alluring power of sexual love';[14] when Plutarch wants Homeric authority for his image of the alluring power of poetry, he chooses two lines from the description of Aphrodite's sex-charged girdle: 'loveliness is figured upon it, and passion of sex is there, and the whispered endearment that steals the heart away even from the thoughtful' (*Iliad* 14.216–17, tr. Lattimore, quoted by Plutarch in *How the Young Man Should Study Poetry* 15c). Peitho's realm also included another closely related metaphorical area for capturing the enchantment of poetry, that of spells and witchcraft[15] (here above all we see that this desire does not simply equal pleasure, but is also a matter of power, and allows for the paradoxical urge to be immersed in fear and anguish). The poet's inspired voice casts a spell over the audience, persuading and convincing with its enthralling art, and the captivated trance into which the ideal audience sinks is already imagined for us by Homer, as he shows us the reaction of the Phaeacians to the tales of Odysseus:

> So he spoke, and all of them stayed stricken to silence, held in thrall [*kēlēthmō(i) d' eschonto*] by the story all through the shadowy chambers.
>
> (Homer, *Odyssey* 11.333–4, tr. Lattimore)

---

13. On seduction in Greek poetics, see especially G. Walsh, *The Varieties of Enchantment: Early Greek Views of the Nature and Function of Poetry* (Chapel Hill, 1984), 14–15, 22; W.G. Thalmann, *Conventions of Form and Thought in Early Greek Epic Poetry* (Baltimore, 1984), 129–30. Modern criticism, even outside Lacanian circles, has begun to show considerable, and varied, interest in the text's seduction or the reader's desire: R. Barthes, *Le Plaisir du texte* (Paris, 1975) (an onanistic version, this); R. Chambers, *Story and Situation: Narrative Seduction and the Power of Fiction* (Minneapolis, 1984), esp. 10, 215–16; B. Rosebury, *Art and Desire: A Study in the Aesthetics of Fiction* (New York, 1988); Currie, *NF*, 200–8, 210–11. A classicist can only register extreme despondency at the modern critics' entire lack of interest in the fact that the beginning of European criticism is so intimately involved with these same issues.

14. R. Buxton, *Persuasion in Greek Tragedy: A Study of Peitho* (Cambridge, 1982), 31.

15. Buxton, op. cit., 40, 51–2.

This is a self-reflexive moment, of course, and a very fine one, as we imagine the singer, Homer, singing these words to his own enraptured audience, stricken to silence in the shadowy chambers.

If seduction and poetic language can be figured as alluring and enchanting, they may also be represented (particularly by hostile parties) as inherently deceitful and oblique, and the *Odyssey*, with its gallery of duplicitous speakers, reveals this awareness too, as we are shown that responses other than assent are possible, and that the invitation to go along with the wishes of the other person may be resisted.[16] Only thirty lines after the passage I have just quoted, we hear Alcinous acknowledging that he and his people can discriminate, since they certainly do not believe everyone they hear out of all the deceivers who visit their island (11.363-8); and his words are picked up in Book 14 by the tough and sceptical swineherd Eumaeus, who likewise tells the disguised Odysseus of the hordes of liars which come to Ithaca (122-5), and who refuses to swallow all of Odysseus' plausible yarn (361-5). The entire episode in Eumaeus' house shows us, as Goldhill puts it, 'a series of conversations . . . that both veil and reveal the two speakers in a complex network of truths and fictions, fidelity and belief'.[17]

It may appear that we are ending up with a polarity between successfully seductive or deceptive speech, which commands belief, and unsuccessfully seductive or deceptive speech, which fails to win it. But such a polarity would obliterate the interplay between belief and disbelief, the way they define each other, and it would make it impossible for us to discriminate between, for example, the different ways in which 'deceit' is practised upon, and sustained by, the audience of, on the one hand, a poet and, on the other, a lying orator. Already in the fifth century, the strangeness involved in allowing ourselves to be deceived by poetry had received explicit (if oxymoronic) attention from poets and critics:

> For the element of deception in [poetry] does not gain any hold on utterly witless and foolish persons. This is the ground of Simonides' answer to the man who said to him, 'Why are the

---

16. See now the full and interesting discussion in ch. 1 of S. Goldhill, *The Poet's Voice: Essays on Poetics and Greek Literature* (Cambridge, 1991), esp. 36–68.
17. Goldhill, op. cit., 42.

Thessalians the only people whom you do not deceive?' His answer was, 'Oh, they are too ignorant to be deceived by me'; and Gorgias called tragedy a deception wherein he who deceives is more honest than he who does not deceive, and he who is deceived is wiser than he who is not deceived.

(Plutarch, *Moralia*, 15c–d,

tr. F.C. Babbitt, Loeb Classical Library)

In this context, being deceived takes wisdom, of a sort. For the game to work it is necessary for the audience to have some sophistication, says Simonides, some knowledge of the techniques which they are giving themselves over to. If self-awareness (at some level) is part of the compact, it seems, further, that the kind of belief required for being a successful reader or audience is necessarily bound up with a kind of *dis*belief, for if we are too ignorant (not disbelieving enough) we will have *too much* belief, and will not be deceived in the right way.

Knowing what (or how) *not* to believe is as integral a part of the experience as knowing what (or how) to believe—otherwise everything collapses. This is easiest to see in drama, as in the legend of the theatre-goer who rushes on to the stage to stop Othello smothering Desdemona,[18] or in the marvellous anecdote (of which Catharine Edwards reminds me) about Nero's performance in the title-role of 'Hercules Mad': 'There is a story that a young recruit on guard in the wings recognized him in the rags and fetters demanded by the part of Hercules, and dashed boldly to his assistance' (Suetonius, *Nero* 21.3, tr. R. Graves). But it is not only in drama that audiences need to have their wits about them even as they are entranced. Here we may introduce Newsom's extremely useful concept of 'duality', which he sees as the key to understanding how we assent to fiction:

in entertaining fictions (or making believe) we divide our beliefs between real and fictional worlds. . . . an essential part of reading stories or of entertaining any kind of make-believe is

---

18. Walton, *MMB*, 192–5 ('Rescuing heroines').

'having it both ways.' It is insisting on our belief in the fictional
world *even* as we insist also on our belief in the world in which
the reading or make-believe takes place.[19]

We may remark in passing that Newsom's 'duality' is one way of
trying to come to terms with the apprehension that art is something
crafted *and* emotionally compelling or immediate. Even the most
enthralling documents of mimetic art may call attention to their own
crafted status, and they may (very strangely) do this in such a way
as to *compound* their power to move us. Think of the scene in
Sophocles' *Trachiniae* where Deianeira repeatedly tries to get the
silent Iole to speak ('Who are you? . . . Tell me, unhappy girl, tell
me out of your own mouth', 307, 320–1). At some level, we are
aware that Iole may not respond because there are already three
speaking actors on stage, but this formal imposition of muteness
will, for most audiences, reinforce, rather than undermine, sympathy
for the passivity enforced upon Iole by her culture and her gender.

If we confine ourselves to the issue of the 'division of belief'
which underpins Newsom's 'duality', it becomes apparent that
duality is something which may tip either way, as may readily be
seen if we consider the techniques of maintaining fictive illusion
which we looked at above. Any aspect of literature which contributes to authentication, to lulling the reader into acquiescence, may
be turned around to become a device of alienation. The provision of
verisimilitudinous detail is perhaps the most obvious illustration. It
was a commonplace of ancient criticism that minute circumstantial
particulars contributed to an atmosphere of veracity,[20] and the
doctrine has been stylishly elaborated by Roland Barthes, in his
essay on 'l'effet de réel'.[21] The 'reality effect' is Barthes' term for the
illusion of reality created by the concatenation of apparently incon-
sequential detail of all kinds: the accumulation of minutiae creates a

---

19. *LS*, 134–5 (Newsom's italics); cf. esp. 128, 135–7, 160. We return to Newsom's
theory below. Only at the last minute before submission did I see Harrison's
extremely interesting book (op. cit. n. 10 above); he has his own ways of
clinching with this duality, or 'gap', as he calls it: see esp. 17, 57–8.
20. See no. 12 above.
21. *Communications* 11 (1968), 84–9.

texture of density, 'reality'.[22] But if a reader concentrates on the authorial manipulation involved in the provision of such minutiae, or if an author insists too strenuously upon his responsibility for them, then scepticism and incredulity may soon follow. Anyone who has read any war novels or thrillers, especially with technology involved, will recognize the kind of effect I mean:

> The rearmost shell of this salvo exploded seventy-one feet from Löwenherz's port engine. The theoretical lethal radius of an exploding 10.5 cm. shell was fifty feet. This one fragmented into 4,573 pieces of which twelve weighed over one ounce, 1,525 weighed between one ounce and a fiftieth of an ounce, and 3,036 were fragments of less than a fiftieth of an ounce. Twenty-eight fragments hit Löwenherz's Junkers. Four pieces penetrated the port motor . . .[23]

The omniscience here has swollen into comedy; there is so much authenticating detail that the narrating act has become radically inauthentic.

Other authenticating techniques are similarly two-edged. We may authenticate utterance by saying 'I saw it myself'; we may authenticate it by saying the opposite: 'this is not my story, but the Muses'— or Phaedrus'—or Marlowe's'. Either of these two techniques may always be hovering in the background to destabilize its twin. We may swear that something is true, but that very act conjures up the suspicion that something underhand is going on, exposing us to the charge of 'lying like an eye-witness'.[24] The sublime and magnificent language of epic or tragedy astonishes us, says 'Longinus', so that we see what the poet sees (*On Sublimity* 15.2), but he has to add

---

22. A recent study of the Victorian novel takes this interest in authenticating detail about as far as it can go: R.D. Altick, *The Presence of the Present: Topics of the Day in the Victorian Novel* (Columbus, 1991).

23. Len Deighton, *Bomber* (London, 1978), 434. I am grateful to Prof. Anthony Snodgrass for the quotation, which he uses in his article 'archaeology', in M. Crawford, ed., *Sources for Ancient History* (Cambridge, 1983), 137–84, at 147.

24. From the epigraph to Julian Barnes, *Talking it Over* (London, 1991): apparently a 'Russian proverb'.

that such visualization in poetry 'has a quality of exaggeration which belongs to fable and goes far beyond credibility' (15.8, tr. D.A. Russell).

The limits of belief appear to be always implicated in the limits of disbelief—to be, even, defined by them. This is why, overall, I find Newsom's approach to fictive belief rather more winning than Walton's, for all its excellence. Newsom's account, concerned with the duality of the experience, would have us remain aware of the way in which we are operating with different sets of criteria simulaneously, which define (and may destabilize) each other, while Walton would have us jump for the purposes of the exercise into a make-believe frame of mind which is then self-contained.[25] If the limits of belief, then, are implicated in the limits of disbelief, it may be helpful to think of the category of fiction coming into play when those limits are triggered. We may look at this historically, as Rösler does, and see fictionality coming into being in response to the competition of other discourses,[26] rather as Marcel Detienne sees 'mythology' as a category or concept which only comes into play at the moment when it is contested.[27] The evolutionary model is, however, potentially misleading in its clarity, since it has a tendency to posit a once and for all 'discovery' of a transcendent category of fiction, when it might be more useful to entertain a model in which various ways of thinking about fictionality evolve over time, each coming into play against a background of other modes, which are themselves evolving and changing over time. Genre theory may provide a provisional analogy.[28] If genres are not reified Platonic essences, then mixing or crossing of genres is not something interesting that happens to pre-existing entities, but instead it is the

---

25. See Newsom, *LS*, 121–7, esp. 124–5, on Walton's approach; Currie likewise speaks of 'a *largely* internalised game of make-believe' (*NF*, 196; my italics). Newsom's approach also has, potentially, more explanatory power over different historical periods, as we shall see below.

26. Rösler, 'Entdeckung'. Similarly Halliwell (*The Poetics of Aristotle*, op. cit. [n. 4 above], 74) speaks of Aristotle responding to 'the need to define a more precise role for poetry in a culture which was rapidly developing other types of discourse (history, philosophy, rhetoric, science etc.)'.

27. *L'Invention de la mythologie* (Paris, 1981).

28. Here I am much indebted to the remarks of Duncan Kennedy in his review of two books on Ovid's *Metamorphoses* in *Journal of Roman Studies* 79 (1989), 209–10.

very phenomenon which constitutes what we take to be those essences, defining them in transgression; to use an analogy within an analogy, we may compare the way structuralists talk of such categories as 'human' or 'cultured' being defined at the limits as they are crossed.

In fiction, then, non-belief would always be as much at issue as belief, with fiction being constituted continually at the borders of assent, defined by the play with other modes of assent, becoming apprehensible at the limits. Each culture will have different limits, not only from other cultures, but also within itself; any given reader will have different limits from the next one, and will have different limits in his or her own head. We may go even further and observe that each culture will have different concepts of what belief itself may be. Belief in literary events was certainly something talked of in the ancient world,[29] but the aura attaching to language of belief in a literary context may be (indeed, we ought to expect it to be) quite different in a Christian culture, even if one does not go all the way with Needham's argument that belief as understood in European culture is entirely specific to that particular Christian culture.[30] By way of example, one reading of John Irving's novel *A Prayer for Owen Meany*, which narrates the incredible yet enthrallingly convincing tale of a bizarre Christ-figure in modern New England, might be to see it as a direct confrontation between the modes of belief proper to the novel and the modes of belief proper to the Christian gospels (which are the daily reading of the narrator of the events of the novel).

Where might classicists seek to find the margins between belief and disbelief? Newsom's subject is the modern novel, and for him the margins between belief in the fictional world and in the real world are patrolled by the modern 'discovery' of mathematical probability (what counts as 'probable' in the 'real world' will itself necessarily be undergoing continual redefinition, even after the great seventeenth-century watershed).[31] Michael McKeon's fascinating study of

---

29. Feeney, *GIE*, index under 'belief/disbelief'.
30. R. Needham, *Belief, Language and Experience* (Oxford, 1972).
31. Currie comes close to this kind of outlook at times (though he appears not to know Newsom): *NF* 119, 207.

the rise of the modern novel traces a long dialectical tussle between 'naïve empiricism' and 'extreme skepticism', originating in 'an epistemological crisis, a major cultural transition in attitudes toward how to tell the truth in narrative';[32] the modes of belief invented by the realist modern novel come to be seen as the product of prolonged contestation among the modes of belief invited by many other forms of narrative.

A fuller enquiry into fiction in the ancient world would do well to follow up Newsom's 'duality' and McKeon's 'dialectic', by concentrating on the various margins between fictive and other narratives, especially the margin between the belief accorded to fictions and the belief accorded to other modes of speech or representation. History, philosophy, rhetoric, science would be in the forefront of such an enquiry,[33] along with travel-narratives, biography and hagiography, governmental despatches and *commentarii*, oracles, dream-literature. Classicists have long been accustomed to cite the ancients' distinction between the modes of belief proper to poetry and to the law-court;[34] Victor Sage's forthcoming study of the relationship between the Gothic horror novel and changing attitudes to legal testimony suggests that this conventional antithesis could be re-examined in a much more dynamic fashion.

The problem of belief is inextricably involved with the problem of authority, and one would also have to investigate the range of techniques by which authority is given to fictional and non-fictional accounts,[35] concentrating especially on the overlap in technique between fiction and non-fiction, and between fiction and forgery.[36] Attributing authority to the Muses becomes increasingly problematical (and is anyway complicated even at the beginning of recorded literature by the claim of Hesiod's Muses to know how to speak 'many lies like authentic things, and true things as well', *Theogony*

---

32. *The Origins of the English Novel, 1600–1740* (Baltimore, 1987), 20.
33. Halliwell, loc. cit. (n. 26 above). Plutarch's essay *How the Young Man Should Study Poetry* shows, for example, the systematic interplay between the assent proper to poetry and the assent proper to philosophy.
34. Feeney, *GIE*, 40 n. 144.
35. An important start already made by Goldhill, op. cit. (n. 16 above).
36. Bearing in mind always the aphorism of H. Kenner, *The Counterfeiters: An Historical Comedy* (Bloomington, 1968), 165: 'The counterfeit . . . does not claim a reality it does not possess, but only an origin—that is, an authorization.'

27–8). The advent of literacy introduces new problems of authority. Plato still authenticates his productions by *oral* links to the 'event' (or else, conversely, distances himself from responsibiity for the account by means of the multiple layers of memory which preserve it); but documentary authentication is already coming in by the end of the fifth century,[37] and becomes increasingly important in fiction, and its twin, forgery, as authors of novels and pseudo-histories come up with ever more elaborate provenances for the 'genuine' documents which are their source. The concept of documentary authenticity in a manuscript culture is itself, of course, a diverting problem: what becomes of the authenticating phrase 'written in his (or my) very own hand' (*manu ipsius scriptum*) when it is copied by someone else's hand?[38] (The transition from manuscript to printing involves a host of new problems of authentication.)[39]

Documents, then, may be 'found' in graves, libraries, and archives.[40] Xenophon of Ephesus obliquely cites a written inscription as the source for his novel (5.15),[41] while Antonius Diogenes offers a truly stupendous multi-layered documentary transmission for *The Wonders Beyond Thule*.[42] We may see the tradition persisting in a wider range of historical settings, through Defoe's and Richardson's 'editorial' prefaces, to Umberto Eco's scholarly introduction to *The Name of the Rose*, where he explains the 'provenance' of the 'manuscript' which is the novel. The bifocal power of the enterprise is illustrated neatly by our complex response to Eco's trick. Although we read the scholarly introduction with our tongues in our cheeks, the authoritative power of the novel as a novel is not exploded, but buttressed, by the device. The parade of learning convinces us that this is an author who does know the world which he is going to recreate for us, and our self-esteem is flattered by the

---

37. W. Speyer, *Die literarische Fälschung im heidnischen und christlichen Altertum: ein Versuch ihrer Deutung (LF)* (Munich, 1971), 75.

38. Speyer, *LF*, 85.

39. Kenner, op. cit. (n. 36), 31–2.

40. Speyer, *LF*, 67–70. Note here, especially, the marvellous tales of documentary discovery attached to the 'eye-witness' accounts of the Trojan war by Dares and Dictys.

41. G.L. Schmeling, *Xenophon of Ephesus* (Boston, 1980), 80–1.

42. Gerald N. Sandy, in Reardon, *CAGN*, 776. My warm thanks to John Morgan for help with these novels and pseudo-histories.

genial impression we derive of an author who knows that we are canny enough to read through his own canny pretences.

I have followed Newsom in making 'duality' the leitmotif of my discussion, but many modern professional readers of fiction (university employees) are not so dualistic, being more inclined to the sceptical side of the enterprise, and wanting persistently to tip the scales towards self-consciousness, and disbelief. I have much more sympathy with these critics, who are at least motivated by an interest in literarity, than with their counterparts in the other pan of the scales, who wish to be charmed and beguiled and leave it at that. But the learned self-awareness of the sceptics can make them commit the opposite fault to that of the doltish Thessalians who were cited above, so that they become too wise to be deceived by the poet, rather than too ignorant. If I had to choose, I would prefer to follow the main ancient poetic and critical tradition, which regarded the spell of fiction as the donnée, the *explanandum*. But the point, I think, is that we do not have to *choose*: we do not want to be too ignorant, like the Thessalians, or the man who rescues Desdemona, or Nero's soldier, but we do not want to be too wise either. Or rather, to play the deceitful game of fiction successfully, we need to be ignorant and wise simultaneously.

Bibliography

Adlington, W., tr., *Apuleius: The Golden Ass*, ed. S. Gaselee (London, 1958)

Altick, R.D., *The Presence of the Present: Topics of the Day in the Victorian Novel* (Columbus, 1991)

Annas, J., *An Introduction to Plato's Republic* (Oxford, 1981)

Annas, J., 'Plato on the Triviality of Literature', in Moravcsik and Temko, eds, *Plato on Beauty*, 1–28

Armayor, O.K., 'Did Herodotus ever go to the Black Sea?', *Harvard Studies in Classical Philology* 82 (1978), 45–62

Armayor, O.K., 'Did Herodotus ever go to Egypt?', *Journal of the American Research Centre in Egypt* 15 (1978), 59–73

Armayor, O.K., *Herodotus' Autopsy of the Fayoum: Lake Moeris and the Labyrinth of Egypt* (Amsterdam, 1985)

Austin, J.L., *Sense and Sensibilia* (Oxford, 1964)

Austin, J.L., *How to Do Things with Words* (Oxford, 1965)

Avenarius, G., *Lukians Schrift zur Geschichtsschreibung* (Meisenheim am Glan, 1956)

Bakhtin, M.M., *The Dialogic Imagination*, tr. C. Emerson and M. Holquist (Austin, 1981)

Barnes, J., *Talking it Over* (London, 1991)

Barthes, R., 'L'effet de réel', *Communications* 11 (1968), 84–9

Barthes, R., *Le plaisir du texte* (Paris, 1975)

Barthes, R., *Roland Barthes par Roland Barthes* (Paris, 1975)

Bartsch, S., *Decoding the Ancient Novel: The Reader and the Role of Description in Heliodorus and Achilles Tatius* (Princeton, 1989)

Bartsch, W., *Der Charitonroman und die Historiographie* (Leipzig, 1934)

Barwick, K., 'Die Gliederung der Narratio in der rhetorischen Theorie und ihre Bedeutung für die Geschichte des antiken Romans', *Hermes* 63 (1928), 261–87

Beerbohm, M., *Zuleika Dobson* (London, 1911)

Belfiore, E., 'Pleasure, Tragedy and Aristotelian Psychology', *Classical Quarterly* 35 (1985), 349–61

Biederman, H., *Handlexicon der magischen Künste* (Graz, 1976)

Booth, W.C., *The Rhetoric of Fiction* (Chicago, 1961, 2nd edn 1983)

Bourdieu, P., *Esquisse d'une theorie de pratique* (Geneva, 1972)

Bowie, A.M., 'Exordia in Thucydides: Homer and Herodotus', in H.D. Jocelyn and H. Hurt, eds, *Tria Lustra: Classical Essays presented to John Pinsent* (Liverpool, 1993), 152–62

Bowie, E.L., 'Early Greek Elegy, Symposium and Public Festival', *Journal of Hellenic Studies* 106 (1986), 13–35

Bowie, E.L., 'One That Got Away', in L.M. Whitby, P.R. Hardie, J.M. Whitby, eds, *Homo Viator. Classical Essays for John Bramble* (Bristol, 1987), 13–23

Bowie, E.L., 'Who Read the Ancient Greek Novels?', in J. Tatum and G.M. Vernazza, eds, *The Ancient Novel*, 150–1

Bremer, J.M., van Erp Taalman Kip, A.M. and Slings, S.R., eds, *Some Recently Found Greek Poems*, *Mnemosyne Suppl.* 99 (Leiden, 1987)

Brock, R., review of A.J. Woodman, *Rhetoric in Classical Historiography*, in *Liverpool Classical Monthly* 16.7 (1991), 97–102

Brunt, P.A., 'Cicero and Historiography', in *Philias Charin: Miscellanea in onore di Eugenio Manni* (Rome, 1979), 311–40

Brunt, P.A., *Studies in Greek History and Thought* (Oxford, 1993)

Burn, A.R., tr., *Herodotus: The Histories* (Harmondsworth, 1972)

Buxton, R., *Persuasion in Greek Tragedy: A Study of Peitho* (Cambridge, 1982)

Calderini, A., 'La *enguesis* matrimoniale nei romanzieri greci e nei papiri', *Aegyptus* 39 (1959), 29–39

Calvino, I., 'Levels of Reality in Literature', in *The Literature Machine*, tr. P. Creagh (London, 1989), 101–21

Carey, C., 'Archilochus and Lycambes', *Classical Quarterly* 36 (1986), 60–67

Chambers, R., *Story and Situation: Narrative Seduction and the Power of Fiction* (Minneapolis, 1984)

Chiasson, C.C., 'Tragic Diction in Herodotus: Some Possibilities', *Phoenix* 36 (1982), 151–61

Clarke, H., *Homer's Readers: A Historical Introduction to the Iliad and Odyssey* (London, 1981)

Connor, W.R., *Thucydides* (Princeton, 1984)

Cornford, F.M., *Thucydides Mythistoricus* (London, 1907)

Cresci, L.R., 'Il romanzo di Longo Sofista e la tradizione bucolica', *Atene e Roma* 26 (1981), 1–25

Currie, G., *The Nature of Fiction* (Cambridge, 1990)

Dällenbach, L., *Le récit spéculaire* (Paris, 1977)

Davies, L.J., 'A Social History of Fact and Fiction: Authorial Disavowal in the Early English Novel', in E.W. Saïd, ed., *Literature and Society* (Baltimore, 1980)

Davies, M., ed., *Poetarum Melicorum Graecorum Fragmenta* 1 (Oxford, 1991)

Davies, R.W., *Soviet History in the Gorbachev Revolution* (London, 1989)

Davis, L.J., *Factual Fictions: the Origins of the English Novel* (New York, 1983)

Day, G., *From Fiction to the Novel* (London, 1987)

Deighton, L., *Bomber* (London, 1978)

Dessau, H., 'Über Zeit und Personlichkeit der Scriptores Historiae Augustae', *Hermes* 24 (1889), 337–92

Detienne, M., *L'invention de la mythologie* (Paris, 1981), tr. M. Cook as *The Creation of Mythology* (Chicago, 1986)

Deutsch, H., 'Fiction and Fabrication', *Philosophical Studies* 47 (1985), 201–11

Dewald, C., 'Narrative Surface and Authorial Voice in Herodotus' Histories', *Arethusa* 20 (1987), 147–70

Di Gregorio, L., 'Sulla biografia di Giamblico e la fortuna del suo romanzo attraverso i secoli', *Aevum* 38 (1964), 1–13

Dover, K.J., 'Thucydides "as History" and "as Literature"', *History and Theory* 22 (1983), 54–63

Duncan-Jones, K., and van Dorsten, J., eds, *Miscellaneous Prose of Sir Philip Sidney* (Oxford, 1973)

Earl, D., 'Prologue-form in Ancient Historiography', *Aufstieg und Niedergang der römischen Welt* 1.2, ed. H. Temporini (Berlin, 1972), 842–56

Eden, K., *Poetic and Legal Fiction in the Aristotelian Tradition* (Princeton, 1986)

Eden, P.T., ed. and tr., *Seneca: Apocolocyntosis* (Cambridge, 1984)

Edwards, M.J., 'Treading the Aether: Lucretius De Rerum Natura 1.62–79', *Classical Quarterly* 40 (1990), 465–9

Erbse, H., ed., *Festschrift Bruno Snell* (Munich, 1956)

Erbse, H., 'Uber das Prooimion (1.1–23) des thukydideischen Geschichtswerkes', *Rheinisches Museum* 113 (1970), 43–69

Everett, W., 'Upon Virgil, Aeneid VI, vss 893–898', *Classical Review* 14 (1900), 153–4

Fairweather, J., *Seneca the Elder* (Cambridge, 1981)

Feeney, D.C., *The Gods in Epic: Poets and Critics of the Classical Tradition* (Oxford, 1991)

Fehling, D., *Die Quellengaben bei Herodot* (Berlin, 1971), tr. J.G. Howie as *Herodotus and his 'Sources'*, ARCA 21 (Leeds, 1989)

Ferrari, G.R.F., 'Plato and Poetry', in G. Kennedy, ed., *Cambridge History of Literary Criticism* (Cambridge, 1989), 92–148

Fiddick, P., 'Facts do Furnish a Story', *The Listener* 124 (25 October 1990), 4–6

Finley, J.H., *Thucydides* (Cambridge, Mass., 1942)

Finley, J.H., *Three Essays on Thucydides* (Cambridge, Mass., 1967)

Fornara, C.W., *The Nature of History in Ancient Greece and Rome* (Berkeley, 1983)

Forster, E.M., *Aspects of the Novel* (Harmondsworth, 1988)

Foucault, M., *Les mots et les choses* (Paris, 1966)

Fowler, D.P., 'On Closure', *Materiali e Discussioni* 22 (1989), 75–122

Fowler, H.W. and F.G., tr., *The Works of Lucian of Samosata* (Oxford, 1905)

Fraser, P.M., *Ptolemaic Alexandria*, (Oxford, 1972)

Free, T., 'Written or Living Culture', *Journal of the Anthropological Society of Oxford* 21.1 (1990), 51–65

Fusillo, M., '‹Mythos› aristotelico e ‹récit› narratologico' *Strumenti Critici* n.s. 1.3 (1986), 381–92

Gabba, E., 'True History and False History in Classical Antiquity', *Journal of Roman Studies* 71 (1981), 50–62

Gabba, E., *Dionysius and The History of Archaic Rome* (Berkeley, 1991)

Garcia, Gaul C., ed., *Apuleyo: El Asno de Oro*, tr. Diego Lopez de Cortegana, 1513 (Madrid, 1988)

Gaskell, E., 'More on Spontaneous Combustion', *The Dickensian* 69 (1973), 25–35

Genette, G., *Narrative Discourse*, tr. J.E. Lewin (Oxford, 1980)

Genette, G., *Seuils* (Paris, 1987)

Genette, G., *Narrative Discourse Revisited*, tr. J.E. Lewin (Cornell, 1988)

Genette, G., 'Récit fictioneel, récit factuel' *Fiction et Diction* (Paris, 1991), 65–93

Gill, C., 'The Death of Socrates', *Classical Quarterly* n.s. 23 (1973), 25–8

Gill, C., 'The Genre of the Atlantis Story', *Classical Philology* 72 (1977), 287–304

Gill, C., 'Plato and Politics: the Critias and the Politicus', *Phronesis* 24 (1979), 148–67

Gill, C., 'Plato's Atlantis Story and the Birth of Fiction', *Philosophy and Literature* 3 (1979), 64–78

Gill, C., ed., *Plato: the Atlantis Story* (Bristol, 1980)

Gill, C., 'Plato and the Education of Character', *Archiv für Geschichte der Philosophie* 67 (1985), 1–26

Gill, C., 'Dogmatic Dialogue in Phaedrus 276–7?', in L. Rossetti, ed., *Understanding the Phaedrus* (St Augustin, 1992), 156–72

Gill, C., *The Self in Dialogue: Personality in Greek Epic, Tragedy and Philosophy* (Oxford, 1994)

Goldhill, S., *The Poet's Voice: Essays on Poetics and Greek Literature* (Cambridge, 1991)

Gomme, A., *A Historical Commentary on Thucydides* (Oxford, 1945)

Goodyear, F.R.D., ed., *The Annals of Tacitus* (Cambridge, 1972–81)

Gould, J., *Herodotus* (London, 1989)

Grafton, A., *Forgers and Critics* (London, 1990)

Gray, V., 'Mimesis in Greek Historical Theory', *American Journal of Philology* 108 (1987), 467–86

Griffin, M.T., 'The Lyons Tablet and Tacitean Hindsight', *Classical Quarterly* 32 (1982), 404–18

Griswold, C.L., ed., *Platonic Writings, Platonic Readings* (New York, 1988)

Grube, G.M.A., tr., *Plato: the Republic* (London, 1981)

Gulley, N., 'Plato on Poetry', *Greece and Rome* 24 (1977), 154–69

Guthrie, W.K.C., tr., *Plato: Protagoras and Meno* (Harmondsworth, 1961)

Hägg, T., *Narrative Technique in Ancient Greek Romances* (Stockholm, 1971)

Hägg, T., *Photios als Vermittler antike Literatur, Studia Graeca Upsaliensia 8* (Uppsala, 1975)

Hägg, T., *The Novel in Antiquity* (Oxford, 1983)

Hägg, T., 'Metiochus at Polycrates' Court', *Eranos* 83 (1985), 92–102

Hägg, T., 'Callirhoe and Parthenope: the Beginnings of the Historical Novel', *Classical Antiquity* 6 (1987), 184–204

Haight, G.S., 'Dickens and Lewes on Spontaneous Combustion', *Nineteenth Century Fiction* 10 (1955–6), 53–63

Halliwell, S., 'Plato and Aristotle on the Denial of Tragedy', *Proceedings of the Cambridge Philological Society* 30 (1984), 49–71

Halliwell, S., *Aristotle's Poetics* (London, 1986)

Halliwell, S., *The Poetics of Aristotle: Translation and Commentary* (London, 1987)

Hammond, N.G.L., 'The Arrangement of the Thought in the Proem and in other Parts of Thucydides I', *Classical Quarterly* 2 (1952), 127–41

Hammond, N.G.L., 'The Particular and the Universal in the Speeches of Thucydides', in P.A. Stadter, ed., *The Speeches in Thucydides* (Chapel Hill, 1973), 49–59

Hansen, N.A., *The Witch's Garden* (Santa Cruz, 1978)

Harrison, B., *Inconvenient Fictions: Literature and the Limits of Theory* (New Haven, 1991)

Harrison, S.J., ed., *Oxford Readings in Vergil's Aeneid* (Oxford, 1990)

Harrison, S.J., 'The Speaking Book: The Prologue to Apuleius' *Metamorphoses*', *Classical Quarterly* 40 (1990), 507–13

Hartog, F., *Le Miroir d'Hérodote: Essai sur la représentation de l'autre* (Paris, 1980), tr. J. Lloyd as *The Mirror of Herodotus: the Representation of the Other in the Writing of History* (Berkeley, 1988)

Hartog, F., 'L'oeil de Thucydide et l'histoire "veritable"', *Poétique* 49 (1982), 22–30

Havelock, E.A., *Preface to Plato* (Oxford, 1963)

Holford-Strevens, L., *Aulus Gellius* (London, 1988)

Homeyer, H., *Lukian: wie man Geschichte schreiben soll* (Munich, 1965)

Hornblower, S., *Thucydides* (London, 1987)

Hornblower, S., *A Commentary on Thucydides* I (Oxford, 1991)

How, W.W., and Wells, J., *A Commentary on Herodotus* (Oxford, 1912)

Hunter, R.L., *A Study of Daphnis and Chloe* (Cambridge, 1983)

Immerwahr, H.R., *Form and Thought in Herodotus* (Cleveland, 1966)

Irving, F., *Metamorphosis in Greek Myth* (Oxford, 1991)

Jensen, C., ed., *Philodemus: Peri Poiematon* (Leipzig, 1923)

Jones, R.M., 'Posidonius and the Flight of the Mind through the Universe' *Classical Philology* 21 (1926), 97–113

BIBLIOGRAPHY

Kannicht, R., 'Die alte Streit zwischen Poesie und Philosophie' *Altertums-Unterricht* 23.6 (1980), 6–36, tr. as *The Ancient Quarrel Between Poetry and Philosophy. Aspects of the Greek Conception of Literature. The Fifth Broadhead Memorial Lecture 1986* (Canterbury, N.Z., 1988)

Kant, I., *Groundwork of the Metaphysic of Morals*, tr. H.J. Paton in *The Moral Law* (London, 1986)

Kennedy, D.F., review in *Journal of Roman Studies*, 79 (1989), 209–10

Kenner, H., *The Counterfeiters: An Historical Comedy* (Bloomington, 1968)

Kerényi, K., *Die griechisch-orientalische Romanliteratur in religions-geschichtlicher Beleuchtung* (Tübingen, 1927)

Kirk, G.S., *Myth: Its Meaning and Function in Ancient and Other Cultures* (Berkeley, 1970)

Knox, B., *Oedipus at Thebes* (Oxford, 1957)

Krischer, T., 'Herodots Prooimion', *Hermes* 93 (1963), 159–67

Kuch, H., ed., *Der antike Roman: Untersuchungen zur literarischen Kommunikation und Gattungsgeschichte* (Berlin, 1989)

Kuch, H., 'Die Herausbildung des antiken Romans als Literaturgattung', in H. Kuch, ed., *Der antike Roman*, 11–51

LaCapra, D., *History and Criticism* (Ithaca, 1985)

Laird, A., 'Person, *Persona* and Representation in Apuleius's *Metamorphoses*', *Materiali e Discussioni* 25 (1990), 129–64

Lanata, G., *Poetica pre-platonica* (Florence, 1963)

Latacz, J., 'Realität und Imagination. Eine neue Lyrik-Theorie und Sapphos *Phainetai moi kenos* Lied', *Museum Helveticum* 42 (1985), 67–94

Lateiner, D., *The Historical Method of Herodotus* (Toronto, 1989)

Lear, J., 'Inside and Outside the *Republic*', *Phronesis* 37 (1992), 184–215

Lee, D., tr., *Plato: The Republic* (Harmondsworth, 1976)

Lewis, C.S., *The Magician's Nephew* (London, 1955)

Lewis, C.S., *Till We Have Faces: A Myth Retold* (London, 1956)

Liebeschuetz, W., 'The Structure and Function of the Melian Dialogue', *Journal of the Hellenic Studies* 88 (1968), 73–77

Loraux, N., 'Thucydide a écrit la guerre du Péloponnèse', *Metis: Revue d'anthropologie du monde grec ancien* 1 (1986), 139–61

Lord, A., *The Singer of Tales*, 2nd edn (New York, 1974)

Lowenthal, D., *The Past is a Foreign Country* (Cambridge, 1985)

Lubbock, P., *The Craft of Fiction* (London, 1921)

Luce, T.J., 'Ancient Views on the Causes of Bias in Historical Writing', *Classical Philology* 84 (1988), 16–31

Luck, G., *Arcana Mundi* (Baltimore, 1985)

MacAlister, S., *The Dream in Greek Romance* (Ph.D. diss., Sydney, 1987)

Macherey, P., *A Theory of Literary Production*, tr. G. Wall (London, 1985)

Mackenzie, M.M., *Plato on Punishment* (Berkeley, 1981)

Macleod, C., 'Thucydides and Tragedy', in *Collected Essays* (Oxford, 1983), 140–58

MacLeod, M.D., ed. and tr., *Lucian: a Selection* (Warminster, 1991)

Macrobius, *In Somnium Scipionis*, ed. J. Willis (Leipzig, 1963)

Maehler, H., *Die Auffassung des Dichterberufs im frühen Griechentum bis zum Zeit Pindars. Hypomnemata* 3 (Göttingen, 1963)

Maehler, H., 'Der Metiochos-Parthenope Roman', *Zeitschrift für Papyrologie und Epigraphik* 23 (1976), 1–20

Marincola, J., 'A Selective Introduction to Herodotean Studies', *Arethusa* 20 (1987), 26–40

Martin, J., *Antike Rhetorik* (Munich, 1974)

Martin, R.H. and Woodman, A.J., eds, *Tacitus: Annals 4* (Cambridge, 1989)

McDowell, D.M., ed. and tr., *Gorgias: The Encomium of Helen* (Bristol, 1982)

McKeon, M., *The Origins of the English Novel, 1600–1740* (Baltimore, 1987)

Meijering, R., *Literary and Rhetorical Theories in Greek Scholia* (Groningen, 1987)

Millar, F., 'The World of the *Golden Ass*', *Journal of Roman Studies* 71 (1981), 63–75

Minton, W.W., 'Invocation and Catalogue in Hesiod and Homer', *Transactions of the American Philological Association* 93 (1962), 188–212

Mittelstadt, M.C., 'Longus' *Daphnis and Chloe* and the Pastoral Tradition', *Classica et Medievalia* 27 (1966), 162–77

Mittelstadt, M.C., 'Bucolic-lyric Motifs and Dramatic Narrative in Longus' *Daphnis and Chloe*', *Rheinisches Museum* 113 (1970), 211–27

Moles, J.L., 'The Interpretation of the "Second Preface" in Arrian's *Anabasis*', *Journal of Hellenic Studies* 105 (1985), 162–8

Moles, J.L., ed. and tr., *Plutarch: Cicero* (Warminster, 1988)

Moles, J.L., review of A.J. Woodman, *Rhetoric in Classical Historiography*, in *History of the Human Sciences* 3.2 (1990), 317–21

Molinié, G., ed. and tr., *Chariton. Le Roman des Chaireas et Callirhoe* (Paris, 1979)

Momigliano, A., *The Development of Greek Biography* (Cambridge, Mass., 1971)

Moravcsik, J. and Temko, P., eds, *Plato on Beauty, Wisdom and the Arts* (Totowa, N.J., 1982)

Morgan, J.R., 'History, Romance and Realism in the *Aithiopika* of Heliodoros', *Classical Antiquity* 1 (1982), 221–65

Morgan, J.R., 'Lucian's *True Histories* and the *Wonders beyond Thule* of Antonius Diogenes', *Classical Quarterly* 35 (1985), 475–90

Morgan, J.R., 'A Sense of the Ending: the Conclusion of Heliodoros' *Aithiopika*', *Transactions of the American Philological Association* 119 (1989), 299–320

Morgan, J.R., 'Reader and Audiences in the *Aithiopika* of Heliodoros', *Groningen Colloquia on the Novel* 4 (1991)

Mossman, J.M., 'Tragedy and Epic in Plutarch's *Alexander*', *Journal of Hellenic Studies* 108 (1988), 83–93

Moxon, I.S., Smart, J.D., and Woodman, A.J., eds, *Past Perspectives: Studies in Greek and Roman Historical Writing* (Cambridge, 1986)

Müller, C.W., 'Chariton von Aphrodisias und die Theorie des Romans in der Antike', *Antike und Abendland* 22 (1976), 115–36

Murray, O., 'Herodotus and Oral History', in A. Kuhrt and H. Sancisci-Weedenburg, eds, *Achaemenid History 3: Method and Theory* (Leiden, 1988), 93–115

Murray, P.A., 'Poetic Inspiration in Early Greece', *Journal of Hellenic Studies* 101 (1981), 87–100

Murray, P.A., 'Homer and the Bard', in T. Winnifrith, P. Murray, and K.W. Gransden, eds, *Aspects of the Epic* (London, 1983)

Myres, J.L., 'Herodotus the Tragedian', in *A Miscellany Presented to J.M. MacKay LL.D.* (Liverpool, 1914), 88–96

Nagy, G., 'Herodotus the *Logios*', *Arethusa* 20 (1987), 175–84

Needham, R., *Belief, Language and Experience* (Oxford, 1972)

Nehamas, A., 'Plato on Imitation and Poetry in *Republic* 10', in Moravcsik and Temko, eds, *Plato on Beauty*, 47–78

Neitzel, N., 'Hesiod und die lügende Musen. Zur Interpretation von Theogonie 27f.', *Hermes* 108 (1980), 387–401

Nelson, W., *Fact or Fiction: The Dilemma of the Renaissance Storyteller* (Cambridge, Mass., 1973)

Newsom, R., *A Likely Story. Probability and Play in Fiction* (New Brunswick, 1988)

Nisbet, R.G.M., and Hubbard, M., *A Commentary on Horace's Odes 1* (Oxford, 1975)

Norris, C., *The Contest of Faculties: Philosophy and Theory after Deconstruction* (London, 1985)

O'Kelly, L., 'It's Dramatic, but it's not True', *The Independent* (12 May 1991), 15

O'Sullivan, J.N., 'The Sesonchosis Romance', *Zeitschrift für Papyrologie und Epigraphik* 56 (1984), 39–44

Ogilvie, R.M., *A Commentary on Livy 1–5* (Oxford, 1965, rev. 1970)

Ogilvie, R.M. and Drummond, A., 'The Surviving Evidence', in F.W. Walbank et al., *The Cambridge Ancient History*, 2nd edn, 7.2 (*The Rise of Rome to 220 BC*) (Cambridge, 1989), 1–29

Page, D.L., ed., *Poetae Melici Graeci* (Oxford, 1962)

Page, D.L., ed., *Further Greek Epigrams* (Cambridge, 1981)

Pandiri, T.A., '*Daphnis and Chloe*: the Art of Pastoral Play', *Ramus* 14 (1985), 116–41

Paul, G., '*Urbs Capta*: Sketch of an Ancient Literary Motif', *Phoenix* 36 (1982), 144–55

Pearson, L., *The Lost Histories of Alexander the Great* (Philadelphia, 1960)

Pearson, L., and Sandbach, F.H., eds and tr., *Plutarch's Moralia 11* (Cambridge, Mass., 1967)

Pelling, C.B.R., 'Truth and Fiction in Plutarch's *Lives*', in D.A. Russell, ed., *Antonine Literature* (Oxford, 1990), 19–52

Perry, B.E., *The Ancient Romances: A Literary-Historical Account of their Origins* (Berkeley, 1967)

Peter, H., ed., *Historicorum Romanorum Reliquiae* (Leipzig, 1906–14, repr. Stuttgart, 1967)

Pfeiffer, R., *History of Classical Scholarship 1*, (Oxford, 1968)

Pfister, F., 'Isokrates und die spätere Gliederung der *Narratio*', *Hermes* 68 (1933), 457–60

Plepelits, K., *Chariton von Aphrodisias. Kallirhoe* (Stuttgart, 1976)

Porter, H., *Lies, Damned Lies, and Some Exclusives* (London, 1984)

Potts, L.J., *Aristotle on the Art of Fiction* (Cambridge, 1953)

Pritchett, W.K., *Dionysius of Halicarnassus: On Thucydides* (Berkeley, 1975)

Pucci, P., *Hesiod and the Language of Poetry* (Baltimore, 1977)

Rawlings, H.R., *The Structure of Thucydides' History* (Princeton, 1981)

Rawson, E., *Intellectual Life in the Late Roman Republic* (London, 1985)

Reardon, B.P., ed., *Collected Ancient Greek Novels* (Berkeley, 1989)

Reardon, B.P., *The Form of Greek Romance* (Princeton, 1991)

Redfield, J.M., *Nature and Culture in the Iliad* (Chicago, 1975)

Reeve, C.D., *Philosopher-Kings: The Argument of Plato's Republic* (Princeton, 1988)

Reeve, M.D., 'Hiatus in the Greek Novelists', *Classical Quarterly* 21 (1971) 514–39

Reitzenstein, R., *Hellenistische Wundererzählungen* (Leipzig, 1906)

Rhodes, P.J., *A Commentary on the Aristotelian Athenaion Politeia* (Oxford, 1981)

Ricardou, J., *Problèmes du Nouveau Roman* (Paris, 1967)

Richardson, N.J., 'Pindar and Later Literary Criticism in Antiquity', *Papers of the Liverpool Latin Seminar* 5 (1985), 383–401

Riffaterre, M., *Text Production* (Columbia, 1979)

Riffaterre, M., *Fictional Truth* (Baltimore, 1990)

Rijksbaron, A., 'Chariton 8,1,4 und Aristot. *Poet.* 1449b28', *Philologus* 128 (1984), 306–7

Robertson, D.S., ed., *Les Metamorphoses*, Tome 1 (Livres 1–3), tr. P. Vallette (Paris, 1972)

Rohde, E., *Der griechische Roman und seine Vorläufer*, 3rd edn (Leipzig, 1914), 4th edn (Wiesbaden, 1960).

Rokeah, D., 'Speeches in Thucydides: Factual Reporting or Creative Writing?', *Athenaeum* 60 (1982), 386–401

Romm, J., 'Novel *contra* Encyclopedia: The Wonders beyond Thule of Antonius Diogenes', in J. Tatum and G.M. Vernazza, eds, *The Ancient Novel*, 49

Romm, J., *The Edges of the Earth in Ancient Thought* (Princeton, 1992)

Roncalli, F., 'Osservazioni sui *libri lintei etruschi*', *Rendiconti dell'Accademia Pontificia* 51–2 (1978–80), 3–21

Rosebury, B., *Art and Desire: A Study in the Aesthetics of Fiction* (New York, 1988)

Rosenmeyer, T.G., 'Gorgias, Aeschylus and *Apate*', *American Journal of Philology* 76 (1955), 225–60

Rösler, W., 'Die Entdeckung der Fiktionalität in der Antike', *Poetica* 12 (1980), 283–319

Rösler, W., 'Persona reale o persona poetica? L'interpretazione dell'io nella lirica greca arcaica', *Quaderni Urbinati di Cultura Classica* 19 (1985), 131–144.

Rösler, W., 'Realitätsbezug und Imagination in Sapphos Gedicht *Phainetai moi kenos*' in W. Kullman and M. Reichel, eds, *Der Übergang von der Mündlichkeit zur Literatur bei den Griechen*, (Tübingen, 1990), 271–287

Russell, D.A. and Winterbottom, M., eds and tr., *Ancient Literary Criticism* (Oxford, 1972)

Ruthven, K.K., *Critical Assumptions* (Cambridge, 1979)

Sacks, K., *Polybius on the Writing of History* (Berkeley, 1981)

Saïd, S., 'La société rurale dans le roman grec', in E. Frézouls, ed., *Sociétés urbaines, sociétés rurales* (Strasbourg, 1987), 149–71

Salmon, P., 'Chariton d'Aphrodisias et la révolte égyptienne de 360 avant J.-C.', *Chronique d'Egypte* 36 (1961), 365–76

Scarcella, A.M., 'Realtà e letteratura nel paesaggio sociale ed economico del romanzo di Longo Sofista', *Maia* 22 (1970), 103–31

Scarcella, A.M., 'Les structures socio-économiques du roman de Xénophon d'Ephèse', *Revue des Etudes Grecques* 90 (1977), 249–62

Schmeling, G.L., *Xenophon of Ephesus* (Boston, 1980)

Scobie, A., *Apuleius: Metamorphoses (Asinus Aureus) 1, A Commentary* (Meisenheim am Glan, 1975)

Scobie, A., 'Storytellers, Storytelling, and the Novel in Greco-Roman Antiquity', *Rheinisches Museum* 122 (1979), 229–59

Scobie, A., *Apuleius and Folklore* (London, 1983)

Segal, C.P., 'Gorgias and the Psychology of the Logos', *Harvard Studies in Classical Philology* 66 (1962), 99–155.

Segal, C.P., 'The Two Worlds of Euripides' *Helen*', *Proceedings of the American Philological Association* 102 (1971), 553–614.

Shakespeare, W., *As You Like It*, New Temple Shakespeare (London, 1934)

Shorey, P., tr., *Plato: the Republic*, in the Bollingen *Collected Dialogues of Plato* (New York, 1964)

Sidney, Sir Philip, *An Apology for Poetry*, ed. G. Shepherd (London, 1965)

Slings, S.R., 'Poet's Call and Poet's Status in Archaic Greece and Other Oral Cultures', *Listy Filologické* 112 (1989), 72–80

Slings, S.R., *The I in Personal Archaic Lyric* (Amsterdam, 1990)

Snodgrass, A., 'Archaeology', in M. Crawford, ed., *Sources for Ancient History* (Cambridge, 1983), 137–84

Speyer, W., *Bücherfunde in der Glaubenswerbung der Antike* (Göttingen, 1970)

Speyer, W., *Die literarische Fälschung im heidnischen und christlichen Altertum: ein Versuch ihrer Deutung* (Munich, 1971)

Stadter, P.A., 'Arrian's Extended Preface', *Illinois Classical Studies* 6.1 (1981), 157–71

de Ste Croix, G.E.M., *The Origins of the Peloponnesian War* (London, 1972)

de Ste Croix, G.E.M., 'Aristotle on History and Poetry', in B. Levick, ed., *The Ancient Historian and his Materials* (Farnborough, Hants., 1975), 45–58

Stock, W., 'Hesiod's lügende Musen', in H. Gorgemann and E.A. Schmidt, eds, *Studien zum antiken Epos* (Meisenheim am Glan, 1976), 85–112

Stoneman, R., tr., *The Greek Alexander Romance* (London, 1991)

Strasburger, H., *Die Wesensbestimmung der Geschichte durch die antike Geschichtsschreibung* (Wiesbaden, 1966)

Strawson, P.F., *Freedom and Resentment* (London, 1974)

Svenbro, J., *La parole et le marbre: aux origines de la poétique grecque* (Lund, 1976)

Syme, R., *Ammianus and the Historia Augusta* (Oxford, 1968)

Syme, R., *Emperors and Biography* (Oxford, 1971)

Syme, R., *Roman Papers* (Oxford, 1979–91)

Syme, R., *Historia Augusta Papers* (Oxford, 1983)

Tatum, J. and Vernazza, G.M., eds, *The Ancient Novel: Classical Paradigms and Modern Perspectives* (Hanover, N.H, 1990)

Taylor, C., *Sources of the Self: The Making of the Modern Identity* (Cambridge, 1989)

Teske, D., *Der Roman des Longos als Werk der Kunst* (Münster, 1991)

Testamentum Latine, ed. J. Wordsworth and H.I. White (Oxford, 1911)

Thalmann, W.G., *Conventions of Form and Thought in Early Greek Epic Poetry* (Baltimore, 1984)

Todorov, T., *Introduction à la littérature fantastique* (Paris, 1970)

Torraca, L., *Duride di Samo: la maschera scenica nella storiografia ellenistica* (Salerno, 1988)

Toynbee, A.J., ed. and tr., *Greek Historical Thought* (London, 1924)

Treu, K., 'Der Realitätsgehalt des antiken Romans', in H. Kuch, ed., *Der antike Roman*, 107–25.

Ullman, B.L., 'History and Tragedy', *Transactions of the American Philological Association* 73 (1942), 25–53

Verdenius, W.J., 'Gorgias' Doctrine of Deception', in G.B. Kerferd, ed., *The Sophists and their Legacy* (Wiesbaden, 1981), 116–28

Veyne, P., *Les Grecs ont-ils cru à leurs mythes?* (Paris, 1983), tr. P. Wissing as *Did the Greeks Believe in their Myths?* (Chicago, 1988)

Voloshinov, V.N., *Marxism and the Philosophy of Language*, tr. L. Matejka and I.R. Titunik (Cambridge, Mass., 1986)

Walbank, F.W., 'Tragic History: a Reconsideration', *Bulletin of the Institute of Classical Studies* 2 (1955), 4–14

Walbank, F.W., 'History and Tragedy', *Historia* 9 (1960), 216–34

Walbank, F.W., *Speeches in Greek Historians*, J.L. Myres Lecture (Oxford, 1965)

Walbank, F.W., *Selected Papers: Studies in Greek and Roman History and Historiography* (Cambridge, 1985)

Walden, J.W.H., 'Stage-terms in Heliodoros's *Aethiopica*', *Harvard Studies in Classical Philology* 5 (1894), 1–43

Walsh, G., *The Varieties of Enchantment: Early Greek Views of the Nature and Function of Poetry* (Chapel Hill, 1984)

Walton, K.L., *Mimesis as Make-Believe: On the Foundations of the Representational Arts* (Cambridge, Mass., 1990)

Wehrli, F., ed., *Die Schule des Aristoteles* (Basel, 1944–59)

West, D.A. and Woodman, A.J., eds, *Creative Imitation and Latin Literature* (Cambridge, 1979)

West, D.A., *The Bough and the Gate* (Exeter, 1987)

West, M.L., *Studies in Greek Elegy and Iambus* (Berlin, 1974)

West, M.L., ed., *Hesiod, Works and Days* (Oxford, 1978)

West, M.L., ed., *Iambi et Elegi Graeci* (Oxford, 1971–2); 2nd edn 1 (1989), 2 (1992)

West, S., 'Herodotus' Epigraphical Interests', *Classical Quarterly* 35 (1985), 278–305

West, S., 'Herodotus' Portrait of Hecateus', *Journal of Hellenic Studies* 111 (1991), 144–60

White, H., *Tropics of Discourse* (Baltimore, 1978)

White, H., *The Content of the Form: Narrative Discourse and Historical Representation* (Baltimore, 1987)

Wilcken, U., 'Ein neuer griechischer Roman', *Hermes* 28 (1893), 161–93

Wilson, J., 'What does Thucydides claim for his Speeches?', *Phoenix* 36 (1982), 95–103

Winkler, J.J., 'The Mendacity of Kalasiris and the Narrative Strategy of the *Aithiopika*', *Yale Classical Studies* 27 (1982), 93–158

Winkler, J.J., *Actor and Auctor: A Narratological Reading of the Golden Ass* (Berkeley, 1985)

Winkler, J.J., *The Constraints of Desire* (New York, 1990)

Wiseman, T.P., *Clio's Cosmetics: Three Studies in Greco–Roman Literature* (Leicester, 1979)

Wiseman, T.P., 'Practice and Theory in Roman Historiography', *History* 66 (1981), 32–50

Wiseman, T.P., *Roman Studies, Literary and Historical* (Liverpool, 1987)

Woodman, A.J., 'From Hannibal to Hitler: the Literature of War', *University of Leeds Review* 26 (1983), 107–24

Woodman, A.J., *Rhetoric in Classical Historiography: Four Studies* (London, 1988)

Wright, M.R., 'How Credible are Plato's Myths?', in G.W. Bowersock, W. Burkert, M.C.J. Putnam, eds, *Arktouros: Hellenic Studies presented to B.M.W. Knox* (Berlin, 1979), 364–71

Zeitlin, F.I., 'The Closet of Masks: Role-playing and Myth-making in the *Orestes* of Euripides', *Ramus* 9 (1980), 51–77

Zeitlin, F.I., 'The Poetics of Eros: Nature, Art and Imitation in Longus' *Daphnis and Chloe*', in D.M. Halperin et al., eds, *Before Sexuality* (Princeton, 1990), 417–64

Ziegler, K., 'Paradoxographoi', in Pauly-Wissowa, *Real-encyclopädie der classischen Altertumswissenschaft* 18.3 (1949), 1137–66

Zimmermann, F., 'Kallirhoes Verkauf durch Theron', *Berliner Byzantinische Arbeiten* (1959), 72–81

Zimmermann, F., 'Chariton und die Geschichte', in H.J. Diesner, ed., *Sozialökonomische Verhältnisse im alten Orient und im klassischen Altertum* (Berlin, 1961), 329–45

Index of Passages
from Ancient Authors

ACHILLES TATIUS
1.2.2–3 217
AELIUS ARISTIDES
33.2 24
ALCAEUS
fr. 6L–P 30
fr. 10V 35
fr. 208V = 326L–P 30
ALCMAN
fr. 21P 25
ANACREON
fr. 358P 31
fr. 359P 31
fr. 360P 35
APPIAN
Praef. 15.62 103
APULEIUS, Metamorphoses
1.1–2 . . . . 147, 156–9
1.8 167
3.21–2 . . . . . 124, 147–8, 156, 162–73
3.23 167
3.24 167
4.28 149
11.1 . . . . 164, 169
ARCHILOCHUS
fr. 4W 29
fr. 13W 29, 30
frr. 88–113W 7–8
fr. 168W 35
frr. 168–71W 32
frr. 172–81W 3, 31
fr. 182W 35
frr. 182–4W 31–2
frr. 185–7W 31
frr. 188–92W 32–3
frr. 196–196A W 32–5
ARISTOPHANES
Clouds 225, 1503 170
Frogs 1008-98 . . . . 72, 73
Wasps 1122ff. 3

ARISTOTLE Poetics
1449b21–8 . . . . 77, 183
1451a36–8 . . . . 76, 182
1451a38–b11 . . 76, 107–8, 109, 117, 233
1451b11–32 . . . . 74n, 76n, 233
1451b21–2 . . . . 3n
1453b22–6 . . . . 76n
1455a16–21 . . . . 76n
1455a22–b16 . . . . 74n
1459a17ff. 183
1460a5–8 211
1460a18–26 . . . . 75n
1460a26–7 . . . . 74–5, 182
1460a28–9 . . . . 75n
1460b15–32 . . . . 75n
ARRIAN, Anabasis
Praef. 1–3 135–7
1.12.5 103
AUGUSTINE
Civitas Dei 18.18 . . . . . . 160–1, 193
Soliloquies 2.9.16 191–2
CHARITON OF APHRODISIAS
1.1.1 205
1.4.11 203–4
2.6.4 202
2.9.3 223
3.2.6 202
3.5–8 213
4.1.11 221
5.8.2 216–7
6.8.6 206
7.4 206
7.6 207
8.1 . . . . 183, 207
CICERO
Ad familiares 5.12 191
Brutus 42–3 . . . . 132–3, 137
De inventione 1.27 . . . . . . 129, 191
1.29 188
1.46 188

De oratore 2.62 126–7
2.63 143
[CICERO], *Rhetorica ad Herennium*
1.12–13 . . . . 129, 189–91
DIODORUS SICULUS
1.2.7 136–7
DIONYSIUS OF HALICARNASSUS
Ad Pompeium 3 94
Antiquitates Romanae 1.1.2–3 94
1.2.1 94
1.39–44 128–9
DURIS OF SAMOS (*FGrH* 76)
fr. 1 184–5
EPHORUS (*FGrH* 70)
fr. 9 142
'FLAVIUS VOPISCUS',
see *HISTORIA AUGUSTA*
GORGIAS
fr. 11D–K (*Helen*) 54n, 172
fr. 23D–K 74, 172, 180–1, 236–7
GOSPEL OF LUKE
1.5 149
HECATAEUS (*FGrH* 1)
fr. 1 93
HELIODORUS
1.2.8–9 202
1.10.2 223
2.21.5 222
2.22.1 210
2.24.4 222
2.24.5 219
2.34–5 222
3.3.5 222–3
4.1ff. 221
4.2ff. 223
4.3.1 223
5.5.2 223
5.22.3 222
7.6ff. 217–8
8.9 . . . . 205, 221
8.15.2 223
9.8.2 210
9.24 220
10.9 221
10.30ff. 221
HERMOGENES
16.22 144–5
HERODIAN
1.10.5 124
HERODOTUS
1 *praef.* 92–4, 205
1.1–5 . . . . 92–7, 136
1.5.3–4 95
1.6.1 114
2.53.2 13
2.116 233
2.143.1 100

3.80.1 118–20
4.30.1 92
6.43.3 119
6.98.2 111–2
7.20–1 . . . . 92, 97
7.152.3 . . . . 95, 135
7.228.3 5
HESIOD
fr 266R = 358M–W 26
Theogony 27–8 . xiv, 20–2, 25, 37, 70–1,
116, 242–3
31–4 . . . . 22, 109
Works and Days 180ff. 3
HISTORIA AUGUSTA
Aurelian 1.1–2.2 . . . 124–5, 137, 146
HOMER
Iliad 1.1 12
1.6–7 113
1.8 . . . . 12, 93
2.484–92 . . . . 10, 13
6.152 114
9.189 93
9.312–3 2
14.216–7 235
Odyssey 1.1 12
1.3 96
1.325–39 16–17
1.351–2 26
8.43–5 14
8.63–4 14
8.73 15
8.83–91 15
8.265 15
8.480–1 15
8.488–91 . . . . . 15–16, 28, 116
8.496–8 15–16
9.39 222
11.333–4 235
11.362–8 . . . . 137, 236
14.122–5 236
14.151 2
14.192 2
14.361–5 236
19.203 . . . . 19, 20, 70–1
22.347 17
HORACE
Ars Poetica 188 193
ISOCRATES
Helen 64 26–7
JOSEPHUS
Antiquitates 20.154–6 . . . . . 127, 137
JULIAN
Epistles 89.301b 178, 186
JUVENAL
15.13–26 . . . . 19n., 132n.
LIVY
Praef. 2 . . . . 100, 103

5.21.8–9 134
'LONGINUS'
13.3 94
15.2–8 239–40
LONGUS, Daphnis and Chloe
Praef. 212, 218
2.27.2 219
4.20.1 219
LUCIAN
Hist. conscr. 7 127
7–13 123
8 117
32 137
39 . . . . 117, 122
45 . . . . 94, 117
51 . . . . 89, 110, 117, 137
True History 1.3 . . . . . 32–3, 131–2
MACROBIUS, In Somnium Scipionis
1.2.7–8 . . . . 155, 177–8
MIMNERMUS
frr. 13–14W 7
OVID
Fasti 4.326 134–5
PHOTIUS
94 194–5
111 196–7
166 195
PLATO
Meno 80a–c . . . . 169n.
Phaedo 107a–b 59
114d 60
Phaedrus 243a 24, 26–7
244a–257b 60–1
246 170
275b–c 58
Republic 376e–392b 42, 44–7, 55
377d 38
380d–383c 45
382a–e 45, 52–6
391a–d . . . . 46n.
392c 191
412e–413c 54
414b–d 38, 52–3, 55, 64–5
514a–517a 60, 61
514a 38
515a 38
595a–608b 42, 47–51
596b–598d 50
598b–c 48–9
598e 49
600e 38
601a–b 48
602c–605c 49–50
605c–606d 51, 78
Symposium 201d–212b 56, 60, 61
Timaeus 20d–26d 65–6
21b 124

26d 38–9
27c–92c 56
29b–d 58–9
PLINY, Natural History
5.3–4 128
PLUTARCH
Moralia 15c–d 236–7
348c–d 74, 172
826a 94
867c 94
Solon 27.1 120
29.7 179
Theseus 1.3 130
28.2 130
31.4 131
POLYBIUS
2.56.2 . . . . 134, 185–6
2.56.6–8 140
2.56.10–12 . . . . 112, 134, 186
3.31–2 144
3.31.11–13 143
3.32.6 143
3.33.17 141–2
3.48.8 135
12.12.4–5 127
16.14.6 94
36.1.7 . . . . 105, 143
QUINTILIAN, Institutio
2.4.2 232
6.2.31–2 145
6.3.32 211
8.3.67 185
10.1.46 154
SALLUST
Bell. Jug. 1.1 103
5.1 103
Catiline 4.2–3 126
Histories 1.6M 126
SENECA
Apocolocyntosis 1.1–2 . . . 123, 137, 138
De vita patris fr. 1P 126
Quaest. Nat. 4.3.1 . . . 135, 137, 140
7.16.1–2 . . . . xv, 122–3, 127
SERVIUS
Ad Aen. 1.235 130
'SIMONIDES'
fr. 6P 5
fr. 37P 6
SOLON
frr. 32–40W 8
fr. 36.3–7W 8
SOPHOCLES
Trachiniae 307, 320–1 238
STESICHORUS
frr. 187–91P (Helen) 23
fr. 191P 25
frr. 192–3P (Palinode) . . . 23–8, 70–1

fr. 216P 25
fr. 223P 23–4
STRABO
2.1.9 (C70) 131
SUDA
4.433 s.v. Stesichoros 27
SUETONIUS
Nero 21.3 237
TACITUS
Annals 1.1.1 . . . . 103, 126
Histories 1.1.1–2 126
THEOGNIS
54–5 . . . . 29, 30
257–8 29
THEON
Progymnasmata 3 180
THUCYDIDES
1.1–23 98–114
1.1.1–3 . . . . 99–100, 205
1.1.3 110
1.10 73–4
1.10.3 . . . . 46n., 100, 101
1.20.1 101
1.20.3–21.2 101–3
1.21 73–4

1.21.1 . . . . 46n., 100–1, 106
1.21.2 110
1.22 103–7
1.22.2–3 110
1.22.4 . . . . . . 107, 110, 113, 117, 143
1.23 110–14
1.24.1 114
1.97.2 113
1.138.4 133
2.1.1 113
3.81.5 108
5.20 113
5.26 98
8.73.3 108
TYRTAEUS
fr. 5.6–8W 7
VALERIUS MAXIMUS
4.7.4 128
VARRO, De gente pop. Rom.
frr. 3–17P 129
XENOPHON OF EPHESUS
4.2.3ff. 203
4.6 221
5.7 221
5.15 243

General Index

Achilles Tatius *Leucippe and Clitophon*
   194, 204, 217
Adlington, W.   173
Alexander the Great as theme of history
   103, 131, 135–6
akribeia ('precision', 'detailed elaboration')
   143, 144–5
animal fables (Aesop's, etc.)   3, 31–2, 178,
   180
Annas, J.   47n., 82–3
Antheus, the first fictional Greek tragedy   3
Antonius Diogenes *Wonders Beyond Thule*
   194–6, 208–9, 225, 243
aphēgēsis ('story')   136–41
Appian   103
Apuleius *Metamorphoses* (*Golden Ass*)
   147–74
   ambiguity of generic status   173
   ambiguity of truth-status and 'the
      fantastic'   161–2
   Augustine on   192–3
   bewitchment of Lucius by Pamphile's
      metamorphosis   167–9
   bewitchment by language   169–72
   metamorphosis of Pamphile   162–7,
      of Lucius   167–9
   prologue   156–61
   two narrative voices?   158–9
   see also novel
Archilochus   7–8, 29–30, 31–5
argumentum/plasma ('theme/invention')
   129–30, 178, 189–91, 232
Aristophanes *Frogs*   72–3
Aristotle *Poetics*
   concept of *mimesis* and fiction   74–7,
      181–3, 232
   in relation to Plato   78–9
   katharsis ('cleansing')   183
   on poetic and historical truth   76–7,
      107–9, 117, 233
   see also probability
Arrian   103, 135–6
Asclepiades   129
Atlantis story, truth-status of   63–6

Augustine   160–1, 170, 191–3
Austin, J.L.   xvii–xviii

Bakhtin, M.M.   228n.
Barthes, R.   238–9
Bartsch, S.   80n., 224n, 229n.
Beerbohm, M. *Zuleika Dobson*   138
bewitchment
   in Apuleius   167–9
   by language (in Gorgias)   172–3, 236–7
   (in Homer)   235–6,
   (in Plato)   169–70
Bradford City stadium fire   138
Bulgakov, M. *The Master and
      Margarita*   165–6
Burn, A.R.   119

catalogue (Homeric)   13–14
Cato   105, 146
Cazotte *Le diable amoureux*   161, 170
Cervantes *Don Quixote*   xiii, 225
charter or foundation myth (in Plato)   65
Chariton *Chaereas and Callirhoe*   183, 187,
      197–8, 199–200, 203–4, 205–8, 212–13,
      214, 216–17, 220, 221, 222, 224, 228, 229
Cicero
   on historiography   88, 102, 132–3, 137,
      143
   rhetorical categories   129, 188–91
Clidemus   142, 146
Clio, Muse of History   138
Clitarchus   112
Coleridge, S.   226
collective memory (*mémoire collective*)   7,
      8–9, 11, 13, 16, 31, 37, 71–2
Ctesias of Cnidos   131–2
Currie, G.   193n., 231n., 234n., 240n., 241n.

'Dares the Phrygian'   155, 209
deception
   and poetry in Gorgias   74, 172–3,
      180–1, 236–7, in Plato   44–55

types of, in Augustine   192
see also historiography, lies, mendacity
Deighton, L. *Bomber*   239
Descartes *Meditations*   170
Detienne, M., 11n., 240.
Dicaearchus   128
Dickens, C. *Bleak House*   205
  Our Mutual Friend   230
'Dictys the Cretan'   155, 209
diēgēsis ('narrative')—*mimēsis* ('repre-
  sentation') distinction in Plato   191,
  211
diēgēsis/narratio ('narrative')   187
Diodorus Siculus   136–7
Dionysius of Halicarnassus   88, 128–9, 135,
  144
docu-drama   141
dramatikon as ancient category for novel
  79, 189
Duris of Samos   112, 184, 211

Eco, U.   224, 243–4
enargeia/evidentia ('vivid illustration')
  145–6, 211, 212, 214, 228, 239–40
Ephorus   142, 143, 184, 211
epitaphs and dedications, 'literary' and 'real'
  5–6
epode   31–5
Euripides   72–3
eye-witness accounts
  and key-holes   166–7
  in ancient historiography   91n., 110
  in narrative   155–6, 164–7
  in real life   138–9

fabula/muthos ('story')   129–30, 155, 156–7,
  171–2, 189–90.
  see also *historia*, novel
faction   141
Ferrari, G.R.F.   42n., 47n., 82–3
fiction
  a concept present in all cultures?   xiv,
    xvii, 69–70, 240–1
  an ancient concept?   3, 40–1, 46–7, 50–1,
    55, 74–81, 154–6, 175, 176–93, 231–7
  and ancient rhetorical categories   8on.,
    129–30, 170–3, 177–8, 180, 189–96,
    231–2
  concept of fiction implied in ancient
    practices?   17–20, 22–3, 25–8, 29–37,
    46–7, 50–1, 55–6, 62, 66–8, 70–3, 80–1,
    156, 170, 197, 215–16, 224–5, 242–3
  English term   xiii–iv
  modern concepts of
    as ambivalent between belief and
      disbelief   195, 215, 224–9, 236–44

as willing suspension of disbelief
  (or willing make-believe)   xvi–xvii,
  64, 226
as mode of imaginative self-extension
  82–3
as self-conscious, explicit make-believe
  215–16
as space of uncertainty   xiv, xvii–iii
interest in fictionality as expression of
  current philosophical positions   84–5
fiction–fact distinction questioned
  151–4, 160–1, 174, 242
types of issue raised by (logical,
  epistemological, moral)   xiv, 234
see also Aristotle, historiography, lies,
  novel, Plato, truth
Foucault, M.   xvii

Genette, G.   149n., 151n., 161n., 164n.
Gill, C.   181
Goldhill, S.   14n., 236
Gorgias, see deception
Gual, C.G.   162n.

Halliwell, S.   45n., 232, 240n.
Harrison, S.J.   158n., 159
Havelock, E.A.   44n., 71–2
Hecataeus   93, 100, 106, 131
Heliodorus, *Aethiopica*   154, 204–5, 210–11,
  213–14, 216, 219–20, 221–2, 222–3, 224,
  229
Herodotus
  as eye-witness   91n.
  as successor to Homer   93–4, 96–8, 233
  attitude to Hecataeus   100
  conception of historiography   91–2
  constitutional debate   118–19
  non-committal stance to truth of account
    95, 135
  prefaces   92–4, 97
  'sandwiched' material   94–7
  travellers' tales   131
Hesiod
  status of Perses in *Works and Days*   23,
    36
  see also Muses
Historia Augusta   124–5
historia/historiē ('history', 'enquiry')
  as 'enquiry'   92, 93, 136, 141, 143
  as rhetorical category (alongside *argu-
    mentum* and *fabula*)   129–30, 189–90,
    232
  and the novel   79, 178
historical truth, ancient concepts of
  in ancient historiography in general   100,
    115–21, 136
  in Aristotle   76–7, 107–9, 117, 233

in Herodotus 91n., 95, 136.
in Lucian 89, 102, 110, 117, 122, 123,
125, 128, 137
in Plato 65–6
in Thucydides 100–2, 105–7, 109–10, 114
historiography, ancient concepts of
aims at pleasure/usefulness 102, 106–7,
117, 139, 143, 184
absence of elaboration 146
ancient debate about 88–9, 122
aphēgēsis ('story') in 136–41
concern with greatness of theme 97, 100,
109, 110–13
encomiastic strand in 94, 117, 123
epic touches in 93–4, 96–8, 100, 103
imitation of previous historians 97–8, 99,
113–14
historiography, modern concepts of 84–5,
125n.
see also historia/historiē, historical truth,
history–literature relationship, history–
myth relationship, mendacity
history–literature relationship
in general 153, 160–1, 170, 174
in ancient historiography 90–1, 94, 103,
111–12, 117–18, 124, 132–41, 184–7
in novel 205–6, 208–9
in Platonic dialogues 66–7
history–myth relationship
in history 128–9
in poetry 6–7, 8–9, 10–11, 13, 16
in rhetorical theory 129–30, 189–90,
192–3, 232
Holmes, Sherlock 148, 150, 151, 159, 197n.,
225
Homeric poems
allusions to, in ancient historiography
93–4, 96–8, 100, 103, in ancient novel
222–3
composition and transmission 9, 17–18
criticized by Plato 49–50
role of bards (selectors/inventors) 14–17,
116
status as traditional truth or invented
fiction 9–20, 37, 70–1, 232–3
see also Muses, collective memory
Horace 193

'I', first-personal mode in lyric 35,
in narrative 155–6
Iamblichus Babyloniaca 194, 209
inventio (plausible elaboration of detail)
142
see also probable
Irving, J. A Prayer for Owen Meany 241

Johnson, Dr. 193
Josephus 127, 139
journalism 139
Julian 178
Justin 139

Kannicht, R. 21
katharsis ('cleansing') 183
Kuch, H. 129n., 176n.

Lactantius 146
Lanata, G. 17
Lewis, C.S. The Magician's Nephew
148–53, 158, 160
lies
in ancient historiography 115, 119,
122–3, 124–5
in Hesiod xiv, 20–2, 71, 116, 242–3
in Homer 19–20
in Plato 44–57, 62–5
in relation to fiction xvi–xvii
in Stesichorus 23–8
see also deception, fiction, historiography,
mendacity, Plato, poetic invention
literacy (and authentication) 243
literate audience 106
see also orality
Livy 102, 103, 134, 139
Longinus 239–40
Longus Daphnis and Chloe 209, 212,
218–19, 222
Lucian
on historiography 88, 89, 102, 110, 117,
122, 123, 125, 128, 137
True History 131–2, 157n., 171
see also mirror
Luke's gospel 149

McKeon, M. 241–2
Macrobius 155, 171, 177, 180
Meijering, R. 129n., 156n.
mendacity, types in ancient historiography
modern debate about 89–90
mythical elements 128–9
plausible elaboration of detail 142–6
(see also probable)
relationship to rhetoric 116–17, 132–3,
144–5
tendentiousness (adulation and malice)
126–7
'tragic history' 112–13, 134–5, 140, 185–7
travellers' tales 131–2, 196
Milesia ('Milesian tales') 157
Millar, F. 153

mimēsis ('imitation/representation')
  as modern category 153
  in the ancient novel 212–15, 218
mimēsis-diēgēsis ('representation'–
  'narrative') distinction in Plato 191, 211
  see also Aristotle *Poetics*, mirror
Mimnermus 6–7
mirror,
  history as (in Lucian) 89, 110, 137
mise-en-abyme (embedded) narratives 152
Murray, P. 17
Muses
  in Hesiod xiv, 20–2, 71, 109, 116, 242–3
  in history (Clio) 138
  in Homer 9–10, 11, 13–14, 15–16, 71

narrative
  ancient poetic types of
    dactylic 23–8
    elegy 6–7
    hexameter (epic) 8–20
    iambic and trochaic 7–8
  ancient rhetorical categories for 8on.,
    129–30, 189–93, 211, 231–2
  see also novel, *diēgēsis-mimēsis* distinction
Needham, R. 241
Nelson, W. 140n., 209n.
Nesbit, E. *The Treasure Seekers* 150
Newson, R. 182n., 193n., 226n., 231n.,
  234n., 237–8, 240, 242, 244
Ninus Romance 187
novel, (ancient) or romance
  absence of ancient literary theory
    about 79–80, 129, 154, 176–8, 190–1
  allusions to other genres 199–200, 205–6,
    208–10, 222–3
  ambivalent in its belief-claims 195, 197,
    215, 224–9, 237–40, 243–4
  as development of historical elaboration
    80–1, 185–7
  energeia/evidentia ('vivid illustration') in
    312–15
  general truths in 202
  geography of 198–9
  realism in 228–9
  religion in 200–4
  self-conscious fictionality of 215–24
  significance of openings 149, 198
  significance of titles 197–8

Odysseus (in Homer)
  teller of false and true stories 19–20
  use of oaths to validate claims 2
oracles, truth status of 4–5

orality
  and fictionality 11–12
  and Herodotus' conception of truth
    115–6
  and the transmission of collective 'truth'
    71–2
  in Serbo-Croatian culture 17–18
Ovid 134–5, 169

Parthenius 216
Peitho (goddess of persuasion) 235
Pelling, C.B.R. 142
Perry, B.E. 80–1, 186n.
Petronius *Satyricon* 154
Photius 194–7, 209, 215, 225
plasma ('invention'), see *argumentum*
Plato
  dialogues
    as modes of search for truth 67–8
    authentication of 243
    fictionality not emphasized 66–9
  myths
    as 'noble lies' 52–6
    as expressions of the (incomplete) search
      for truth 56–62
    Atlantis story a pseudo-historical
      'charter-myth' 62–6
  Phaedrus 58, 60–1, 171n.
    and Stesichorus' palinode 24, 26–7
  Republic
    concerned with truth-falsehood not
      fact-fiction distinction 39–40, 43–55
    distinction between *diēgēsis* ('narrative')
      and *mimēsis* ('representation') 191,
      211
    implicit recognition of fictionality of
      poetry 46–7, 50–1
    on 'story-telling' (*muthologia*) 52–6
    truth-status of myth of cave 60–2
  pleasure
    as function of poetry 14–15, 235,
      (combined with instruction) 12
    as function of ancient historiography
      102, 139, 184
Plutarch 157, 159, 172, 179, 235
  on historiography 88, 112, 120–1,
    130–1, 135
poetic invention
  in archaic Greek poetry 37
  in Homer 16–20, 70–1
  in Pindar 70
  in Stesichorus 23–8, 70
  in sympotic poetry 28–36
poetry
  as vehicle of communal truth 65, 84
  see also collective memory

Polybius 88, 102, 105, 112, 127, 134, 135
    136, 140, 141–2, 142–3, 144, 146, 185–6
probable
    in Aristotle 74–7, 181–3, 228
    in Cicero 188
    and rhetorical verisimilitude 142, 187
    and rhetorical categories 189–91
psuchagōgia ('leading of mind') 170–1
    see also bewitchment
psyche, falsehood and truth in 45–6, 52–5

Quintilian 145, 154, 185, 211

Reardon, B.P. 41n., 79n., 80n., 176, 178,
    181, 232–3
Riffaterre, M. 149n., 215
Rhetorica ad Herennium 129, 189–91
Rösler, W. 11–14, 22, 36, 230n., 240
Ruthven, K.K. 227n., 231n.

Sage, V. 242
Sophocles 238
Sallust 103, 126
Seneca 122–3, 125, 127, 135, 137, 140, 146
Servius 130
Sextus of Chaeronea 159
Shakespeare As You Like It xiii
Sidney, Sir Philip 216, 233–4
Simonides 5–6
Slings, S.R. 35–6
Solon 8, 179, 181, 185, 215, 216, 225
Stesichorus (Palinode) 23–8, 70
'story world' 147, 151–4, 160–1, 174
Strabo 131
Suetonius 237
Svenbro, J. 12n., 71n.
Syme, R. 125–6
sympotic poetry
    elegy 28–30
    lyric 30–1
    epode 31–6

Tacitus 103, 126–7, 136
tekmēria ('evidence') 101, 102
Theognis 29–30
Theon 180
Theophanes 140
Theophrastus 184
Theopompus 128, 184, 211

Thespis, inventor of tragedy 179–80, 216,
    225
Thucydides
    attitude to time 109
    conception of historiography 91–2, 136
    greatness of theme 100, 109, 110–13
    his histories useful rather than pleasant
        106–7, 117, 143
    on speeches in historiography 104–5
    preface 99–114
    response to Herodotus 98–100, 101–2,
        106, 111–14
    response to Homer 73–4, 101, 103
    response to predecessors in general
        101–2, 106
    saphes ('clearness') of historical truth
        107, 109–10
    tension between general and specific 108
Timaeus 140
Todorov, T. 161–2
tragedy (Greek)
    echoes of in ancient novel 223
    'tragic history' see mendacity
travellers' tales see mendacity
truth
    as precondition of normal communi-
        cation 1
    as facts and as interpretation 55, 58,
        105–10, 115–21, 136
    in psyche 45
    types of (literal and figurative etc.) 39
    see also historical truth
truth–falsehood distinction (not identical
    with fact–fiction distinction) 39

Valerius Maximus 128, 131
Varro 129

Walton, K.L. 193n., 234n., 237n., 240
West, M.L. 23
Winkler, J.J. 2, 219n.
White, H. 85, 125n.
Woodman, A.J. 90, 116, 119, 126–7, 133,
    139, 234n.

Xenophon of Ephesus Ephesiaca 203, 209,
    216, 243
Xenophon (historian) 80, 206